THE CALLANDER &
OBAN RAILWAY

Oban station (demolished 1987)

THE HISTORY OF THE RAILWAYS
OF THE SCOTTISH HIGHLANDS:

Vol 1 – *The West Highland Railway*
        by John Thomas

Vol 2 – *The Highland Railway*
        by H. A. Vallance

Vol 3 – *The Great North of Scotland Railway*
        by H. A. Vallance (updated by the Great North of
        Scotland Railway Association)

Vol 4 – *The Callander & Oban Railway*
        by John Thomas (updated by John Farrington)

Vol 5 – *The Skye Railway*
        by John Thomas (updated by John Farrington)

Note   The line drawings in the prelims and on pages 28, 48,
          72, 98, 134 and 166 are from the collection of the
          Friends of the West Highland Railway Society.

THE
CALLANDER & OBAN
RAILWAY

The History of the Railways
of the Scottish Highlands – Vol 4

by

JOHN THOMAS

Additional material by John Farrington

LOCH AWE   JOHN HAY '89

DAVID ST JOHN THOMAS
DAVID & CHARLES

British Library Cataloguing in Publication Data

Thomas, John *1914–1982*
The Callander & Oban railway. – (The history of the
railways of the Scottish Highlands; 4)
1. Scotland. Railways services, history
I. Title   II. Farrington, J. H. (John Hugh) *1945–*   III.
Series
385.09411

ISBN 0-946537-46-1

First published 1966

John Thomas 1966,

John Farrington 1990

Printed in Great Britain by Redwood Press Limited,
Melksham, Wiltshire for David St John Thomas
Distributed by David & Charles plc
Brunel House   Newton Abbot   Devon
Published in the United States of America by
David & Charles Inc
North Pomfret   Vermont   05053   USA

Contents

Just before the age of the 'Sprinters' No 37014 climbs from the former Callander & Oban route on the spur to the West Highlands at Crianlarich. R. Kitching

Author's Notes and Acknowledgements

When I first set out to write the story of the Callander & Oban my previous book, *The West Highland Railway*, was enjoying flattering reviews in the lay and railway press and selling merrily in the shops, and I wondered if a c & o history could begin to live up to the reputation of the West Highland. Hitherto the story of the Callander & Oban had only been scratched; there was nothing in print except a few conventional, superficial articles in the files of the railway journals. Yet I sensed that beneath the surface there was a story waiting to be discovered. Little did I realise how remarkable that story was to be.

Fortunately, the men who ran the offices of the old Scottish railway companies had magpie minds. They kept papers and documents, letters and minute books, and like MacEwan of the Killin they locked them away in strong-boxes. Decades later, and with the railway scene changed beyond recognition by amalgamation and nationalisation, the documents made their way by devious routes to a Victorian building in Waterloo Place, Edinburgh. There, the Custodian of Records, British Railways Board, by the flick of a card or the turn of a page can reveal to the inquirer just what his treasure vaults contain on any particular subject. Minutes later the requested documents are on the student's desk—and more often than not there is a cup of tea at his elbow.

The most valuable single find was John Anderson's letters, thousands and thousands of them. Day by day his clerk copied on the thinnest of tissue every letter that his master wrote and preserved them in the order in which they were written. Many of the copies have faded to a pale yellow or a faint grey; some, alas! are indecipherable. The character of John Anderson leaps out; he wrote as the story of the railway was unfolding.

Minute books at the best of times are stilted and scrappy, and the c & o's are no better than average. But the company's affairs were bound up with those of the Caledonian and West Highland and to a lesser extent with the North British, and at Waterloo Place the minute books of all three are available for cross-reference; it is interesting to learn what was said in other board rooms about current c & o topics.

A railway history of course needs local colour, a flavour of contemporary feelings. And here again I had a lucky break. At the time of the coming of the railway a lively newspaper, the *Oban Telegraph*, was published in Oban. It has long since disappeared, but as recently as 1960 a dozen or so bound volumes of it were presented to the Mitchell Library in Glasgow. The volumes covered the years immediately before and after the arrival of the railway, and their pages yielded lucid descriptions of the contemporary scene.

To supplement the descriptive matter with contemporary photographs seemed a forlorn hope. Railway photographers were few in 1880, and most of the pictures taken then have faded from the paper. Again luck favoured the c & o project. My good friend and elder statesman of Scottish railway enthusiasts James F. McEwan turned up with a massive tome that could have been mistaken for a family Bible had it not been for the inscription 'Callander and Oban Railway, 1880' on its scarred leather covers. Inside, faded and mildewed, but not beyond recovery, were pictures taken in 1879-80, the best of which are included in this book.

On the very day that I signed my publisher's contract for this book, quite unknown to me my young friend Alisdair M. Macdonald was in the Edinburgh office of Blyth & Blyth (successors to Blyth & Cunningham) gathering data for an architectural study of Callander station. So Alisdair has contributed drawings and sketches to the book and, through the courtesy of Blyth & Blyth, I have been able to consult drawings of c & o features as supplied to MacKay the contractor nearly a hundred years ago.

Most of the sources on which this book is based are housed in the British Railways Board archives at 23 Waterloo Place, Edinburgh, and I am most grateful for the generous help given by the Custodian of Records, Robert M. Hogg, and his staff. Sincere thanks are also due to Mr C. W. Black, City Librarian of Glasgow and the staff of the Mitchell Library. Many friends of the railway enthusiast fraternity have provided information or turned up with clues to the whereabouts of facts and photographs. Among those not acknowledged below are Lt-Cdr Black, H. D. Bowtell, E. Craven, Dr N. A. McKillop, Douglas McMillan, Montague Smith and Dudley Whitworth. I also express appreciation for the help and hospitality so readily given by Alastair R. Thompson, then Provost of Callander, and the Callander 'worthies' George Pywell, Jock Sutherland and Archie McLaren.

Publisher's Note

After twenty two years it is a privilege to be able to offer this title again. How well I remember the enthusiasm of the late John Thomas in researching and writing it in those quite different days of the mid 1960s.

John Farrington has kindly added another chapter dealing with the still colourful history of the line in recent times. The original remains unaltered, an historic document in its own right yet as relevant today as in 1966. Because of this I have decided to retain the original selection of illustrations even though they were printed letterpress and their quality re-taken for the lithography age will suffer a little. We· cannot find sufficient of the old prints to remake John Thomas's selection without damaging it. But there are many extra illustrations including colour.

D St J T

CHAPTER I

The 'Glenmutchkin' Lines

THE ORIGINAL GLENMUTCHKIN

The Glenmutchkin Railway was conceived round a fourteen-gallon cask of Oban whisky. The year was 1845, and the Railway Mania was at its height. As one of the promoters of the line was to say:

> These were the first glorious days of general speculation. Railroads were emerging from the hands of the greater into the fingers of the lesser capitalists. Two successful harvests had given a fearful stimulus to the national energy; and it seemed perfectly certain that all populous towns would be united and the rich agricultural districts intersected by the magical bands of iron. The columns of the newspapers teemed every week with the parturition of novel schemes, and the shares were no sooner announced than they were rapidly subscribed for.

Augustus Dunshunner and Robert McCorkindale were lesser capitalists: they had £300 between them. But that did not deter them from promoting a £240,000 railway. These two young Glasgow men-about-town dedicated themselves to providing a service for that class of citizen who was for ever complaining that he never could get an allocation of shares, no matter how soon he applied after publication of a railway prospectus.

A preliminary board meeting was held in Dunshunner's lodgings and McCorkindale, the only other person present, was elected secretary. The task was to decide where the railway was to be built. Alcantara was considered but rejected because neither promoter was sure whether it was in Spain or Portugal. The obvious solution was to choose the current fashionable hunting-ground of the railway promoters, the Scottish Highlands. The papers were full of schemes for railways in the Highlands mainly because all the reasonable (and unreasonable) places in more hospitable parts of the country had already been earmarked twice over by rival promoters. In Glenmutchkin, Dunshunner and McCorkindale found the perfect answer to their quest—here was a site crying out for a railway. Glenmutchkin, in the north-west of Scotland, was a bare, bleak valley, 12 miles long, slanting down to a derelict fishing village on the coast. The local landed proprietor, an enthusiastic supporter of the Highland Clearances, had swept every man, woman and child out of the glen and packed them off to America from the village pier to make the place safe for sheep.

It only remained for Dunshunner and his partner to draw up a list of provisional directors. They leant heavily for style and content on the numerous railway prospectuses then appearing in the daily press, and for inspiration on the whisky cask at their elbows. Without a titled gentleman to head the list the prospectus would scarcely be noticed. Sir Polloxfen Tremens, lately the recipient of an obscure baronetcy in Nova Scotia, was willing to oblige; after all, he had nothing to lose. At least one Highland chief was obligatory for the list: the only Highlander Dunshunner knew was McGloskie, a drunken porter who frequented Jamaica Street; with his agreement his name was added to the list in the pretentious style favoured by the clan chiefs: The McGloskie. Dunshunner was elated to find a second *bona fide* Highland chief rejoicing in the name of Mhic-Mhac-Vich. (His grandfather had an island to the west of the Hebrides, but it was not laid down on the maps.) Samuel Sawley, coffin-maker, a vociferous supporter of the no-Sunday-travel movement then occupying more space in the papers than the Corn Laws, readily joined the provisional board on being assured that the Glenmutchkin would not run trains on a Sunday. And the promoters were fortunate indeed in being able to name as their engineer one Walter Solder, a gas-fitter by trade.

In drawing up the prospectus the promoters used the by now well-tested formulae: profits from tourists, sheep and whisky, prominent use in the title of the evocative word *direct*, assurances that engineering difficulties were non-existent and, of course, a mention of Bonnie Prince Charlie. The prospectus was duly completed, the whisky being reduced to a quart-and-a-half in the process, and published in the Scottish Press.

DIRECT GLENMUTCHKIN RAILWAY
In 12,000 shares of £20 each. Deposit £1 per share
Provisional Committee

Sir Polloxfen Tremens, Bart of Toddymains.
Tavish McTavish of Invertavish.
The McGloskie.
Augustus Reginald Dunshunner of St Mirrens.
Samuel Sawley, Esq., Merchant.
Mhic-Mhac-Vich, Induibh.

Phelan O Finlan, Esq., of Castle Rock, Ireland.
The Captain of McAlcohol.
Factor of Glentumblers.
John Job Jobson of Glenscarse and Inveryewky.
Joseph Hickles, Esq.
Habbakak Grabbe, Portioner in Rannoch-Drumclog.
Engineer: Walter Solder, Esq.
Interim Sec.: Robert McCorkindale, Esq.

The necessity of a direct line of Railway communication through the fertile and populous district known as the *Valley of Glenmutchkin* has been felt and universally acknowledged. Independent of the surpassing grandeur of its mountain scenery which shall immediately be referred to, and other considerations of even greater importance, *Glenmutchkin* is known to the capitalist as the most important *breeding station* in the Highlands of Scotland and indeed as the great emporium from which the southern markets are supplied. It has been calculated by a most eminent authority that every acre in the strath is capable of rearing twenty herd of cattle and as has been ascertained after a careful admeasurement that there are not less than *Two Hundred Thousand* improveable acres immediately contiguous to the proposed line of Railway, it may confidently be assumed that the number of cattle to be conveyed along the line will amount to *Four Millions* annually which, at the lowest estimate would yield a revenue larger to the proportion of the capital subscribed than that of any Railway in the United Kingdom. From this estimate the traffic in sheep and goats, with which the mountains are literally covered, has been carefully excluded, it having been found quite impossible (from its extent) to compute the actual revenue to be drawn from that most important branch. It may however be roughly assumed as from 17 to 19 per cent upon the whole, after deduction of working expenses.

The population of Glenmutchkin is extremely dense. Its situation on the west coast has afforded it means of direct communication with America of which for many years the inhabitants have actually availed themselves. Indeed, the amount of exportation of live stock from this part of the Highlands to the Western continent has more than once attracted the attention of Parliament. The manufactures are large and comprehensive and include the most famous distilleries in the world. The minerals are most abundant and among them may be reckoned quartz, porphyry, felspar, malachite, manganese and basalt.

At the foot of the valley, and close to the sea, lies the important village known as the *Clachan of Inverstarve*. It is supposed by various eminent antiqueries to be the site of the Capital of the Picts, and among the busy inroads of commercial prosperity it still retains some interesting traces of former grandeur. There is a large fishing station here to which vessels from every nation resort, and the demand for foreign produce is daily and steadily increasing.

As a sporting country Glenmutchkin is unrivalled; but it is by the tourists that its beauties will most greedily be sought. These consist of every combination which plastic nature can afford—cliffs of unusual magnitude and grandeur, waterfalls only second to the sublime cataracts of Norway, woods of which the bark is a remarkably valuable commodity. It need scarcely be added, to rouse the enthusiasm inseparable from this glorious glen, that there in 1745 Prince Charles Edward Stuart, then in the zenith of his hopes, was joined by the brave Sir Grugar McGrugar at the head of his devoted clan.

The railway will be twelve miles long and can be completed within six months after the Act of Parliament is obtained. There are no viaducts of any importance, and only four tunnels along the whole length of the line. The shortest of these does not exceed a mile and a half.

In conclusion the projectors of the railway beg to state that they have determined as a principle to set their face *against all Sunday travelling whatsoever* and to oppose *every bill* which may hereafter be brought with Parliament unless it shall contain a clause to that effect. It is also their intention to take up the case of the poor and neglected STOKER for whose accommodation and social, moral and intellectual improvement a large stock of evangelical tracts will speedily be required. Tenders of these, of quantities of not less than 12,000, may be sent in to the interim secretary. Shares must be applied for within ten days from the present date.

The promoters were not unduly surprised to find four railway prospectuses at least as outrageous as their own in the same issues of the papers as published their announcement. Nor were they surprised to find that the Glenmutchkin shares were oversubscribed four times by mid-afternoon and a premium of 7/6 a share was being charged on allotment. Dunshunner was inundated with letters from strangers pleading with him to use his influence in getting them some shares. When a Press advertisement announced that Glenmutchkin had been oversubscribed ten times 'a simultaneous groan was uttered by some hundreds of disappointed speculators'. At this point the public-spirited promoters sacrificed their own holdings for hard cash so that more gentlemen could participate in the enterprise.

Plans were presented to the Board of Trade who 'reported handsomely' on what they called 'the Glenmutchkin scheme'. The engineer returned to Glasgow with the results of his first survey. 'Our engineer,' wrote Dunshunner, 'returned along with an assistant who really appeared to have some remote glimmerings of the science of practical mensuration. It seemed from a verbal report that the line was actually practical.' In his description of Glenmutchkin, Solder himself reported:

Ever since the distillery stoppit—and that was twa year last Martinmas —there wasna a hole whaur a Christian could lay his head, muckle less get white sugar for his toddy; forby the change house at the clachan, and the auld luckie that kepit it was sair forfochen wi' the palsy, and maist in the dead thraws. There was naebody else living within twal miles o' the line barring a tacksman, a lamiter and a bauldie.

(The promoters refrained from publishing this report as they thought it might interfere with the preparation of the traffic tables.)

The presentation of the Glenmutchkin bill to Parliament was the signal for Dunshunner to resign from the board and take up residence in Glenmutchkin at a cost of £5 5s a day to the company. This qualified him to go to London as a witness. 'I still recollect with lovely satisfaction,' he wrote,

the many pleasant days we spent in the metropolis at the company's expense. There were just a neat fifty of us and we occupied the whole of an hotel. We fought for three weeks a most desperate battle and might in the end have been victorious had not our last antagonist at the very close of his case pointed out no less than 73 fatal errors in the Parliamentary plans deposited by Solder.

The opposition could have routed the Glenmutchkin on the first day, but they were as anxious as anybody to enjoy the London fleshpots as long as possible. All that remained was for Dunshunner to go back to Glasgow, wind up the company, and pay off the shareholders at sixpence a share.

THE LURE OF ARGYLL

Professor Aytoun's hilarious pasquinade, 'How we got up the Glenmutchkin Railway, and how we got out of it,' appeared in the issue of Blackwood's *Edinburgh Magazine* for October 1845. William Edmonstoune Aytoun was a Writer to the Signet, a member of the Scottish Bar, and professor of rhetoric and *belles lettres* at the University of Edinburgh; Blackwood's was one of the most respected and influential journals of the age. The lampoon attracted wide attention; it was the most distinctive and one of the most significant pieces of writing to come out of the Railway Mania. It added a new adjective to railway vocabulary: forty years later leader writers and historians still talked of Glenmutchkin lines. A lawyer representing a railway being promoted in the West Highlands in 1883 admitted that he had a copy of Glenmutchkin in his bag, and John Anderson, who became secretary and manager of the first railway to penetrate the West Highlands, declared that Glenmutchkin set back railway development in that area by twenty years. Professor Aytoun wrote: 'It contains a deep moral if anyone has sense enough to see it; if not I have a new project in my eye for next session of which timely notice shall be given.'

The prudent heeded Aytoun's warning, but there were still Glenmutchkin schemes in plenty to tempt the imprudent. Indeed, the very month in which the Blackwood article was published, October 1845, was a vintage one for Highland railway projects, most of them every bit as bizarre as the Glenmutchkin. There was the Caledonian Canal & Great North & West of Scotland Railway, 'a line from Inverness along the southern bank of the Caledonian Canal to Fort William thence through Argyllshire, Perthshire and Dumbartonshire direct to Glasgow uniting the Moray Firth and the German Ocean on the east and the Clyde and the Atlantic on the west'. The Scottish Midland Junction Railway with its thirty-nine directors, including the requisite baronets and Right Hons, among other things aimed to 'open up the Central Highlands and connect them with the Low Lands'.

The Scottish Western Railway, widely acclaimed in the technical as well as the lay press, was promoted to connect the cities of Edinburgh and Glasgow and the East and South West of Scotland with the County of Argyll, and the other North Western parts of Scotland. The Scottish Grand Junction Railway had a marquis heading its thirty-four-strong committee. The Caledonian Northern Direct had a duke for a chairman, to say nothing of two lord-lieutenants of counties, two Royal Navy officers and five Members of Parliament. Both lines were intended to confer the benefits of railway communication on Argyll.

Argyllshire loomed large in the railway prospectuses of 1845. The county stretched from Loch Leven in the north to the Mull of Kintyre in the south, and from Dunoon in the east to the Atlantic seaboard and the islands beyond. Its few small towns were widely scattered and served by rudimentary roads. It had one small coal mine and a lead mine that produced spasmodically. Of its 2,432,000 acres only 308,000 were under cultivation. Nevertheless, the *Scottish Railway Gazette* saw Argyll as an El Dorado—'a valuable tract of country which only requires the aid of railway accommodation to render it not merely a source of almost inexhaustible wealth to the proprietors and inhabitants, but the means of adding immensely to the general resources of the county'. The journal listed the minerals from copper to cobalt said to be awaiting exploitation among the mountains of Argyll and added, 'There is even coral on the coast of Kintyre and in the Island of Colonsay'. Dunshunner could not have done better. The writer was of the opinion that the Scottish Western scheme 'comes before the public in a most satisfactory shape, bearing as it does every mark of

mature deliberation and careful investigation of practical details'.
Prospectuses and press were as one in proclaiming that there were no difficulties to be encountered in taking railways through the West Highlands. The SWR was described as being

> remarkably free from difficulties. The whole country traversed by the railway has recently been most minutely examined and levels taken by the engineers who have given a most favourable report on its practicability. The gradients along most parts of the line are of the easiest description. There are no tunnels and no works of difficulty involving an unusual expense.

The Grand Junction described its route through one of the most formidable mountain passes in Scotland thus: 'For the most part it is a dead level, and the surface is so regular that the cost of construction will be much below the average of railway undertakings.' The SGJ intended to get over any mountains in its path by means of atmospheric railways working on 1 in 40 inclines. The Scottish South Midland Junction proposed to cross the Tay and other rivers by using Rendel's Steam Bridge.

Oban was the focal point of both the SWR and the SGJ. Both companies had visions of turning this quiet village, nestling round its little bay of extraordinary beauty, into a cargo and fishing port serving the trade of the Western Isles and even Ireland. Both lines were to have made their way eastwards from the coast across Argyll, first by the south shore of Loch Etive and then by the Pass of Brander and Loch Awe to Dalmally. From there the railways were to run through Glen Lochy into Strathfillan. From Crianlarich, at the foot of the strath, there were two routes open to the Lowlands. The first was eastwards through Glen Dochart, down the rocky defile of Glen Ogle, then by the Pass of Leny to Callander and on to a junction with the north-south trunk line, the Scottish Central Railway. Access to Glasgow and Edinburgh would be gained by using Caledonian and Edinburgh & Glasgow metals respectively. An alternative route from Crianlarich was southward down Glen Falloch, thence by Loch Lomond to Glasgow. The Caledonian Northern Direct planned to run a second line from the south up Glen Falloch to connect at Crianlarich 'with an intended railway called the Scottish Grand Junction Railway or with another intended railway'.

THE SCOTTISH GRAND JUNCTION

For a time it looked as though the SGJ would succeed, especially when the SWR withdrew from the contest and put some of its

B

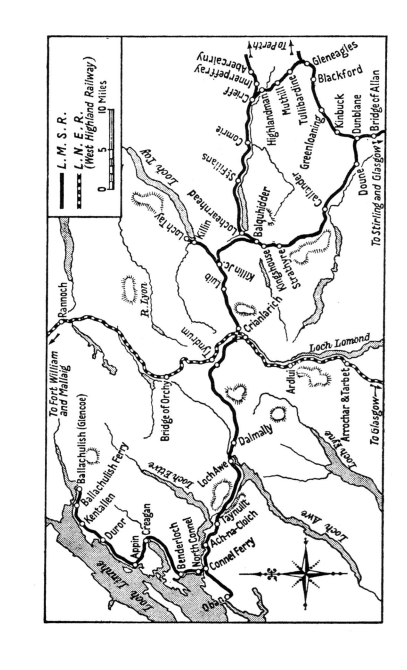

subscriptions at the former's disposal. The Corporation of Glasgow passed with 'unanimity and cordiality' a motion calling for official support of the line. At a single meeting in Glasgow the gentlemen present subscribed upwards of £100,000. The Caledonian Northern Direct took 1,500 shares in the SGJ and paid £3,750 in cash towards their cost. By the early autumn it had been decided that the SGJ would build an east-west line from Callander to Oban, and the CND would build a north-south line from the SGJ at Crianlarich down to Glasgow.

Professor Aytoun's warning came too late to halt the flow of capital to the 'October' railways; not everybody agreed with him. On the day after the October 'Blackwood' containing the lampoon was on sale, the *Glasgow Argus* published a leading article on the 'Progress of Railway Speculation':

> We think those who sound the alarm of an approaching railway crisis have somewhat exaggerated the danger. It may seem wise to the careless or to the ignorant to trace resemblances between the South Seas Mania and the Railway Mania of the present day, and to auger for the latter the same disastrous results as attended the former. Those, however, who look more deeply into the matter and think for themselves cannot discover sufficient resemblance of cause to anticipate a similarity of effect; but, on the contrary, so much difference as to lead to the very opposite conclusion from that reached by the alarmist. We ought not to expect or wish for any diminution of the present excitement until the length and breadth of the land is ribbed with iron, and horse and coach traffic has entirely disappeared. With railways the foundation is broad and secure. They are a necessity of the age.

In such a climate it was no wonder that speculators supported the Highland schemes in true Glenmutchkin style. The Scottish South Midland opened its subscription list on the day the *Argus* leader appeared and closed it four days later, the shares having been subscribed 'to an extent very far exceeding the number to be allocated'. On 15 October the SGJ announced that all its shares had been subscribed, and ten days later the promoters announced that notwithstanding the greatest exertion of the allocation committee they had been unable to complete the investigation of their lists and issue letters of allocation.

By November the SGJ and the CND had survey parties out in the West Highlands. And at this point in the story comes an extravagance that even Professor Aytoun would not have dared to introduce in his Glenmutchkin tale. The Grand Junction was led by the Marquis of Breadalbane, the Caledonian Northern Direct by the

Duke of Montrose. These gentlemen were rival chiefs and Glen Falloch was Breadalbane territory. The appearance of the CND (Montrose's men) in Glen Falloch was a signal for the resurgence of clan warfare, in a new form. Breadalbane's supporters, most of them workers from the lead mines at Tyndrum, surged down Glen Falloch in force, overwhelmed the CND party and threw them, complete with their theodolites, into a ditch. 'We hear it was a well-fought battle,' reported the *Perthshire Courier*, 'gallantly sustained by the engineers against fearful odds, where the assailants were ready to go to any extremity after the Highland fashion to please the laird.' The Montrose men thereafter confined their line of operation to the public road.

Not surprisingly the survey proved to be imperfect, and the surveyors went back to Glen Falloch the following week, this time armed with an interdict to prevent interference by Breadalbane's men. Only one surveyor and an attendant were present and for a time they went unnoticed. The *Perthshire Courier* duly reported, 'The hated theodolite, however, was at length recognised and the fiery cross was again dispatched through Strathfillan and the Clifton miners brought down in full force.' But there was no open warfare. The Breadalbane men contented themselves by removing their plaids and holding them in the line of vision of the theodolite operator.

But for the 1845 schemes the writing was on the wall. In England railway schemes were disappearing like snow off a dyke. Aytoun's message made an impact at last. By April 1846 the CND found that less than half the shares for which the public had so willingly subscribed had been taken up, and out of their fifty-three directors only thirty-one had paid cash for their shares. Deposits were returned to the shareholders and the project was wound up. The same fate overtook the rest of the Glenmutchkin lines, and in a few months of all the bold schemes that had been promoted to serve Argyll not one remained. Some thirty-four years were to pass before steel rails got within a stone's-throw of the distillery that had supplied the inspiration for the original Glenmutchkin.

One railway that survived the holocaust of 1845 was the Scottish Central. To savour in full the story of the Callander & Oban the reader must first acquaint himself with the story of 'the Central'.

CHAPTER II

'The Central'

A BRIDGE LINE

More than a hundred years have passed since Alexander Allan's light-green engines of the Scottish Central Railway trundled over the timber bridges between Stirling and Perth, and 'the Central' was a household phrase in Scotland. To the twentieth-century student of railways the Scottish Central is a long-forgotten, will-o'-the-wisp line that flourished briefly among the pioneer companies of the middle nineteenth century only to be swallowed up in the great amalgamations of 1865-66. But 'the Central' in its day was a fine railway whose officers could speak on equal terms with their counterparts on the Caledonian, Edinburgh & Glasgow and North British. The Scottish Central was barely five years old when Alexander Allan saw fit to leave his job as second-in-command to Trevithick at Crewe to take over the SCR locomotive workshops at Perth: an imposing tribute to the status of the railway and its future prospects. Barely a decade later the Scottish Central owned or controlled from its Perth headquarters railways, existing or projected, that stretched across Scotland from coast to coast—from Dundee in the east to Oban in the west. And the railway was paying the second-highest dividend of any line in Scotland—7 per cent.

The Scottish Central certainly was *central*. The 45-mile main line in the heart of Scotland ran due south from the Tay to the Forth to link the bridge towns of Perth and Stirling and extended 12 miles further south to end on a moor at Greenhill. Authorised in 1845 and opened in 1848, it was built on the cheap; most of the bridges, including a major one over the Forth at Stirling and another across the Allan at Dunblane, were of timber on stone piers. One of the proprietors admitted that with one terminus on an empty moor and the other in a quiet town 'which however we may admire and love it cannot be called a great emporium of trade', the outlook for traffic was not promising.

The Scottish Central's fortunes improved as the Scottish railway network took shape. It linked at Greenhill with the Caledonian coming up from Carlisle, which put Perth in direct communication with London. The Scottish Midland and the Aberdeen Railway continued the great trunk route northwards from Perth to Aberdeen, while the Dundee & Perth put the Scottish Central in direct contact with the busy port on the Tay. The Central owned the only railway bridge across the Forth and the only direct rail link between the systems in the north and those in the south. All traffic from Inverness, Aberdeen and Dundee converged on Perth to be funnelled down the Scottish Central to Greenhill, where it fanned out over the Caledonian, Edinburgh & Glasgow and North British. So the Central became a strategically-placed bridge line, indispensable to the country's north-south rail communications.

Since the Scottish Central's fortunes were so closely linked with its neighbours it was not surprising that it was involved in a series of treaties and agreements with other lines. The most important of these established the Caledonian Central Confederation, a quadruple link-up involving the Caledonian, North British, Edinburgh & Glasgow and Scottish Central in a joint-purse agreement; the members had to pay a fixed proportion of their revenue to the Confederation.

The Central steadily extended its influence. It serviced the locomotives of the Scottish Midland and the Aberdeen lines, and it seemed but a matter of time before it would absorb the northern systems. When Alexander Allan arrived in Perth from Crewe in 1853 he had control of forty-four passenger engines and thirty-four goods engines, 288 passenger coaches and 1,340 goods vehicles. The company consolidated its position by winning the right to run its trains into Edinburgh and Glasgow over Edinburgh & Glasgow and Caledonian metals, and established its own passenger offices and goods yards in these cities. In 1863, in spite of opposition from the Confederation, the Central acquired 31 more miles by absorbing the ailing Dundee & Perth. 'The Caledonian Railway cannot refrain from expressing its aversion to the Dundee and Perth obtaining a new lease of life within the reviving embraces of the Scottish Central,' commented the *Railway Times*. The Caledonian threatened to withdraw from its agreement with the Central, but was placated by an offer from Perth to extend the joint-purse agreement for thirty years from 1 February 1866.

Again, the Scottish Central owned a very profitable tunnel south of Perth. Foreign railways sending traffic through it had to pay tunnel tollage, and this revenue came to about £8,000 a year. It was little wonder that a financial journal could report 'The (Scottish

Central) company appears to be getting into excellent condition. We fully expect it will become one of the very few remunerative railways we have.'

THE DUNBLANE, DOUNE & CALLANDER

The Central had penetrated to the east coast and had spread its influence north to Aberdeen and south to Edinburgh and Glasgow. The west remained to be conquered. The central valley up which the main line ran extended no more than 10 miles to the west before it ended against the foothills of the Grampians. Passes threaded the Perthshire Highlands to reach a series of mountain-girt lochs of great beauty: Loch Katrine, Loch Lubnaig, Loch Earn, Loch Tay, Loch Dochart. Scott had made the country famous in his Waverley novels; it was the land of the Fiery Cross, of Rob Roy and the Lady of the Lake. Tourists were seeking it out in increasing numbers, but travel by the few regular stage coaches over the inadequate roads was tedious and expensive.

Ten miles west of the Scottish Central station at Dunblane, and at the point where the fertile plain ended and the mountains began, stood the weaving village of Callander. It was served by one coach a day from Stirling. The first attempt to take a railway to Callander was made in 1845, when the Stirling, Callander & Tillicoultry Junction Railway published its prospectus. The people of Callander were hard pressed to find any similarity between their placid village and the metropolis described in the railway prospectus. 'There are numerous and valuable Limeworks and Slate Quarries of the first quality in the vicinity of the Western Terminus,' said the prospectus, and it went on to promise 'enormous traffic in cattle from the great markets of Doune and Cockhill.' Of the highway between Stirling and Callander the prospectus declared: 'There are few roads in the kingdom more frequented by private conveyances.' The SC & TJR went the way of the other Glenmutchkin lines.

The Dunblane, Doune & Callander Railway was promoted in July 1846 to build a ten-mile line from a junction with the Scottish Central at Dunblane to Callander. The scheme was supported by local business men, including Donald McLaren whose name is perpetuated in McLaren High School, Callander, and John Stirling, laird of Kippendavie. An Act was obtained, but there was insufficient financial support and the scheme lapsed. A new Act was obtained in 1856 and the DD & C was opened on 1 July 1858. The line, which included all its stations in its title, offered a service of

five trains a day in summer and two in winter. At last Callander and
its lovely surroundings were placed within easy reach of tourists
and the village's rising prosperity spurred the railway promoters to
explore the possibility of taking the railways into the Perthshire
valleys—and beyond.

THE CALLANDER & OBAN

Several small railways were promoted by independent companies
to serve the fertile valleys and lochsides of the Central Highlands,
and the Scottish Central or the Scottish North Eastern (which had
been formed by an amalgamation of the Scottish Midland and the
Aberdeen Railway) usually had a close interest in their affairs. The
Crieff Junction had been opened on 16 March 1856 to connect the
Scottish Central with Crieff, the thriving market town in Strathearn.
The Perth, Almond Valley & Methven, built under the influence of
the SNE, also struck westwards towards Crieff, but a separate company, the Crieff & Methven Junction, provided the link.

Yet another independent company, the Crieff & Comrie, took
the railway a further six miles westward to a terminus in the village
of Comrie. The Scottish Central and the Scottish North Eastern,
both now in Crieff by virtue of their satellite lines, jousted for
control of the Crieff & Comrie. The Comrie promoters rejected an
SNE offer to take up £20,000 worth of shares and accepted an offer
from the Scottish Central, thus giving the Central control of the
line leading into the heart of Perthshire.

Beyond Perthshire lay Argyllshire and the Western Seas. Oban on
the west coast was 71 miles from the Callander railhead; 71 miles
of bleak mountain passes with only a few hamlets along the route.
But it was twenty years since Glenmutchkin had made ridiculous
the idea of taking a railway through this territory. The Scottish
Central boardroom had its sights fixed on the Hebridean seas with
their legendary shoals of prime fish, and on the supposedly rich
cattle trade of Argyll—all waiting, so it was said, the magic touch
of the railway to spark off its development.

The routine meeting of shareholders of the Scottish Central
Railway held in November 1864 was dragging to its close when
the chairman said, almost as an afterthought: 'There is just one
other matter that I would like to bring to your notice,' and proceeded to give the momentous news of a great new railway to the
west coast, the Callander & Oban; the Scottish Central was to contribute £200,000 to it and work it on completion. 'We considered

WINTER GRANDEUR

(1) *John Anderson's railway in Strathfillan*
(2) *8 a.m. Glasgow-Oban train approaching Crianlarich (Lower)*

C & O ENGINES—1

(3) 2—4—2 *radial tank No. 164 at Oban in 1880*
(4) *McIntosh rebuild of Brittain 4—4—0 No. 181 at Oban in 1914*

C & O ENGINES—2

(5) *McIntosh 4—6—0 No. 53 leaving Oban with a passenger train for
Glasgow in 1914*

(6) *McIntosh '918' class 4—6—0 No. 921 and Oban bogie No. 58 about
to leave Oban with southbound train in 1914*

THE C & O SCENE

(7) *Connel Ferry viaduct. Railway operation ceased on the viaduct on 26 March 1966*

(8) *A southbound train entering the Pass of Brander in 1937*

the line so desirable,' explained the chairman, 'and so bound up with our interests, that we could not without being open to the charge of great remissness to our duties, have avoided taking an active part in it.'

The first intimation of the Callander & Oban Railway had reached SCR headquarters in Perth towards the end of June 1864 in the form of a letter from the promoters' representatives.

> 186 West George St.
> Glasgow.
> 22 June 1864.
>
> Dear Sir,
>
> We have been requested by this Committee of the promoters of the proposed Railway to Oban at a meeting held here this day to request the favour of your informing us whether your Company would be inclined to support their proposed undertaking and supposing them inclined to do so to any considerable extent, whether there is any particular route which they should consider it expedient for the Oban line to adopt as a condition of their support. As we have to report your reply to an adjourned meeting of the promoters to be held here on the 8th proximo we request the favour of an early reply.
>
> We are, Sir,
> Henry Inglis, Writer to the Signet, Edinburgh.
> James Keydon, Glasgow.

The Callander & Oban was a revival of the Scottish Grand Junction of 1845. Like the Grand Junction the line was to run from Oban along the south shore of Loch Etive, through the Pass of Brander, thence by Dalmally and Glenlochy and Strathfillan to Crianlarich. And like their SGJ forerunners, the C & O promoters were in doubt where to go from there. Either they could go east by Glen Dochart, Glen Ogle and the Pass of Leny to link up with the Dunblane, Doune & Callander at Callander and so reach Glasgow over Scottish Central and Edinburgh & Glasgow metals, or they could go south by Glen Falloch and Loch Lomond to link up with the Edinburgh & Glasgow, the Forth & Clyde Junction or the Blane Valley Railways.

The promoters of the Callander & Oban were for the most part landed proprietors of modest means. The area in which the proposed railway route lay was thinly populated. There were few potential shareholders, and none could be considered rich. The most likely source of the £600,000 needed were the big established railways of the south. Therefore, a route to the Western Seas, and a voice in its planning, was offered to the railway or combination of railways that made the C & O the best offer. The letter sent to the Scottish Central went also to the Caledonian, the North British, the Edinburgh & Glasgow, the Forth & Clyde Junction Railway, and the Blane Valley Railway.

But 1864 was a year of turmoil on the Scottish railway scene. Amalgamation was in the air. The North British was firmly established in the east, the Caledonian in the west, and both were planning to extend their power by absorbing smaller companies. The Edinburgh & Glasgow, as yet powerful and independent, was the special object of their attentions. In answer to the Callander & Oban letter the Caledonian, North British and Edinburgh & Glasgow sent good wishes but no money; their boards had enough business pending without venturing into such risky territory. Only the Scottish Central on the one hand, and the Forth & Clyde Junction and the Blane Valley on the other, showed an active interest.

At the c & o meeting held in Glasgow on 8 July 1864, twenty-six gentlemen were present, many of them with homes in the territory to be served by the new railway. As the Duke of Montrose declined an invitation to take the chair, a Mr Macrae officiated, and assured his listeners that 'a vigorous prosecution of the enterprise is all that is necessary to ensure success'. The Forth & Clyde and Blane Valley companies teamed up to secure the Glen Falloch route for the Callander & Oban, offering to contribute £70,000 between them. The case for the Glen Falloch route was presented by Mr McCall and Mr Forman, Glasgow engineers whose firm was to plan the West Highland Railway thirty-five years later.

The Scottish Central on the other hand produced a letter from the great Thomas Brassey to say that he would build a railway from Oban to Callander to link with the Scottish Central (via the Dunblane, Doune & Callander) if the Central would put up one-third of the capital. The Central, as already related, agreed to find £200,000, on condition that the Callander & Oban promoters found the remaining £400,000. Money talked, and the c & o men decided to take their line east from Crianlarich to Callander. But a Mr Inglis was unwilling to surrender the Glen Falloch route without a fight, and he moved that Forman should be sent to interview the North British and get them to better the Scottish Central offer, and so ensure that the line came down Glen Falloch. The amendment was rejected—but only by ten votes to eight—and a committee was appointed to wait on the Scottish Central directors.

An agreement between the Scottish Central and the Callander & Oban was duly signed on 17 December 1864, affirming that the Scottish Central would subscribe capital to the extent of £200,000. The c & o was to have nine directors, five appointed by the Scottish

Central and four by the promoters. The line was to be 'made, constructed and completed in a good, substantial sufficient and workmanlike manner, and without the adoption of timber bridges or culverts'. (The Central had had enough of timber bridges.) The rails were to weigh 75 lb per yard and were to be laid in 24 ft lengths on larch sleepers placed at an average distance of 3 ft.

When not less than 20 miles of line directly connected with the Dunblane, Doune & Callander had been constructed and passed for opening by the Board of Trade, the Scottish Central undertook to work it in perpetuity, supplying all plant and having the power to appoint and dismiss staff. Railwaymen on the Callander & Oban would be paid and exclusively controlled by the Scottish Central, but the c & o would be allowed to appoint and pay a secretary, treasurer and any other officer required to manage its finance, capital and directorial aspects. For its services the Scottish Central was to receive one-half of the gross revenue.

The Callander & Oban Railway bill was drawn up and presented in Parliament in January 1865. The directors were named as John Wingfield Malcolm, Farquhar Campbell, Robert Macfie and Robert Tennant for the promoters, and Alexander Macduff, Sir Alexander Charles Gibson Maitland, Bart., James Ferguson Wyllie, James Falshaw and John Wilson for the Scottish Central. Plans were deposited at Dunblane, Perth and Inveraray, a town never to see the c & o or any other railway. The bill sought:

First, a Railway commencing about Five Furlongs South-westwards from the Schoolhouse in the Town of Oban called the Oban Industrial School, and terminating by a Junction with the Dunblane, Doune and Callander Railway, about One and a Half Furlongs Eastward from the Booking Office of the Callander Station of the Railway.
Secondly, a Tramway commencing by a Junction with the Railway above described about One Furlong South-westwards from the said Schoolhouse, and terminating on the Pier on the East Side of the Harbour of Oban about Two Chains Eastward from the South-western end of the said Pier.

During a mammoth Parliamentary sitting extending over two days, 148 railway bills were passed, and one of them was the Callander & Oban. Another bill passed on the same day was the Dingwall & Skye. This scheme had the same object as the c & o, to give an outlet to the Western Seas. It ran across country 100 miles north of the c & o, from Dingwall on what was soon to become the Highland Railway to a point on the Kyle of Lochalsh opposite Skye. Both railways undertook to build harbours: whereas the Callander & Oban's proposed harbour installations at Oban seemed makeshift, the Dingwall & Skye Railway Act specified

> a pier with all proper wharves, landing places, rails, sidings, cranes, sheds and other works and conveniences necessary for facilitating traffic in connection with the intended railway at or near the terminus of the same intended railway at Kyle of Lochalsh in the parish of Lochalsh or on the soil or bed of the sea adjacent thereto.

The Callander & Oban Railway Act was passed on 8 July 1865. The first sod was not cut for over fourteen months. Five years were to pass before a revenue-earning wheel was to turn on the line (and on only 17½ miles at that), and it would be fifteen years before a train entered Oban.

But even before the Act was passed sweeping changes had transformed the railway political scene. Ten days earlier, on 29 June, the Scottish Central had won permission to take over the Dunblane, Doune & Callander as from 31 July 1865; and the Central had enjoyed its new-found gains for one day. On 1 August 1865 the Central itself had been absorbed by the Caledonian, which acquired all its assets and liabilities including the obligation to finance and operate the Callander & Oban. At the outset the c & o directors found themselves with formidable new masters.

Oban station signal box, demolished 1988

CHAPTER III

Difficult Days

CALEDONIAN MISGIVINGS

The Callander & Oban had looked attractive to the Scottish Central. It was not at all attractive to the Caledonian, whose shareholders had no stomach for squandering cash among the Perthshire hills. The amalgamations of 1865 firmly established the Caledonian as the National Line, and the company stood on the threshold of an era of vigorous expansion. There was the Scottish North Eastern to be absorbed and welded into a unit of the Caledonian trunk route that was to stretch from Carlisle to Aberdeen. There were plans for the exploitation of the rich Lanarkshire coalfields and the towns they supported. Glasgow was a city of 400,000 souls and its population was rising rapidly. The 1861 census had shown that Oban and Callander between them possessed fewer than 3,000 inhabitants, and the scattered hamlets between the two could produce barely a thousand more. The certain dividends lying in the coal and iron traffic of the Clyde Valley were infinitely preferable to the nebulous rewards from the fish and sheep of the West Highlands.

From the beginning there was an implacable anti-Callander & Oban lobby in the Caledonian boardroom. This faction would have dropped the Oban line there and then, but the terms of the SCR-Caledonian amalgamation agreement forbade such a course. And there was another reason, if a negative one, why the Caledonian should use caution. The amalgamations of 1865 had given the Edinburgh & Glasgow to the North British, which as the result had now penetrated deep into traditional Caledonian territory—Glasgow and the Clyde coast; and the North British already possessed and exercised running powers into Callander. If the Caledonian abandoned its awkward foster-child on the Callander doorstep, it was reasonable to suppose that the North British would attempt to pick it up.

The Callander & Oban directors had undertaken to find £400,000 along the route of the railway, a task which the hard-headed financiers of the south considered impossible. The Caledonian shareholders feared that they would be called upon again and again to meet deficiencies in the Callander & Oban finances; and they were. The West Highland landowners supported the line to the best of their ability: Breadalbane took 2,000 shares (at £20 a share), the Duke of Argyll took 600, and the company's directors, Malcolm and Macfie, took 300 each. But landowners with money to spare were few in the West Highlands. The small people of the district were assiduously canvassed and thirty-one of them bought one share each, including the sisters Betsy and Jessie McGregor, servants in a Killin villa, and the village shoemakers Malcolm and James McNaughton. When the parish minister at Killin took three shares the free-kirk minister, not to be outdone, also bought three. Innkeepers along the route were liberal subscribers, and a special canvass carried out at Tobermory on the Isle of Mull bore fruit. When the barrel had been thoroughly scraped it was found that 201 individuals had subscribed for £56,360 worth of shares.

THE COMPLEAT RAILWAYMAN

The Callander & Oban might well have gone the way of its Glenmutchkin predecessors had it not been for the arrival on the scene of a man full of energy and original ideas. John Anderson had been assistant to the general manager of the Edinburgh & Glasgow Railway, and the changes that followed the 1865 amalgamations prompted him to try his luck with this new railway in the West Highlands. He accepted the post of secretary to the Callander & Oban at a salary of £250 a year, from which he had to pay his clerk's wages. He was given a small office at 48 Dundas Street, Glasgow.

Anderson sought to supplement his income by becoming secretary of the Glasgow Shale Oil Company Ltd, and for the privilege of conducting that company's affairs on c & o premises the railway board charged him £7 7s annual rental. Yet he was to stay with the c & o for forty-two years. The story of the line revolves round his remarkable personality.

The Callander & Oban boardroom was not a happy place. There was a clear division between the Caledonian directors and the original promoter's directors. (Anderson came to refer to them as the 'West Highland' directors.) The 'West Highland' directors had promised that if local subscriptions did not reach £100,000 they would make up any difference out of their own pockets; the Caledonian directors had no such obligation. The 'West Highland'

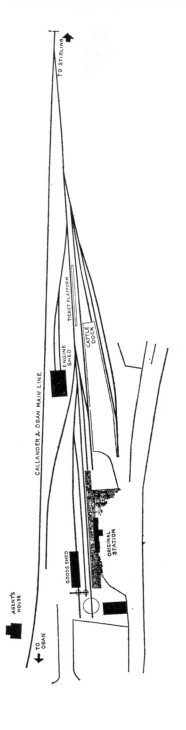

This sketch is based on an official drawing supplied by the Caledonian in September 1868 so that the C & O could plan its junction with the parent line. The drawing shows the layout of Callander old (the original DD & C) station. The old station was closed shortly after the opening of the C & O station and the site was used until 1965 as a goods and mineral depot

directors had little idea of how to run a railway, and most of them had interests at Westminster and elsewhere; the Caledonian directors barely tolerated the whole scheme. The upshot was that Anderson was left to conduct the line's affairs single-handed. An income-tax return of the period shows him as the only paid employee; no treasurer was appointed—probably because there was nothing to treasure!

Money was Anderson's biggest worry. When he issued the first 'call' for a £2 cash payment per share from the line's supporters, he discovered that some of the people who so helpfully had signed subscription application forms now had second thoughts. A Mr McDonald of Killin, on receiving his 'call', wrote in indignation to Anderson denying that he had ever put his name down for fifty shares. 'I beg you will be so good as to erase my name from the list of those to whom shares have been allotted,' he implored. The response from the expected subscribers in Mull was particularly poor.

Meanwhile, Blyth & Cunningham of Edinburgh had been appointed engineers of the line, and on 16 August 1865 Benjamin Blyth, annoyed because no orders had been received to begin the survey, wrote to Anderson:

> As there is to be a meeting of directors on 30th inst we wish you to bring before them the necessity of giving us immediate orders to proceed with the surveys if it is contemplated to begin any of the works in spring as details will require very careful consideration for which it is desirable we should have as much time as possible, and when winter sets in we can scarcely work in such a country except at great disadvantage.

When Blyth was informed of the company's financial difficulties, he suggested to Anderson that a contract should be let for the first 17½ miles from Callander to the head of Glen Ogle. This was 2½ miles short of the *minimum* length of line the Caledonian had agreed to work. Nevertheless, Anderson recommended to his board that Blyth be instructed to prepare plans, so that a contract could be advertised.

Anderson then embarked on a campaign to attract money. First he drew up a list of defaulting subscribers: the thirty-nine names were headed by that of the Marquis of Breadalbane. Anderson wrote to them appealing for their goodwill and support, using a selection of stock letters slanted to suit the various types of recipient. He wheedled, pleaded or threatened as the occasion demanded, hinting that his correspondent was letting the West

Highlands down, or holding out the promise of rich rewards to come. A note of desperation rings in his letter to Angus Gregorson, solicitor, Oban: 'Is there no way you can approach any of the Trustees of the first and second Earls of Breadalbane? If they cannot take shares they might agree to favourable terms as to land.' To a minister of the kirk who had failed to take up his promised thirty shares Anderson pleaded for a deposit of £6 towards the cost of his £600,000 railway.

Anderson also set off on a tour of the West Highlands to prod the laggards and attempt to get new shareholders. In Oban he peddled shares round the shops: he sold only thirteen. 'Almost every small shopkeeper has already taken an interest in the railway,' he reported to his directors. 'There is nothing more to hope for from Oban as the place has been thoroughly canvassed.' But he had better luck with a circular he sent to prominent West Highlanders; this sold seventy-five new shares.

Nor, in his search for money, was Anderson averse to poaching on the preserves of the rival Dingwall & Skye Railway. He assured a prospective shareholder in Skye that there was little hope of a connection being made between the Kyle of Lochalsh and the Highland Railway and urged him to throw in his lot with the C & O: 'Several proprietors who had applied for shares in the Kyle Akin (sic) line have now become shareholders with us, and I will be glad to have your application on the enclosed form.'

Another of Anderson's preoccupations about this time was the odd little affair of the Ardrishaig & Lochawe Railway. This company was promoted to build a line from Ardrishaig on Loch Fyne to join the Callander & Oban at Dalmally. In a letter to one of the 'West Highland' directors on 20 November 1865, Anderson pointed out that the Ardrishaig & Lochawe bill was to be presented in Parliament the following week, and noted 'This will do no good.' But in a stock letter sent to James McKenzie *on the same day* Anderson added, 'A new line is projected from Ardrishaig to join us at Dalmally which cannot fail to benefit this line.' Whatever his real thoughts, Anderson at once organised a petition against the Ardrishaig project, although Blyth advised against this course, and the Caledonian gave him no support. His petition received Callander & Oban approval and was presented to Parliament, only to be withdrawn on the urgent representations of the C & O solicitors. The Ardrishaig & Lochawe was the first of several similar projects to fall by the wayside.

C

CONSTRUCTION OF THE LINE

When the C & O came to letting the contract for the Callander to Glen Ogle section there was, of course, no talk of Thomas Brassey, who had offered to build the line when it was first promoted. That gentleman was in the process of losing a million pounds in the financial troubles of 1866. Ten contractors submitted tenders ranging from £124,000 to £233,800, the successful one of £124,218 coming from John MacKay. At a board meeting on 25 September 1866, when the contract was presented for signing, the official seal of the company was delivered, impressed on the contract, and placed in a special box, the key of which was handed to John Anderson amid applause. In the excitement of the moment nobody noticed that the contract had not been signed. The first sod of the railway was broken on 29 October 1866. The contract was signed on 6 November.

The long series of financial crises, and the consequent delay in letting the contract, meant that MacKay was starting work in winter. He established camps along the route, and put a large labour force and teams of horses to work between Callander and Lochearn-head. Progress was rapid at first. The soil in the Pass of Leny was light and sandy and presented no serious problems to the navvies. The absence of stone proved an embarrassment: all stone required in the construction work had to be taken by cart from Callander. When, beyond Strathyre, local stone was found, the owner demanded so high a price that MacKay found it cheaper to continue bringing it from Callander. Later, when he reached the rocky slopes of Glen Ogle, he found all the stone he wanted!

The navvies were well-behaved by the standards of the time. MacKay paid them once a month on the sites where they worked, so that they did not congregate in large groups. One constable patrolled the line, and when the local police authorities announced that a second was to be appointed (at the railway company's expense) Anderson protested that the conduct of the navvies was such that the man was not required. He toured the works, asking local inhabitants if they had been disturbed by the navvies; he heard of only one complaint—a minor disturbance at Strathyre.

In the initial stages the Callander & Oban was buffeted by the tea-cup storms so common in the stories of new railways. It was necessary, as the Act put it, 'to give notice of taking of Houses of the Labouring Classes' when the properties had to be removed to make way for the line; this was done by exhibiting notices a reasonable distance from the houses concerned. But a notice stuck on a tree would not have been acceptable to Sir Malcolm MacGregor, Bart, of Edinchip near Balquhidder. Sir Malcolm wanted the C & O to tunnel under his estate at a cost of £9,000; but Parliament considered that an extravagance. Nevertheless, the Act forbade the company to deviate from its centre line or to take land for temporary work in Edinchip estate; there must be no side cuttings and no spoil banks. The Callander & Oban had to take its pound of flesh, no more, no less. In addition to paying a fair price for the land, it had to agree to handing over an additional £2,500 as compensation for loss of grazing as soon as ground was broken on Edinchip estate.

Blyth's surveyors had no sooner staked out the ground when Sir Malcolm's agents wrote to Anderson claiming the cash. Anderson replied that the surveyors had only passed through the estate and had not broken ground. But he cautioned Blyth, 'Do nothing that could be construed as taking possession. These people seem very anxious to have money from us.' John Stuart McCaig of Oban, a shareholder, wrote asking for a station to be built near his house, and Campbell of Dunstaffnage demanded a £2,500 deviation. But Oban was far away geographically, and even further financially; these requests had only an academic interest for Anderson.

The company lived a hand-to-mouth existence. The fruits of successive calls were never enough to meet current expenditure. When a proprietor from whom land had been purchased agreed to become a shareholder, Anderson confessed to a friend that he hoped he would pay as much in deposit as he charged for his land. He told one of the 'West Highland' directors: 'I am depending on the Caledonian £10,000 for the next contractor's payments.' To MacKay, when he asked to be allowed to proceed with the works more quickly, Anderson explained, 'The company are most anxious to move as slowly and cautiously as possible in all cases where money payments are required.'

He particularly asked MacKay to delay as much as possible in pressing for possession of Edinchip, for the company had not the money to pay the owner's ransom. But in February 1867 MacKay asked Anderson to get possession of Edinchip as a matter of urgency; the permanent way was formed on either side of the estate, and the contractor was having to take plant and materials round the unbroken 1¼ miles of forbidden ground by road. It was not until August of that year that MacKay was allowed to put

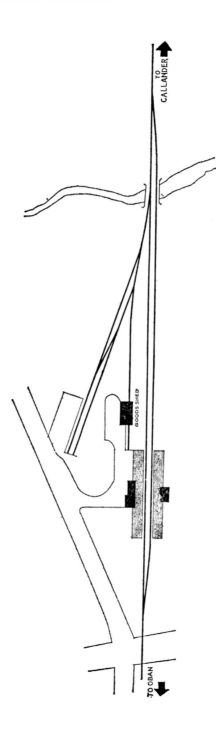

TO CALLANDER

TO OBAN

GOODS SHED

Original layout suggested for Strathyre. Although this layout was suggested the C & O finances stretched only to a single platform, a loop and a short siding. As traffic and revenue built up a second platform and additional sidings were added. The station was burned down in 1893 and rebuilt about four years later

men in Edinchip. The navvies were told not to damage as much as a single tree, and the proprietor's factor was on the spot to see that the instruction was obeyed.

In the summer of 1867, 2,250 tons of rails were delivered at £6 11s 9d per ton and 78 tons of fishplates and bolts at £13 15s per ton. The rails, manufactured by the Rhymney Iron Company, were of assorted lengths: 1,127 were 24 ft long, 97 were 23 ft 9 in , 95 were 23 ft 7 in., 27 were 21 ft and 20 were 18 ft. They were laid on locally-produced larch sleepers. When the Callander & Oban was asked to provide an inspector to supervise the manufacture of the rails in accordance with accepted practice, Anderson declined on the grounds of expense. He considered that his resident engineer, Mr Kerr, who had been appointed in November 1866, could inspect the rails when they arrived. The secretary also thought that if he sent an inspector to the works he 'would not have good grounds for refusing any that were found defective at Callander'.

MacKay was well satisfied with the summer's work and he set his labour force and over 60 horses to preparations for his winter programme. At this point the Caledonian decided that work on the line must stop *for the winter*. The decision was taken at a Callander & Oban board meeting in November 1867 at which only the Caledonian directors were present. Anderson was aghast; far from expecting what might well turn out to be the abandonment of the railway, he had hoped that the meeting would authorise the letting of a contract for the continuation of the railway to Crianlarich or Tyndrum. But on this subject the Caledonian directors were cold and uncompromising: no more money for the Callander & Oban this year. Writing about the fateful meeting to one of his 'West Highland' directors, Anderson said: 'You will notice that none of the promoters was there, and the Caledonian, I believe, had come to a decision in their board room.'

MacKay, of course, shared Anderson's indignation, pointing out that his men did more work in winter than in summer, in proportion to the time employed. 'Being in a Highland district,' he wrote, 'I have a greater command of men than on any other works at present proceeding.' Anderson was not the man to accept the Caledonian dictate without a fight. He argued that postponement of the work would damage the credit of the company, and make it more difficult than ever to get 'calls' honoured, let alone attract new subscribers. And he pointed out that if MacKay was forced to withdraw his plant and labour, the company would be faced with a heavy claim for compensation.

The Caledonian issued an ultimatum: either Anderson must persuade the contractor to accept a token payment for his work, the balance to be paid with interest at an unspecified date in the future, or all work on the line must cease. Anderson explained the

Callander West signal box

position to MacKay, asking him to phase his work so that expenditure was spread over as long a period as possible. Bowing to the inevitable, the contractor accepted the lesser of two evils. Work on the line went on. MacKay had no sooner been placated than Blyth asked for £1,000 due to him. 'Postpone payment until after the next call,' was the instruction recorded in the minute book.

The winter brought storms and floods, but MacKay made progress. After an official inspection of the works in March 1868, Blyth reported that three-fifths of the cuttings and three-quarters of the masonry had been completed, and four major bridges were in a condition to carry the contractor's traffic. 'The contractor,' wrote Blyth,

> has been considerably hampered by wet and stormy weather during the last three months, but has nevertheless made satisfactory progress; upwards of one half of the entire work is now complete. The severe storms of January-February, which did so much damage to other lines, did no injury whatever to these works although in an unfinished state, and the flood of 1 February was 10 inches higher at Callander and about one foot higher in Loch Lubnaig than any of which we could obtain record from the oldest inhabitant when we designed the works. These results are most satisfactory to us as they must be also to the directors. We have studied throughout to make the works substantial yet with a due regard to economy. The line while passing through a difficult country will be made in all respects secure and will be undoubtedly the most beautiful in Scotland.

This confident report pleased the 'West Highland' directors, but left their Caledonian colleagues uncomforted. When 1868 dragged into 1869 and the little railway among the hills was no nearer opening for traffic the anti-Callander & Oban faction campaigned vigorously for the total abandonment of the line beyond Tyndrum. The Callander & Oban Railway (Abandonment) Bill was framed, seeking to limit the company to building 34 miles of line between Callander and a point 300 yards west of Tyndrum Inn, and extending the time allowed for completion to Tyndrum. The original authorised capital was to be reduced from £600,000 to £243,000, of which the Caledonian was to have the privilege of contributing £162,000. The bill relieved the Caledonian of its obligation to continue the railway beyond Tyndrum, but if any other company should extend it to Oban the Caledonian claimed the right to work and maintain it. It sugared the bitter pill by offering to work the completed Callander & Tyndrum Railway at cost.

On 2 February 1870 the boards of the Callander & Oban and the Caledonian Railways held separate meetings in Glasgow to discuss the implications of this Bill. The c & o shareholders were given a glowing description of the progress of their railway and promised that it would be opened for traffic between Callander and Killin at an early date. One of the shareholders had the temerity to ask 'Where is Killin?' He was told that it was three miles from Killin village 'but coaching arrangements are in progress'; he was not told that Killin station was 600 ft above Killin village, at the end of a narrow, winding mountain road.

Meanwhile, half-a-mile away, the shareholders at the Caledonian meeting were hearing that the terminus of the railway was on a

Callander railway station gas lamp

bare hillside and utterly useless. 'The capital expended has been thrown away; the railway is so much waste paper and will never pay for the oil to grease its wheels.' The Caledonian chairman explained that the only solution was to continue the line to Tyndrum, where it would link with the roads from the west and north, from which some traffic could be expected. The meeting approved the decision to stop at Tyndrum, and the chairman declared himself 'very happy'.

The Callander & Oban Railway (Abandonment) Act became law in May 1880. *Abandonment* had an ominous ring. The 'West Highland' directors felt that they were breaking faith with their Oban supporters, but John Anderson had no doubt that the setback was temporary.

THE LOCHEARNHEAD COAL TRAFFIC

On 26 April 1870, *The Scotsman* published an article speculating on the benefits that the railway would bring to residents and tourists alike. 'It will be a great accommodation to tourists and enable them to pass through moor and meadowland, up defiles, over rivulets, lakes and torrents into the very heart of one of the most picturesque and attractive districts in the kingdom.' The writer went on to prophesy that the railway would solve the district's most pressing problem—the transport of heavy goods, particularly coal, at reasonable rates. He then made this intriguing observation: 'Already, and indeed for nearly a year, the inhabitants of Lochearn-head have obtained coal at 13/- per ton whereas formerly the price varied from 18/- to 20/- per ton.' *Already, and indeed for nearly a year*—how had a railway still five weeks short of its opening date been able so long to confer such benefits?

As early as 1867 the irrepressible Anderson had tried to establish revenue-earning traffic on the unfinished line: 'We would only require the use of it so many times a day, and the contractor would be left the free use of it the remainder of the time.' A coal depot was opened at Lochearnhead in August 1868 and a local coal merchant was appointed its manager. The Caledonian worked the coal into Callander, where its agent supervised the handing-over of the traffic to the C & O. MacKay's engine moved the coal over the C & O, the contractor being paid 9d per mile for this service; the records suggest that he brought loads of timber in the reverse direction.

The people of the district were quick to appreciate the advantages of rail transport, and soon residents at Strathyre were petitioning for a parcels service. 'Decline meantime,' Anderson noted in his minute book. There is some evidence that passengers were carried clandestinely. Mr Forbes, a coach operator, made a complaint 'as to parties travelling on the contractor's engine', but Anderson retorted that what MacKay did with his engine was his own business. A stronger communication must have arrived from a source that could not be ignored, for early in 1870 Anderson was instructed by his board to 'intimate to Mr MacKay that the coal traffic must cease at once'.

Anderson had recorded in detail the monthly statistics of the Lochearnhead coal traffic, down to the owners and numbers of the wagons used. In June 1869, 144 tons 19 cwt of coal were railed from Callander to Lochearnhead; in August, 100 tons 14 cwt were handled, and in September 38 wagon loads—making 230 tons 13 cwt. If the Callander & Oban profited from this seemingly lucrative enterprise, it omitted to record the fact in its accounts.

SUCCESS IN SIGHT

The Act of 1865 had specified that the Caledonian would take over the working of the Callander & Oban on the completion of a length of not less than 20 miles. The Callander-Killin stretch was only 17½ miles, and Anderson became anxious when the reply to his request that working should begin was long delayed. However, the Caledonian did eventually agree to work the railway, reserving the right to withdraw its locomotives, rolling-stock and staff at any time. Anderson had difficulty in persuading the Caledonian to form a junction with the c & o at Callander; many letters passed on the subject, but at last, on 3 November 1869, the parent company informed Anderson that it had no objection to the junction being formed 'if the Callander & Oban board desired that the junction should now be made'.

Four stations were planned for the line. In 1867, Blyth had urged Anderson to establish some sort of passenger accommodation behind the Dreadnought Hotel at the west end of the town. (The Caledonian terminus, formerly the terminus of the Dunblane, Doune & Callander, was at the east end.) About the same time Mr Buchanan Smith waited on the c & o directors on behalf of the townspeople with a petition 'praying that a station for Callander be placed behind the Dreadnought Hotel'. The board replied politely, but no firm promise was given. In the event Callander's c & o station was built on the suggested site, and the company extended its line eastwards by 61 chains to link with the Caledonian near the old station. The name 'Dreadnought station' never appeared in public or working timetables, but was used frequently in internal correspondence.

The first intermediate station was at Strathyre, and the second was named Lochearnhead although it was two miles from that village. Killin was situated in open country at the top of Glen Ogle, 950 ft above sea level and close to a small mountain loch, Lochan Larig Eala. There were single platforms at Strathyre, Lochearnhead and Killin, and two platforms, one very short, at Callander.

When John Anderson called on Blyth to produce designs for station buildings he was furnished with an intriguing document. It was labelled at the top 'Portpatrick Railway, 1860', but this was scored out and 'Callander and Oban Railway, 1870' substituted in pencil. Below drawings showing substantial station buildings in stone was the legend 'Crossmichael, Parton, New Galloway, Kirkcowan'. These names had been crossed out and replaced with 'Killin station'. But the grand stone stations of the Portpatrick Railway were beyond the purse of the Callander & Oban. Simple wooden structures were provided at Callander and Killin, and a wooden booking office and porter's lodge had to suffice for Strathyre and Lochearnhead. David McNiven of Doune offered to build Killin station for £193 5s and Callander for £183 10s. The minute book notes 'Accept McNiven if respectable for Callander'.

When it became clear that the railway would be ready for public traffic in early summer, Anderson busied himself providing necessary trappings, such as signals and turntables. Steven & Sons signalled the whole line, with the staff and ticket system, for £466 9s 3d. Cowans Sheldon supplied the Killin turntable for £260 and MacKay the masonry for £133 10s. The chronic shortage of money of course dominated such transactions. When an engine shed at Killin was needed, Anderson demanded 'a rough shed' at a cost not exceeding £50; when McNiven offered to build a shed of rough timber with wood and felt top for £57, he was told to use sacking for roof and sides at a cost of £30; when 12 ft platform seats were offered at 34s each, Anderson opted for 7 ft seats at 22s. In shopping for station furniture he looked for 'cheap grates and wooden chairs or benches'.

Serious negotiations for the employment of Caledonian engines did not begin until eighteen days before the opening of the line. On 13 May 1870, Anderson sent Benjamin Conner, locomotive superintendent of the Caledonian Railway, a rough, thumb-nail sketch of a typical C & O overbridge, with dimensions pencilled in 'from which you will be able to see the size of carriage that will pass through'. Anderson had already informed Conner that the cope of the platform walls was 2 ft 6 in. from the outsides of the rails. He asked the Caledonian to provide him with what any other railway would have been content to call a timetable but what the C & O insisted on calling a *Scheme of Trains*. The Caledonian planned out a service of four trains each way per day between Callander and Killin, but this was too elaborate and too expensive for Anderson, and the timetable that came into force on opening day provided two daily return trains.

Anderson was painfully aware that his isolated station on the hillside would starve of passengers unless he made some arrangement with the coach operators of the Central Highlands. In May he

c & o waiting shed

met the coach proprietors at Crieff, the main outcome being that Forbes of Aberfeldy agreed to run *Queen of Beauty*, 'a well appointed, fast, four-horse coach', between Aberfeldy and Killin, connecting with both Highland Railway and c & o trains. The coach terminated at Killin village, but Anderson persuaded a local coach hirer to provide a service between the village and the station; this vehicle subsequently became celebrated as 'McPherson's bus'.

INSPECTION AND OPENING

On the day that Anderson wrote to Conner about the locomotives he also notified the Board of Trade that his line was ready for inspection, and that he had asked the Caledonian to supply two heavy locomotives for the occasion. 'I suppose this will be sufficient for a single line,' he wrote. 'If not, will you please advise me.' Captain Tyler replied that he would require three engines and a first-class carriage, and that he would leave London for Callander by the Limited Mail on 17 May. A flurry of tidying-up began along the line. Anderson, instructing Galloway, who had taken over from Kerr as resident engineer, to lop branches from a tree to give an improved view of a signal, explained: 'If the Government Inspector finds everything done when he starts it is likely to keep him in a better humour.' With the same end in view Tyler was to be lodged in luxury at Edinchip. Breakfast was arranged for him in a private parlour at the Dreadnought Hotel on the day of his arrival, and the proprietor informed who his guest was and why he had come to Callander.

Tyler was met at Stirling on the morning of 18 May, and spent that day and the next going over the line with Anderson, Ainslie and MacKay. He departed on the second evening without expressing an opinion either way. Meanwhile, Anderson immersed himself in preparations for the opening day. By 20 May neither tickets, dating-machines nor tables of fares had arrived, and Anderson wrote the Caledonian urgently requesting these items. To the Caledonian stores department he wrote: 'I will feel obliged by your sending me a few posters of the opening of our line as I wish to send them to a few friends in the Highlands.'

In spite of his preoccupation with the affairs of the railway in those hectic pre-opening days, the files show that Anderson took time to answer correspondence unconnected with the C & O. A namesake, Robert Anderson, whom he had know in his Edinburgh & Glasgow days, asked for a reference; Anderson composed a long eulogy ending, 'You are qualified for a very much more important charge. Your suavity of manner and gentlemanly address are well fitted to aid you in the conduct of the business of a Railway Company, and I shall be glad to learn that you have been successful in receiving the appointment of Locomotive Superintendent of the Highland Railway Company.' He did not get the job.

Another correspondent asked for information on the working of Villa Tickets. This referred to a scheme that Anderson had thought up for the E & G, whereby people who built houses at Lenzie near Glasgow, and other places on the line, were given free season tickets to Glasgow for periods depending on the value of their houses. To a Highland Railway stationmaster who asked that a friend should be given a job on the C & O, the secretary replied ruefully, 'My experience is that he should not expect much from railway service.'

When by 24 May no word had come from the Board of Trade, Anderson despatched a polite note to the secretary inquiring if the line had met with approval. By the same mail he sent a letter to his chairman, Wingfield Malcolm, who was in London, asking him to use his influence with the Board of Trade. The correspondence files speak eloquently of the flutter that ensued when late on 25 May the stationmaster at Callander received a telegram from Golspie to say that Tyler was on the way south and would visit Callander on the following evening to take another look at the line. Urgently-phrased telegraphs brought Anderson, Ainslie, Galloway and MacKay to the scene. But all that Tyler wanted was a check rail put in on a 15-chain curve. After a very quick look he left Callander, hinting to Anderson that he could safely advertise the opening of the railway for 1 June. On 30 May the long-awaited telegram arrived from the Board of Trade: 'The opening of the Oban and Callander (sic) Railway is allowed; the official papers will be sent this evening.' A grateful Anderson wired back, 'Many thanks for your very kind attention.'

On 1 June more than a hundred people turned up at Killin to ride on the 7.15 a.m. train to Callander. Some came by coach and carriage, but most of them walked up to the hillside station in the dawn hours from Killin village and from places further afield. There was a holiday mood in the district, and the local population set out to enjoy a novel experience. It was regrettable that the Callander & Oban directors did not share their enthusiasm: invitations to the opening ceremony were sent to all nine of them, but the Caledonian representatives ignored the occasion, and only one of the 'West Highland' directors attended—Daniel Ainslie who lived in Callander.

About 11 a.m. a special train set off from Callander with local dignitaries and invited guests. They had an exhilarating trip. Never before had they travelled in such country in such a fashion. The Pass of Leny opened in the mountains west of Callander and the train climbed up its lush green floor with the broken brown-and-white waters of the Leny churning alongside. The railway crossed and re-crossed the tumbling river on slender, single-span, bowstring-girder bridges. (What a headache they were to present to future locomotive designers.) At the head of the pass the line skirted St Bride's, where the messenger of Roderick Dhu in Scott's tale thrust his dramatic signal into the bridegroom's hand as he left the church. There was a swift change of scene as the railway picked up Loch Lubnaig and wound along its shore at water level, with the mountains rising steeply on the opposite side of the carriages. This was the route of the fiery cross:

> Ben Ledi saw the cross of fire,
> It glanced like lightning up Strathyre.

The villagers of Strathyre were at the station to welcome the train, which after a brief halt trundled on up the narrow valley by Kingshouse and the Braes of Balquhidder and across the MacGregor stronghold of Edinchip to Lochearnhead station. Then came the highlight of the trip. The train emerged on the mountain-face above Loch Earn, climbing steadily all the time and giving exciting views out over the loch; in the years to come experienced travellers were to say that this was the finest view obtainable from a British train.

The line turned into the rocky defile of Glen Ogle, and clinging to the narrow ledge that MacKay had blasted out of the mountain, climbed further and further up the west wall of the glen. On the other side of the glen, far below, was the coach road, and on the floor a broken, eroded track, the work of General Wade who had first brought transport to this remote pass.

All too soon the train reached the summit of the pass and stopped at Killin station. Coaches were waiting to take some of the passengers down to Killin village and back. Most wandered over the mountainside until departure time, but a few of the bolder spirits walked down Glen Ogle and rejoined the train at Lochearnhead.

When Anderson was back in Glasgow that night he went to his office and wrote identical letters to the three absentee 'West Highland' directors.

> 1 June 1880
> 8 p.m.
>
> Dear Sir,
>
> I have just returned from Callander. We have had a very successful opening. It was made quite a holiday in the Killin district, and about 120 passengers left there by the first train in the morning. The day was fine and really the district looked magnificent. Mr Ainslie was the only director present. He had a number of his Callander friends with him.

The secretary took time that evening to write to A. & W. Smith of the Cook Street Engine Works, Glasgow. 'Please forward the weighing machines for the Callander and Oban Railway *at once*,' he urged. 'We are feeling the want of them very much.'

Like the Callander & Oban, the Dingwall & Skye Railway had been thwarted in its efforts to reach the Western Seas. Financial and engineering difficulties brought abandonment of the last ten miles to the Kyle of Lochalsh. But on 19 August 1880 the 53 miles between Dingwall and Strome Ferry on Loch Carron were opened for traffic. The Skye line had spent £227,081 in getting there. In the same period the Callander & Oban had spent £195,694 in pushing its line 17½ miles to Glen Ogle. At least the *Skye* railway had reached salt water; the Callander & Oban still had 54 miles to go. And there was only £24,204 in the bank.

Glen Cruitten summit

OBAN

(9) *Oban Bay about 1890 showing railway pier, station and North Pier.
One plan was to take the railway across the bay to the North Pier.*
(10) *The approach to Oban station and pier in 1880, showing the
'commodious signalling station'*

CALLANDER STATION

(11) *Coaches awaiting the arrival of the train, about 1895*

(12) *A busy morning in 1959. A diesel excursion, No. 45153, on 9.18 a.m. Oban-Glasgow, and No. 45213 on an up freight*

CHAPTER IV

John Anderson's Railway

THE FIRST MONTHS

If the people of the district had been reluctant to part with money for C&O shares, they showed no reluctance in applying for free passes once the railway was opened. Ministers, doctors and hotel-keepers seemed to think they were entitled to travel free of charge. Such applicants received short shrift. 'Offer him a season ticket at the normal rates,' was the board's instruction to Anderson when a Killin doctor applied for a pass. Most applications were filed with the word 'reject' scrawled across them. The editor of the *Perthshire Advertiser* was told that he would get a pass on special occasions only. But an application from John Bett, the factor of the Marquis of Breadalbane's estates, was granted with alacrity: it was important to keep on the right side of Breadalbane's man.

The first complaint against the Callander & Oban reached Anderson's office on the railway's second working day. Consignments of freight for John McPherson and Charles Stewart of Killin which were to have been sent up the line on 1 June, were still lying at Callander station on 2 June, apparently because the Caledonian had neglected to supply a table of freight rates to the stationmaster. Anderson was annoyed, for Charles Stewart was a faithful supporter of the railway; the Callander stationmaster was wired to forward the freight at once.

On the fourth day Anderson insured his stations against fire: Callander for £230, Strathyre for £175, Lochearnhead for £250, and Killin for £240. Fires were in fact distressingly frequent at C&O stations: at a later date a firemaster was to describe Callander station, with its pinewood and paint, as the worst fire hazard in the county.

Callander station was C&O property, as was the 61-chain extension of the line to Callander Junction. Until 1891 the Caledonian paid the C&O £1,700 a year for services provided at Callander station, and from 1 August 1891 the parent company contributed £800 annually towards the cost of repairs and maintenance. Two-

D

thirds of the stationmaster's wage was paid by the C & O and one-third by the Caledonian; the wages of booking and parcels clerks, ticket collectors and porters, were chargeable to the C & O. The signalman at the junction box was appointed by the Caledonian and paid by the C & O. (It was a twenty-seven lever box, eleven levers working to the goods yard, eleven to the main line, and five spare.) The cost of running the goods department was apportioned between the two companies in accordance with tonnage handled.

Passengers could book at Callander for destinations on the Caledonian and beyond. The first 61 chains of their journey on C & O metals was reckoned for accounting purposes as two miles, which meant that the C & O took 2d to 4d for every Caledonian passenger booked. This length of C & O track was, incidentally, described in the Caledonian Junction Arrangements Book as being 'between Dreadnought Station and Callander Junction'.

The gibe was levelled at the C & O that it went to nowhere. Nevertheless it was a showpiece. In an hour visitors were whisked from the serenity of Callander to the rocky grandeur of Glen Ogle. Anderson himself wrote the advertisements for the first excursions, promising to take his passengers to 'the Khyber Pass of Scotland'. In the Caledonian public timetable that summer, among the more conventional operating footnotes appeared the following: 'The view of Loch Earn and the impressive wilds of Glen Ogle as seen from the railway is one of the grandest in Scotland.' In July, Anderson felt justified in adding another train each way to the timetable which now read:

Callander	9.35 am	11.10	6.0 pm
Strathyre	10.20	11.42	6.32
Lochearnhead	10.40	11.53	6.48
Killin	11.0	12.10	7.0

Killin	7.15 am	2.40 pm	6.20 pm
Lochearnhead	7.34	3.10	6.43
Strathyre	7.45	3.25	6.55
Callander	8.15	4.0	7.30

Saturday afternoon excursions were run from Glasgow to Killin at 4s 6d return and to Strathyre and Lochearnhead at 4s 3d. The single fare by coach from Killin station to Killin village was 9d for railway ticket holders and 1s for ordinary passengers. From Killin station to Luib hotel the fare was 1s 8d plus the coachman's fee of 6d. All trains stopped at Laggan Farm House on Loch Lubnaig by request, mainly for the benefit of trout and salmon fishers. During the summer a coach left Killin station daily for Oban and Balla-chulish, giving a connection from the 6.30 am from Edinburgh Waverley and the 6.50 and 7.10 from Glasgow Buchanan Street; the coach in the opposite direction connected with the 6.20 pm from Killin. This through coach was operated by Dr Campbell of Balla-chulish, and the fares for the single journey were 11s inside and 17s outside. Coach operators in the Killin area resented Campbell's appearance and refused to accommodate his horses at Killin. An appeal for help to Anderson brought the reply, 'I have found it almost impossible to fight against the powers in the district if they are dissatisfied, but I cannot see why any person should be offended on account of your coach.' Anderson was most anxious to maintain the link with Oban and he found accommodation for the horses in the contractor's stables; when these became disused the c & o built a special hut.

The people of Kingshouse, between Strathyre and Lochearnhead, were disappointed at being given no station of their own, and in October 1870 they petitioned for a platform. Anderson told them to build one themselves, but to the satisfaction of the railway company —which they did. It was opened on 21 June 1871. Drivers were instructed to stop when anybody was waiting there. The c & o must have had a poor opinion of the people of Kingshouse: an instruc-tion in the working timetable concerning passengers boarding trains at the platform read 'Guards must point out such passengers to the stationmasters at Strathyre or Lochearnhead so that the fares may be collected and the passengers rebooked.' When, at one stage, the local people asked the c & o to extend the platform, the board agreed provided the petitioners supplied the timber free. The good people of Kingshouse decided to accept this condition if the railway company would carry a daily mail-bag for them. This the c & o considered blatant blackmail: 'We cannot come under such an obligation as concessions would involve,' Anderson told them.

With the end of summer the excursion traffic vanished, and two short trains a day were sufficient. By the end of six months the line's gross earnings were £2,511—enough to enable the company to declare a dividend of 1 per cent and carry forward £368. Anderson must have longed for the passing of that first winter. With the coming of summer 1871 he was writing to the Caledonian 'I wish a few good excursions could be got over our line before the next half-yearly balance comes on.' He pleaded with the Caledonian to run regular trips to the line on Saturdays: 'Were this worked well I am satisfied that our balance sheet would be improved.'

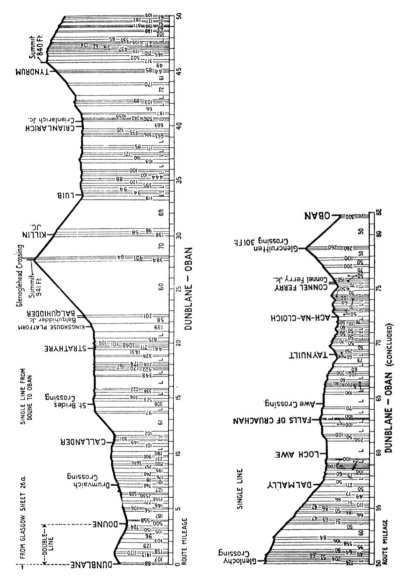

Gradient profile : Dunblane-Oban

A BRUSH WITH THE NORTH BRITISH

A minute with the alarming heading 'Reported occupation of Callander station by the North British Railway' reflects a brush Anderson had with the North British in the early days over the running of that company's trains into Callander station. The North British did not have running powers into the c & o station, but they had a special agreement with the Caledonian to terminate a specified number of trains there. The Callander & Oban received a few pence for every North British passenger. Anderson kept a close watch on North British traffic, and he found that the trains were arriving in Callander with only one or two passengers, so the revenue was insufficient to pay for their servicing. Anderson complained to Archibald Gibson, the secretary of the Caledonian : 'The N.B. Railway Company's trains run into our station under your company's authority, and I must protest against the continuance of the present state of matters.' Anderson wanted payment per carriage, not per passenger, with a fixed minimum for each train. The North British promptly withdrew its service.

In the late autumn of 1870 the c & o secretary heard a rumour that the North British was considering making a branch line from Callander (old station) to the Trossachs. 'This would leave us outside altogether,' he wrote to a friend. 'There is not much time to lose if we are to occupy the ground first.' He at once set about promoting the Trossachs Railway, and the first his directors knew about it was when they received a prospectus, along with the notice of the next routine half-yearly meeting.

The branch was to leave the c & o a mile west of Callander station and run for 8¼ miles by the north shore of Loch Vennacher to Loch Katrine. Anderson and Galloway, in October 1870, trudged round the shores of Loch Vennacher themselves looking for the best route. The proposed line ran for six miles through Lord Murray's policies, the rest of it being in Montrose territory. Lord Murray's factor was hostile, and the Duke of Montrose showed no enthusiasm, but the secretary was confident that he could win them over. Baird, of the Trossachs hotel, near the proposed terminus of the railway, spoke in glowing terms of the lucrative tourist trade; and Anderson enlisted the support of influential local people, notably Walter Buchanan, the Callander banker.

A setback came when the Caledonian sent Anderson its estimate of tourist traffic in the Trossachs, based on through tour bookings :

this was much less optimistic than Baird had been. Anderson pleaded with Baird to produce accurate figures, not only of the coach traffic but of the steamer traffic on Loch Katrine. He also told him to canvass local residents and submit a list of subscribers.

The Trossachs Railway was considered at the next meeting of the board, but a decision was deferred on the grounds that a bill could not be prepared in time for the next parliamentary session. But the c & o had enough worries without adding the problems of an unnecessary branch line; when the North British made no further sortie towards Loch Katrine, the plans were quietly dropped. The Trossachs Railway reappeared in various guises now and then, but the Trossachs remained railless for all time.

ON TO TYNDRUM

The Caledonian, in spite of protests from outraged shareholders, put up enough money for the Tyndrum contract to be advertised. Nine contractors tendered for the job; MacKay's offer was £79,458 16s 11d. The c & o board was much attracted by the lowest offer of all, £69,108 from Granger of Strathpeffer; but Granger wanted an extra £792 for a cutting which though described in the plans as through soil he insisted would be through rock. Easton Gibb of Cardiff offered to do the job for £69,261 with no extras. Anderson was instructed by the board to let to Gibb on condition that the works progressed fast enough to appear to the engineer likely to be finished within the stipulated period, 'or failing then the Company to have the option of reletting the contract risk and expense'. If Gibb declined these conditions Anderson was to accept Granger's offer, provided he could beat him down to £260 10s for the rock cutting. Gibb accepted, but when a few weeks later he discovered an arithmetical error of £100 in his estimate, the c & o board expressed extreme annoyance. Nevertheless, he launched out with the contract, work commencing in October 1871.

The route from Killin to Tyndrum was 17 miles long. The line dropped from the summit at Glen Ogle on a gradient of 1 in 69 to reach the slopes flanking the south side of Glen Dochart; then it passed westwards through Luib to Crianlarich before turning north up Strathfillan to Tyndrum. No special engineering problems arose in this hill grazing country, though there was trouble over the threatened despoilation of a salmon pool: the board placated the hostile owner by taking a wide curve round the pool. The line was opened to Tyndrum in August 1873. Oban was still 36¾ miles and a five-and-a-half-hour coach journey away.

Anderson now had a 34½-mile railway at his command. He had entered into an elaborate series of agreements with coach and steamboat operators to attract every possible tourist. Much of the Scottish holiday traffic in those days was concentrated in the far-away Firth of Clyde resorts, and this was potentially a rich source of revenue. Some of the vessels plying their complex system of sailings from Helensburgh, Greenock, Dunoon, Rothesay and other Firth towns penetrated far up the sea lochs into the heart of Argyll, and the *Chancellor* sailed to Arrochar at the head of Loch Long. Anderson arranged for a new coach to pick up passengers disem-

LOCH DOCHART.

barking at Arrochar pier, to go on to collect those from the Loch Lomond steamer at Ardlui, and to deliver them at the C & O Crianlarich station. From there they returned to Glasgow or the Firth of Clyde *via* the C & O and Caledonian railways, through tickets being issued for the tour.

Through tickets were also issued by MacBrayne's steamer *Iona*, which sailed up to Ardrishaig in Loch Fyne; from here a coach connection ran to Tyndrum *via* Dalmally. Tickets were also issued from Callander & Oban stations to Glasgow *via* Loch Lomond; passengers by this service travelled from Crianlarich to Ardlui by coach, from Ardlui to Balloch at the foot of Loch Lomond by steamer, and thence by train to Glasgow. Although this route took Glasgow passengers away from the Caledonian, Anderson asked the company to exhibit at Dunblane a board inscribed 'Passengers for Loch Lomond via Crianlarich change here.' 'It might help us against Loch Lomond via the Trossachs,' he explained.

Anderson went to extraordinary lengths to attract excursion traffic. To be a success an excursion over c & o metals had to originate in Glasgow, Edinburgh or some other southern centre of population, and the Caledonian needed much prodding before it would initiate a train. When the secretary proposed to run an excursion to Killin on the Queen's Birthday holiday in May 1875, he wrote to Irvine Kempt of the Caledonian : 'I hope you will have this carried out *and advertise it well and in good time.*' On 11 May he had received no reply and wrote to Kempt again : 'I hope you have got all arrangements for this. I would like to see it advertised early.' Two days before the holiday the Caledonian indicated that the train would run; on the same day Anderson wrote to the hotel proprietors along the line :

> Thursday first the 20th inst is to be a holiday here, and we are to try an Excursion train as far as Killin. I write you this note to warn you that you may have an extra number of people. I have suggested that a bill may be sent to you so that you may have particulars.

Letters also advised coach proprietors to meet the train at Killin. On the day after the excursion Anderson told Kempt : 'This to my mind was a success seeing that the public had only two days' notice.'

The Caledonian agreed to issue excursion tickets every Saturday from Glasgow, Larbert, Stirling, Bridge of Allan, Dunblane and Callander to all stations on the c & o. Anderson's determination to build up his excursions is again revealed in his correspondence with the proprietor of Crianlarich Hotel, whom he *instructed* to employ a guide to meet the trains on Saturdays and take the passengers to the summit of Ben More. With the letter Anderson enclosed a draft advertisement which the hotel keeper was told to insert in the newspapers *at his own expense* :

> I cannot offer to pay any part of the advertisement as other parties in that case would ask us to do the same, but a few advertisements in the Glasgow and Stirling papers and a hand bill at the railway

stations would not amount to much. I hope you will go into it as I have had some difficulty in carrying it and am anxious for its success.

Anderson added that he hoped the Marquis of Breadalbane and his factor, John Bett, would not object to the excursionists wandering over their mountain.

The advertisement itself read:

Mountain Climbing and Fishing

Joseph Stewart, Hotel Keeper, Crianlarich, begs to inform the public return tickets are now issued at single fare from Glasgow and other stations to Crianlarich, and that he has arranged for a guide conducting the excursionists to the top of Ben More, 3,843 feet high, on arrival of the first train from the South, and that he has also arranged to have boats in readiness for parties fishing on Loch Dochart.

LOCH AWE.

At the time when Anderson was struggling to popularise his railway, the Caledonian was making much of Bridge of Allan as a spa-type resort. Anderson considered that Strathyre had a climate at least as good as Bridge of Allan's, but he had no proof. So he set up a weather-observation station at Strathyre, and in July 1874 the stationmaster was provided with a specially-ruled meteorological register with instruction on how to measure rainfall. On 30 September, Anderson wrote to the stationmaster:

I send you Thermometer by Passenger Train today which I hope you will receive all right. You must not be frightened for it. Should it at any time get fixed tap it on the side with your hand or give it a sharp swing by your side and you will find that it will at once come all right again. I have seen the optician and he says that the one now sent you is one of the very best kind in existence for the purpose wanted, and is so easily put right at any time. I shall be glad to hear that you get on all right with it.

But the stationmaster seems to have had some difficulty with his thermometer; some of the readings suggested that the equator must have slipped. At the end of the first year Anderson sent a summary of the Strathyre records to Alexander Buchan, secretary of the Meteorological Society and an international authority on thermo-metrical analyses, explaining:

> I instituted these observations believing that Strathyre was equally as mild as Bridge of Allan. If not asking too much I would be glad to receive your observation on return. There are some blanks in the Registration on account of our stationmaster not thoroughly under-standing the workings of the instruments and on several occasions the thermometer was broken, but now the registration goes on satis-factorily.

The coach that linked Tyndrum with Oban passed along the south shore of Loch Etive and through Connel Ferry. Across the water the districts of Benderloch and Appin were linked to the south shore and the coach road by a small ferry operating at irregular intervals. If a coach could take passengers from Appin to the north shore of Loch Etive, and a ferry could then take them across the loch in time to pick up the Oban-Tyndrum coach, Anderson felt that some of the people would eventually reach the trains. Some of the mails from the north, which were then conveyed from Ballachulish by Hutchison's steamers, might also be captured. Dr Campbell of Ballachulish was asked if he could provide the Appin-Connel Ferry connection, 'even a horse-trap'. Macfie, one of the 'West Highland' directors, lived in Appin, and Anderson's letter to him, urging that a boat should be stationed on each side of Loch Etive, gives a glimpse of passenger communication in the Highlands before the railway age. 'I will not detail all the miseries that have been stated to me as you may know them well, such as waiting two or three hours on the north side waiting the boat coming, shouting, whistling, making bonfires, etc.' Also 'the dreadful inconvenience for the greater part of the year in waiting upon Hutchison's boats would make people seek our route'.

Anderson made it his business to find out at first hand the public reaction to his railway's services. A local resident was asked:

> Will you be good enough to let me know how the trains are pleasing the folk up about your quarter this month, whether or not you have heard of any complaints or if it could be advantageous to have the

goods train leave Tyndrum at half-past two o'clock with a composite carriage attached so as to give a later outing from the country?

In the midst of his bustle Anderson found time to design notice-boards for the 'Ladies' at Luib, Tyndrum and Crianlarich. He sent a sketch of what he wanted to the stores department of the Caledonian, with instructions that the boards must be 'nicely painted and with gilt letters. I consider this better than sending a man away up there to paint it on the doors.'

'THE CALEDONIAN PEOPLE'

To a friend who had criticised the C & O winter timetable of 1874, Anderson's comment was, 'I am not much surprised at your complaint,' and he went on to castigate 'the Caledonian people', ending 'Please do not quote this letter in any way.'

The timetable concerned was as follows:

Callander	9.40 am	6.35 pm
Strathyre	10.10	7.2
Lochearnhead	10.27	7.16
Killin	11.0	7.45
Luib	11.22	8.5
Crianlarich	11.44	8.25
Tyndrum	12.0	8.40
Tyndrum	5.45 am	1.30 pm
Crianlarich	6.2	1.47
Luib	6.22	2.7
Killin	6.47	2.34
Lochearnhead	7.7	2.55
Strathyre	7.20	3.10
Callander	7.45	3.35

After a few weeks the up trains were timed to leave Tyndrum at 5.30 a.m. and 2 p.m. respectively. The down morning and the up afternoon trains were mixed, and connected with the coaches to and from Oban. A coach connection was also given to Fort William by the Glencoe and Glenorchy coach on alternate days in winter and daily in summer. The coach left Fort William at 5.30 a.m., Ballachulish at 7.45, and arrived at Tyndrum to connect with the 2 p.m. train for the south.

Anderson knew the requirements of the community; the Caledonian, on the other hand, ignored local needs, and imposed on the C & O a timetable which suited its own engine workings. The 5.30 a.m. departure time was a bone of contention; Anderson thought 5.30 was absurdly early to start a train from a small West Highland

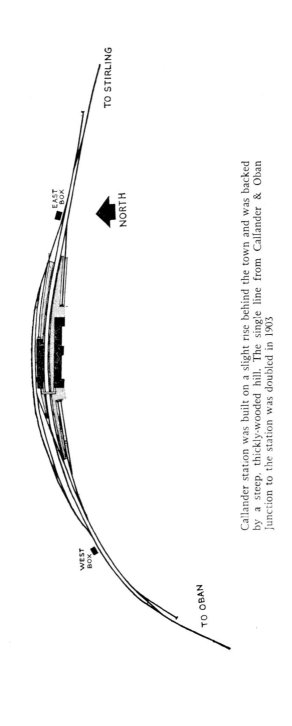

TO STIRLING

EAST
BOX

NORTH

WEST
BOX

TO OBAN

Callander station was built on a slight rise behind the town and was backed by a steep, thickly-wooded hill. The single line from Callander & Oban Junction to the station was doubled in 1903

railhead, especially in the depths of winter, and asked for the time to be advanced to 8 a.m. But the 5.30 departure allowed the engine to do certain purely Caledonian chores in the neighbourhood of Dunblane before returning to Tyndrum on the afternoon down train, and the Caledonian insisted on it. 'Practically money thrown away,' was Anderson's verdict. His request for a 3 p.m. afternoon departure was similarly rejected.

As in the railway's first winter, traffic justified only the two trains each way per day, each consisting of two carriages and a van when required. There was no goods train. Anderson kept a close watch on the format and loading of the trains; if the Caledonian sent more coaches than were required—and for which the c & o had to pay—he lost no time in complaining. Winter traffic was indeed so sparse that Anderson considered reducing the service to only one mixed train daily between Callander and Tyndrum, and one return service between Killin and Callander, but the idea had to be abandoned because neither engines nor men could now be housed at Killin. The engine-shed and turntable had been moved bodily to Tyndrum.

When 'the Caledonian people' proposed raising their charges to the c & o for the use of engine power from the originally agreed 8d per mile to 1s, Anderson of course fought back. He pointed out that the cost of running an engine on the Caledonian, Glasgow & South Western and North British was, respectively, $10\frac{3}{4}$d, 9d and $8\frac{1}{2}$d per mile—an average of $9\frac{1}{2}$d. Why was the c & o to be charged 1s? 'If you say that the c & o line has stiff gradients I grant it, but the answer is that the trains are generally light and your company neither supply water nor light, which is an item in your locomotive expenditure, and we provide stabling.' Smithells of the Caledonian was extremely hurt because Anderson introduced the Glasgow & South Western and the North British into the dispute and he protested strongly. Anderson retorted, 'As you object to me seeking to base cost upon the figures of any other line I have looked at the average cost per day of your own engines,' and proceeded to catalogue the results of his researches among the Caledonian Railway half-yearly reports.

He told Smithells that out of 620 engines owned by the Caledonian, 475 were in traffic on any one day; the cost of operating them, according to the accounts, was £240,449 for a half year or £3 11s 6d per engine per day. The c & o timetable called for 140 engine miles a day per engine, which at 1s per mile meant £7 a day per engine. But the same engine, in addition to its Callander & Oban duties, did

48 miles wholly on Caledonian metals, at a presumed cost of £2 8s. The apparent cost of running the engine allocated to the C & O was £9 8s per day compared with the Caledonian average of £3 11s 6d per day. In the year ending 30 September 1874 the C & O paid the Caledonian £620 0s 2d for carriage mileage and £223 1s 4d for wagons, a total of £843 1s 6d.

Anderson calculated that the capital value of all the Caledonian stock used on the C & O was not more than £2,000 : 'Your company is certainly entitled to interest, depreciation and repairs, but I believe you will agree with me that a sum which would recoup your railway for original cost in about three years is excessive.' And he added : 'At the same time you inconvenience our traffic by arranging times of trains for us to save engines in steam.'

Anderson's most celebrated skirmish in his running battle with the Caledonian was over the lateness of trains. This, he maintained, was due to slipshod Caledonian operating methods between Larbert and Callander, which resulted in trains being handed over late at Callander. Anderson's directors told him to record the following minute : 'Trains from Edinburgh to Callander are systematically detained between Larbert and Callander and desire that a remonstrance should be made to the Caledonian Railway Company.' The *systematically detained* stung James Smithells into replying, on 18 November 1873 :

> I am instructed by my Directors to say that they very much regret that a report so unjust to this company should have been made by a Director of the Callander and Oban Company.
> On referring to the records of the running of the trains between Edinburgh and Callander during the month of October last, I find that on an average they were handed over by the North British Company at Larbert 19 minutes behind time, while the average time lost on the Caledonian lines between Larbert and Callander was 8 minutes, the distance hauled being in both cases about the same. With the large traffic we have to work on the Central Section it is impossible to run the trains to time when once they are late and out of proper order, as other trains get in their way, and the lines become otherwise occupied, and I am satisfied that anyone practically acquainted with the working of Railway Traffic will admit that as the trains are never delivered to us on time at Larbert, this Company ought not and cannot be expected to run them punctually north of Larbert.
> In the circumstances my Directors consider that the 'remonstrance' referred to in the Minutes of your Board ought to have been directed against the North British Company, and they desire that this letter be submitted to your Board at their next meeting, and that it be recorded upon your minutes as the Official reply of the Company to your minute of 31st ultimo.

And the Caledonian had not finished with the matter. In the next few weeks it took the trouble to study the timings of c & o trains, and on 3 December Smithells wrote to Anderson:

> I find that during the month of October last the trains from Edinburgh to Tyndrum regarding which the complaint was made against the Caledonian Railway, arrived at Tyndrum on the average nearer the time than they were handed over to us at Larbert, so that in no way has the C and O Company's trains been delayed by this Company.

The Caledonian correspondence was duly inscribed in the Callander & Oban minute book and Ainslie, one of the 'West Highland' directors, 'professed his satisfaction in finding that the detention complained of originated with the North British and not with the Caledonian Railway Company'.

DALMALLY

On 3 February 1874 the c & o board received the assent of its shareholders to frame a bill for the extension of the line from Tyndrum to Oban. Recent results had been poor. Passenger and livestock receipts were up, but other revenues had dropped. After the last half-year's expenses had been paid the company had £480 in hand—not enough to pay ½ per cent dividend. The board thought that only the completion of the line through to Oban would bring an end to difficulties. The Callander & Oban Railway (Tyndrum and Oban) Act received the Royal Assent on 11 July 1874, but it was not until March 1875 that construction tenders were invited; and even then only for the first 12 miles.

The new venture of course involved John Anderson in another round of money-raising. He made a special effort to tap the people who would benefit directly from the extension, and some of his letters were surprisingly curt: he *ordered* the locals to subscribe. To Fraser, of Dalmally Hotel, near which the extension would pass, he wrote:

> I feel very much that the West Highland directors on the board may get soured altogether, for they really have not got the support they deserved, and they have frequently had to take heavy burdens on themselves. I would like to see a respectable sum opposite your name and I must ask you to let me put down your subscription at £300. The money will not all be required at once, and I feel certain that you will be the first to feel the advantage from the extension, and you will soon recoup yourself the amount I have named. Be good enough to let me have an answer, and a favourable one, by Saturday.

Fraser took twenty shares at £10 each.

Breadalbane gave the ground on which the railway was to be built, in exchange for shares—at least, he sent his factor Bett to tell Anderson that he intended to do so. But Anderson was not content with a verbal contract, and he insisted in getting the agreement in writing. Two months later the marquis still had not returned his subscription contract: 'Could you wire asking its return to me as a great favour?' inquired Anderson of Bett.

The long-suffering Caledonian had the honour of making the largest single contribution to the extension. In May, when the extension was discussed, a shareholder described the C & O as 'a blister on the company', and worse trouble was expected at the July meeting, on the announcement that the Caledonian had subscribed £20,000. But the chairman began by telling his audience that the Caledonian dividend was up from 2 per cent to $6\frac{1}{4}$ per cent, that traffic was on the increase, that ordinary stock had risen from 75 to 130 in eight years, and that all would get a bonus in the shape of new stock. All this good news must have acted as a soporific, for there was not a murmur of dissent at the news of a further investment in the withered western arm. The meeting, reported a financial columnist, was 'numerously attended, was perfectly unanimous and harmonious, and almost as perfectly silent'.

John MacKay got the job of building the 12 miles of railway from Tyndrum westward to Dalmally. The line ran for the first five miles through almost treeless Glen Lochy on a gently-falling gradient, then plunged for seven miles on an average gradient of 1 in 55 down to Dalmally. There were no intermediate stations. A new two-platform station was built three hundreds yards west of the existing station at Tyndrum.

At this point occurred the curious episode of Henry Dübs and the steel rails. In May 1875, Anderson asked the Caledonian stores department for the names of manufacturers of steel rails, these being required for the Dalmally extension. Tenders were duly invited from recommended firms. But in the same month Anderson and Henry Dübs, famous as the proprietor of the Glasgow Locomotive Works (later part of the North British Locomotive Company), engaged in a curious correspondence on the subject of steel rails; curious because Dübs had hitherto in no way been associated with the supply or manufacture of rails. The letters suggest that Anderson was most anxious for Dübs to get the contract, and Dübs was equally anxious to do so. He offered to accept payment by bill, but

STRATHYRE

(13) *Strathyre station about 1890. The station buildings were destroyed by fire in 1893*

(14) *Class 5 No. 45496 at Strathyre with the 11.50 a.m. Glasgow-Oban, on 12 August 1961*

TOWARDS TAYNUILT

(15) *The line under construction in the Pass of Brander, 1879*
(16) *Awe viaduct newly completed, 1880*

Anderson answered that the C&O always paid in cash; however 'your kind offer will be appreciated'. Letters were exchanged twice during May, and at least one meeting took place in Glasgow, when the secretary told Dübs that the directors had not yet decided whether to use iron or steel rails. In the end Dübs failed to get the contract. Anderson wrote formally to the unsuccessful tenderers, but more cordially to Dübs:

2 June 1875

Steel Rails

I am sorry to inform you that the order for the above has been given to another maker.

An offer was voluntarily made to us last Friday by one of the offerers which was lower than yours, and as the maker's name stands well in the market it has been accepted.

I am sorry that a small difficulty took the order away from you.

The only civil engineering feature of note on the extension was the masonry viaduct at Succoth on the descent to Dalmally. It was finished by November 1876. On a raw Monday afternoon a party of ladies and gentlemen were taken up the line on a contractor's wagon to see Mrs Dinnie, wife of the builder, set the keystone; flags fluttered from the hilltops above the bridge, and the navvies' huts were decorated with flags and bunting. A reporter from a local newspaper noted that Mrs Dinnie did the job 'in a very graceful and workmanlike manner'. The party then adjourned to a wooden platform which the contractor had built above one end of the viaduct and on which he had installed a whisky cask and a piper. In this bizarre and chilly setting the whisky flowed, the bagpipes skirled, and the guests danced until the gathering darkness drove them back to their train.

The line was opened to Dalmally on 1 May 1877. The Oban & Dalmally Coach Company provided services described as connecting with the trains of the Callander & Oban, Caledonian and London & North Western Railways. Through tickets to Oban, including the coach journey, were issued from the principal LNW stations.

Passengers for Oban on the late-afternoon train stayed overnight at Dalmally, resuming by coach at 7 next morning. Those travelling south by the 7 p.m. coach from Oban also stayed overnight, and caught the 5.45 train in the morning.

Dalmally, standing at the head of Loch Awe and on the road to Inveraray on Loch Fyne, provided Anderson with wonderful scope for circular tours. He held a joint meeting with coach and steamer operators, including the proprietor of the Loch Awe steamer, and a complex system of tours was worked out. One example involved

E

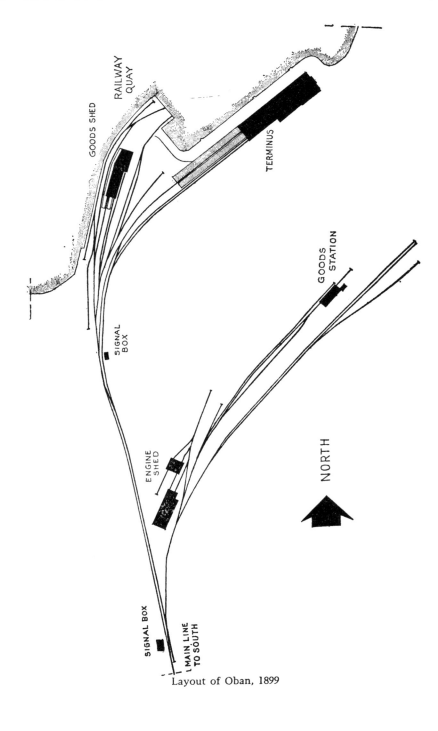

GOODS SHED

RAILWAY QUAY

TERMINUS

GOODS STATION

SIGNAL BOX

ENGINE SHED

NORTH

SIGNAL BOX

MAIN LINE TO SOUTH

Layout of Oban, 1899

a sail from the Clyde through the Kyles of Bute and up Loch Fyne to Inveraray, thence by coach and Loch Awe steamer to Dalmally; return was by rail over the Callander & Oban and Caledonian. Through day fares for this tour were quoted from points as far distant as Carlisle—the round trip from Carlisle, third class, including coachmen's fees, costing £1 12s 2d. Passengers left Carlisle at 3.50 a.m. and arrived back at 11.55 p.m.

The combined timetable was as follows:

Up

Oban		9.20 am	1.0 pm	7.0 pm
Connel Ferry		9.50	1.30	
Taynuilt *arr.*		10.50	2.30	8.35
Taynuilt *dep.*		10.55	2.35	8.40
Dalmally *arr.*		12.50 pm	4.25	10.35
Dalmally	5.45 am	1.30 pm	5.0 pm	
Tyndrum	6.15	2.1	5.30	
Crianlarich	6.28	2.15	5.42	
Luib	6.43	2.31	5.56	
Killin	7.0	2.48	6.11	
Lochearnhead	7.14	3.3	6.25	
Strathyre	7.24	3.13	6.35	
Callander	7.45	3.35	6.55	
Stirling	8.36	4.45	8.7	
Glasgow	9.30	5.53	9.15	
Edinburgh	9.50	6.30	9.45	

Down

Edinburgh		6.5 am	8.30 am	3.35 pm
Glasgow		7.0	9.0	4.5
Stirling		8.18	10.18	5.5
Callander		9.20	11.7	6.10
Strathyre		9.41	11.28	6.35
Lochearnhead		9.52	11.40	6.47
Killin		10.7	11.55	7.5
Luib		10.21	12.10 pm	7.21
Crianlarich		10.36	12.25	7.38
Tyndrum		10.50	12.40	7.54
Dalmally		11.20	1.10	8.25
Dalmally	7.0 am	11.35	1.25 pm	
Taynuilt *arr.*	8.55	1.25 am	3.15	
Taynuilt *dep.*	9.0	1.45	3.40	
Connel Ferry		2.40	4.30	
Oban	10.35	3.20	5.10	

THE LAST LAP

Almost exactly a year passed between the opening of the line to Dalmally and work beginning on the final 24½ miles to Oban. There had to be the usual money-gathering pause. This time the London & North Western Railway came to the rescue with the purchase of £50,000 of 4½ per cent preference stock. The English company was given the right to appoint one director to the c & o board. In practice this meant that Breadalbane resigned, and was at once reappointed to represent the LNW; there is nothing to suggest that the LNW as such exercised directorial power.

Beyond Dalmally the engineer faced his hardest task. The railway had to be taken along the wooded shores of Loch Awe, and round the flank of the great granite hulk of Ben Cruachan. Escape to the salt water of Loch Etive was by the Pass of Brander, a narrow defile through which the coach road and the river Awe jostled in close company. A cleft had to be cut in the mountainside above road and river to take the railway, and a high bridge had to be constructed to carry the line across the gorge of the Awe. A seven-span, lattice-girder bridge was required at the Lochy crossing and one of three spans at Falls of Cruachan. West of Taynuilt the railway had to twist and turn round the outcrops of rock to reach the shore of Loch Etive and Connel Ferry. The promoters had hoped to take it round the coast on an easy course through Dunstaffnage and Dunollie to Oban; vested interests had forced them to turn inland and climb steeply up and over a ridge before starting on a final exciting, twisting descent of Glencruitten to emerge on Oban Bay.

The route was re-surveyed by John Strain of Glasgow, who became its engineer. The Dalmally-Oban section was let in two contracts of almost equal length, that for Dalmally-Taynuilt going to W. & T. Adams and the Taynuilt-Oban contract going to Ireland & Company of Montrose. Work started at both ends in May 1878. The navvies blasted granite boulders left on the slopes of Ben Cruachan since the Ice Age, and these, crushed, became part of the concrete—then a new medium—with which Strain built his culverts and retaining walls.

Oban had pleaded for a railway for years, but now that the contractor's men were in the streets some of the inhabitants showed no pleasure. The c & o Act of 1865 had visualised a tramway running from the proposed terminal station on the south side of the bay to the existing north pier on the north side of the bay, crossing on the way the town's main square and skirting one of the principal streets. This line, to carry freight from station to pier, and known variously as the Oban Tramway and the Oban Town Railway, engendered a great heat when first mooted. Its opponents did not get the tramway removed from the Act, but they had severe restrictions placed on its use; the Callander & Oban was forbidden to employ on it 'locomotive engines or carriages propelled by steam or by atmospheric agency', or stationary engines and ropes. Presumably the wagons had to be horse-hauled or manually operated.

The Act which finally gave the C & O the right to enter Oban also restricted the tramway's route: 'It shall not be lawful for the company to take or use or encroach upon any part of the public place in the town of Oban called Argyll Square, or that portion of the road or street in the said town called Shuna Street.' George Street was similarly protected. But the site of the station still had to be decided.

The local concern was understandable, because between the site of the proposed railway terminus and the pier the bay swept round in a crescent, and one of the main streets followed its contour. The view across the bay to the island of Kerrera and the mountains of Mull was one of the most pleasing in the Highlands; and the railway planned to run across the bay from the south shore to the pier on an embankment that would cut off the famous outlook from the street. Some thought the line should be confined to the south shore, or even relegated to Lochavullin at the back of the town. But a rival faction, and it was powerful, positively wanted an embankment. Which side you took depended on whether you read the *Oban Times* or the *Oban Telegraph*: the *Times* was anti-embankment, the *Telegraph* pro-embankment.

The supporters of the embankment insisted that railway and steamers *must* be brought together. They also claimed that Oban Bay, far from being a tourist attraction, was little more than a cesspool: the Black Lynn, which served as a channel for the town's untreated sewage, emptied into the bay in front of the main street. Writers spoke of the 'filthy and offensive foreshore polluted with town sewage and every nameless abomination', of the 'most fetid effluvium that ever frightened away a tourist', and of a 'dirty, sloopy strand which gives forth both smells and sights to disgust the pure-eyed and pure-nostrilled promenaders of George Street'.

A section of the community had seen a chance to have the bay filled in and the sewage piped further off-shore at the C & O's expense. The embankment seemed preferable to a sewage farm. 'The passing and re-passing of trains should not institute an eyesore in any sense,' the *Telegraph* assured its readers.

> If the iron horse is to come to our coast he will come laden with valuable commodities for the public benefit, and we ought therefore to receive him in no churlish spirit. Instead of restricting him to a shed outside our walls let us give him free access to an ornamental stable in the very heart of the burgh.

And *The Highlander* cautioned: 'Oban and the railway must not be afraid of each other. On the contrary, the nearer they can be brought to each other the better; and the nearer the terminus and the pier are the better.'

The opponents of the embankment included local men who had been good friends to Anderson and the railway, among them Angus Gregorson of Oban and Dr Campbell of Ballachulish. Campbell wrote in the *Oban Times*:

> A more insane and preposterous scheme could hardly be conceived. It will convert our Obanian Princes street into a low back street and our Alexandra Parade into a Broomielaw. It would be far better that Oban should never see the railway than that it should see it only to become extinct.

The rival factions organised public meetings in the town. There was due consternation when only a handful of people turned up at the pro-embankment meeting—but it was discovered that Macmillan, the town crier, who recently had discarded his cracked bell and been supplied with 'an article of superior volume with which to accomplish his tintinabulation', had failed to announce the meeting. For his lapse he was hauled before the Town Council and severely reprimanded.

The railway solved the problem by negotiating to purchase some ten acres of land—some of it recently reclaimed—at the south side of the bay, on which it proposed to construct its own pier, adjacent to the station. This news was heard with dismay by the owner of the North Pier, John McCaig. Addressing a meeting of Scottish railway shareholders in Glasgow, he lambasted the new scheme as being extravagant: the reclaimed land was a stage projecting into the bay, and

> on this stage a beautiful station whose Grecian columns will be taught to support springing Roman arches full of life and vitality, a splendid sea esplanade with plate-glass verandahs along the side of the station —the whole affair variously estimated at from £50,000 to £100,000— will be built.

McCaig's picture of the proposed station was fanciful in the extreme. Oddly enough, he himself contributed an exotic note to the setting of the modest terminal that was eventually constructed: the striking round tower on the hill behind the town, which dominates views of the station looking towards the platform ends, was built by McCaig. It was intended to be a replica of the Colosseum at Rome, but was never finished.

The pro-embankment *Oban Telegraph* was incredulous when news of the railway pier was announced, and claimed that the scheme was a clever ruse on the part of the C & O to lull opposition; when it became plain that the plan was authentic the *Telegraph* condemned it as 'branded with the mark of insanity. It involves a wanton destruction of the amenity of the town. . . . *To arms, countrymen and townsmen.*'

The C & O had won something of a Pyrrhic victory. The ground on which it proposed to build the station and pier belonged to its own director, Macfie of Airds. He had reclaimed the land with a view to building a new street of houses, and he wanted £20,000 for it. The C & O's offer of £2,950 had to rise to £5,389 4s, which was an arbitrator's estimate of the value.

Work on the railway went on. An unaccustomed glare in the sky behind Oban marked the place where the navvies were working by floodlight in Glencruitten. There were setbacks. In the Dalmally section severe frosts interfered with the concrete work, and floods damaged the foundations of new bridges. In the winter of 1878 the *Earl of Carrick*, bringing steel rails from Workington to Bonawe for the Taynuilt section, ran on rocks at the entrance to Loch Etive; the vessel broke in two and became a total wreck, though some of the rails were salvaged. In August 1878 a vessel arrived at Oban with two locomotives for Ireland & Company. When the second engine was being removed by crane the chains snapped and the engine nearly crashed through the bottom of the boat. Subsequent attempts to remove it in one piece failed, and the engine had to be dismantled, and reassembled on the pier.

Sedate Oban was content to accept the economic benefits bestowed by its famous distillery, but it was indignant at the effects on the railway navvies of the product of the distillery. Over 400 men were employed between Taynuilt and Oban, the majority of whom, according to a local newspaper report, were 'considered to be the lowest type of men, and capable of committing any evil action'. A typical news item of the time read: 'The navvies had a big pay on Saturday and the police station was in consequence well patronised. In the evening some of the coaches had great difficulty in passing along the public road from the number of drunk men falling or lying about.' The local lodge of the Good Templars started in Oban the British Workman Public House, a peculiarity of this establishment being that it did not supply alcoholic drinks. From this idea came a series of Navvies' Rests which were set up at camps along the line and staffed by volunteer social workers. From these institutions came reports of navvies singing the Auld Hundredth, signing the pledge and handing their spare cash to the representative from the Post Office Savings Bank.

With the coming of the spring weather of 1880 work was pushed ahead at all parts of the contracts to ensure a summer opening. By June the *Oban Telegraph*, unsure of railway terminology, was able to report that a commodious signalling station had been completed at Drimvargie and that the landing platform was ready. At long last the railway was coming to Oban.

Taynuilt station

CHAPTER V

'Prosperity and Financial Sunshine'

GALA PERFORMANCE

During the afternoon of 29 June 1880 the LNW Holyhead-Dublin mail steamer *Lily* paddled northwards at reduced speed into the unfamiliar waters off the west coast of Scotland. At 3.30 that morning *Lily* had left her home port with a party of LNW officials and their friends bound for Oban, where next day they hoped to take part in the opening ceremony of the Callander & Oban Railway.

The voyagers had anticipated a pleasant cruise in surroundings famous for their beauty. They were to be disappointed; fog and heavy rain not only obliterated the Scottish coast and the islands of the Inner Hebrides, but delayed the ship so that the scheduled 5 p.m. arrival could not be met. It was 7 o'clock on that dripping grey evening when *Lily* slipped into Oban Bay and joined the congregation of ships that had gathered for the occasion. The surrounding hills were barely visible through the murk; even a local paper admitted that the rain was 'thick and relentless''. A few of the visitors must have reflected gloomily on that snell day last January when they had picked their way on a tour of inspection through unfinished, snowbound stations and over icy sleepers. They would have been even less warmly disposed had they known that the secretary of the LNW presently would receive from their Scottish hosts a bill for what the C&O board considered to be the LNW's share of the opening day's festivities—an amount carefully calculated in accordance with the proportion of C&O stock held by the English company.

Those guests who ventured ashore that evening found Oban busily preparing for one of the most important days in its history. The Queen's Birthday normally was celebrated in May, but the magistrates of Oban had decided to postpone the holiday until the day the railway opened. As the *Oban Telegraph* so indelicately put it, the holiday was 'nominally in honour of the birthday of Her Majesty, but in reality in celebration of the greatest local event in the history of the burgh'. John Anderson was still superintending as workmen put the finishing touches to the new station. The celebration banquet was to take place in the station circulating area, hung for the occasion with red and white draperies and decorated with evergreens, including a 'welcome' sign in flowers wrought 'by the fair and willing hands of Mrs Anderson'. Oddly enough the purvey was in the hands of the Glasgow & South Western Railway Company, whose St Enoch Hotel (Glasgow) staff were laying the tables.

Oban was astir early on the morning of 30 June. Crowds watched the ladies and gentlemen of the LNW leave the *Lily* and enter the special train that was to convey them to Dalmally, leaving Oban at 9 a.m. As the forenoon advanced people flocked into the town on foot, and by coach and steamer. MacBrayne's *Chevalier* arrived laden from Fort William, which town had declared a holiday in honour of the opening of the railway 40 miles away. At 11 o'clock a procession of magistrates, militia, freemasons and others formed up outside the station before setting off on a triumphal circuit of the town. The procession was back in good time to greet the returning LNW visitors, who brought with them guests from Edinburgh and Glasgow whom they had met at Dalmally. The double-headed special rolled into Oban to the sound of cheers, martial music and exploding fog signals.

The speeches that followed the inaugural banquet included some choice gems of railway luncheon oratory. A member of the Callander & Oban board in proposing the continued success of the Caledonian Railway Company said: 'That company (the Caledonian) is governed by honourable, straightforward, intelligent gentlemen, and they have officials who are not to be excelled for kindness and civility.' One would have given much for a sight of Anderson's face at that moment. In his reply Thomas Hill, chairman of the Caledonian, was honest enough to refer to the 'hours of darkness when the board was almost overturned' on the question of the C & O. He added the hope (unfulfilled) that that day would see the end of feuding between parent and adopted child.

The C & O officer charged with proposing the toast to the Magistrates and Town Council of Oban chose as his after-luncheon theme the open sewer that bordered the station frontage, and 'stagnates through a great part of the town'. In the next breath he exhorted those members of his audience who came from Edinburgh to go home and tell their friends to 'try for themselves the salt water and pure air of Oban'.

Another speaker was of the opinion that the railway had been created by the stroke of a magic wand, but Breadalbane, expressing his disbelief in fairies, said: 'I prefer the stroke of the piston. I think it is a more palpable means of getting to Oban.' It was left to Breadalbane's fellow-nobleman, the Duke of Sutherland, to deliver the day's prize platitudes. He was certain that the LNW directors were sorry that they had not *doubled* their contribution to the C & O. 'The stations are marvels of taste and convenience, and the railway is beyond doubt a first-class line. I am glad to hear that the Government proposes to send their young engineers at Woolwich to see here what a line ought to be. (Applause.) I am sure that some of our LNWR friends will be able to get a wrinkle from what they have seen.' (Applause.) The guest from the Board of Trade, Major Marindin, who had lately inspected the line, might have well choked over his port at that point. The distinguished guests later found time to toast John Anderson. The secretary was not a man for platitudes: in a brief reply he spoke of 'the lukewarm friends and open foes' he had encountered during his fifteen-year struggle to push the railway through to Oban.

The railway had cost £645,000, including the price of the pier (still under construction), the company's own gas and water works, new streets in the vicinity of the station, and a decorative esplanade wall that was an asset to the town. Two engineers and five contractors—including Duncan Watson who was working on the pier—had been involved. The station had a double-line bay and a single-line bay, one line in the double bay normally being used by goods trains.

The completion of the C & O brought Anderson his just reward at last: he was made the company's secretary and traffic manager at a salary of £700 with £50 expenses. His office was moved from Glasgow to Oban, the company paying the cost of his domestic removal. Among the business chattels moved up the line were the tissue copies of over 20,000 letters that Anderson had written by hand during the construction of the line. The notepaper supplied for use in the new office was headed: The Caledonian Railway, Callander and Oban Line.

Anderson was to make his home in Oban for twenty-seven years, and he quickly established himself as a leading member of the community. He was a man who stood out in a crowd. In the picture in Plate 19 he is seen clean-shaven and pugnacious in an age when men masked their facial expressions behind the universal beard.

The timetable offered in 1880 was as follows:

	Up						
	am	am	am	am	pm	pm	pm
Oban *dep.*		5.40	8.20	10.0	12.45	1.0	6.15
Connel Ferry		5.57	8.35	10.19	1.0	1.25	6.30
Taynuilt		6.15	8.50	10.35	1.17	1.55	6.46
Loch Awe		6.36	9.7	10.56	1.37	2.30	7.4
Dalmally		6.44	9.17	11.5	1.45	2.50	7.11
Tyndrum		7.11	9.45		2.15	3.30	7.39
Crianlarich		7.23	9.58		2.28	3.52	7.51
Luib		7.36	10.12		2.43	4.17	
Killin		7.53	10.27		3.0	4.45	8.16
Lochearnhead	7.25	8.7	10.41		3.14	5.5	8.30
Strathyre	7.35	8.17	10.51		3.24	5.20	8.40
Callander	7.53	8.37	11.13		3.45	5.45	8.58

The 5.40 a.m. departure from Oban ran as a mixed train to Dalmally, and the 8.20 a.m. departure from Oban became a mixed train from Dalmally to Callander. The 10 a.m. was not in the original timetable, but was added after the first few weeks to cater for visitors to Oban who wanted a day out at one of the stations on the line. It was announced as 'a short train'.

	Down					
	am	am	am	pm	pm	pm
Callander *dep.*		9.25	11.15	3.0	6.35	11.48
						am
Strathyre		9.48	11.38	3.25	6.57	12.22
Lochearnhead		10.1	11.51	3.38	7.9	12.40
			pm			
Killin		10.25	12.8	4.0	7.24	1.10
Luib		10.38	12.23	4.15	7.38	1.32
Crianlarich		10.52	12.38	4.31	7.52	1.54
Tyndrum		11.5	12.52	4.45	8.5	2.18
Dalmally	6.58	11.32	1.23	5.13	8.35	2.55
Loch Awe	7.4	11.40	1.36	5.22	8.43	3.7
Taynuilt	7.20	11.57	1.53	5.39	9.2	3.42
		pm				
Connel Ferry	7.36	12.12	2.9	5.45	9.18	4.8
Oban	7.55	12.28	2.25	6.10	9.35	4.35

The working timetable for the down direction did not show a goods train, but the 3 p.m. from Callander ran mixed. The 11.48 p.m. from Callander was given the title 'West Highland Mail' in the working but not in the public timetable. It made a conditional stop at Tyndrum to drop passengers from south of Carlisle. When no stop was made the driver was instructed to pass through the station at reduced speed 'to throw off mails'.

Steamer and coach services in the West Highlands were re-organised to connect with the Callander & Oban trains. During the latter part of 1879 Anderson had once again convened a conference of interested proprietors to devise a new pattern of transport for the West Highlands. He also made a point of seeing Thomas Cook, to ensure that the Oban line's tourist attractions were not over-looked.

An express service was provided by MacBrayne's steamer *Iona* between Oban and Fort William. The steamer left Fort William at 9.30 a.m. and arrived at Oban at 12.30 to connect with the 12.45 train departure for the south. The return sailing was at 1 p.m., conveying passengers who had arrived by train at 12.28, and regaining Fort William at 4.30. The steamer called at Port Appin, Balla-chulish and Corran Ferry in each direction. Railway and steamer combined thus gave a vastly improved service to North Lorn and Lochaber.

The steamer connection from Mull left Tobermory at 8 a.m., called at Aros, Lochaline and Craignure, and arrived at Oban at 11.30. The return trip left Oban at 1.30 and reached Tobermory at 5 p.m. During the summer a large selection of circular day excur-sions was offered, these involving travel to Pass of Melfort, Loch Awe, Pass of Brander, Glen Etive, Glencoe and Ballachulish. A steamer, the *Glen Etive*, plying on Loch Etive, connected with the trains at Connel Ferry.

John Anderson in his most optimistic moments could not have envisaged the surge of traffic that came to the railway that first summer. The annual trades holidays were beginning in Scotland's industrial south, and the public turned out in their hundreds to sample the new railway. Islanders came into Oban for the same purpose. Hotel and boarding-house accommodation was at a prem-ium. A trip down to Dalmally and back was a favourite ploy, and was many people's first experience of rail travel.

The rail-coach-steamer trips were fully booked day after day. The people of Argyll, many of whom had never considered going more than a mile or two beyond their own villages, ventured as far as Callander and Stirling and even to Edinburgh and Glasgow on day trips that cost 5s or less. They came to the stations in families and even communities, and they brought bands with them that played in the station concourse as they bought their tickets and entered the trains. In the first week a goodly proportion of the population of Easdale came up to Oban by special steamer, and soon were 'snugly ensconsed in comfortable railway carriages thundering along the new highway to Dalmally'. And oh! the excitement at Glenorchy School when John Cameron lined up his sixty-nine pupils in the playground and marched them to Dalmally station, with a piper at their head, to embark on a train journey to Oban.

The largest and most lucrative excursions came from the populous centres of the south. During the Glasgow Fair week a twenty-coach train brought 1,000 trippers into the town; Edinburgh sent 1,200 in one train, Airdrie 400 in another. It was a far cry from the

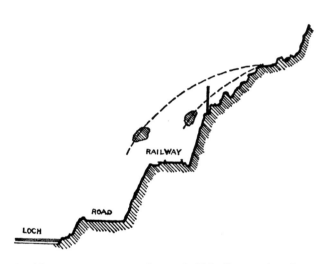

Boulder screen to protect the track. This diagram, based on a sketch in the official memorandum, shows the railway in cross section. The diagram is not to scale

days of the two-coach Tyndrum trains. The first sea-to-sea train trip took place within a fortnight of the opening, a special running from Dundee to Oban in five hours; the excursion was organised by John Leng, the proprietor of the *Dundee Advertiser* and the *Dundee Telegraph*, as a reward to his staff for their excellent and arduous work in connection with the recent Tay Bridge disaster and the subsequent inquiry. The excursionists were greeted like pioneers of trans-continental travel, and dined in the Argyllshire Gathering Hall, several town and railway officials, including Anderson, being present. Then in August came the first-class traffic. Ladies and gentlemen with their families and servants commandeered first-class carriages, and gaily-painted coaches, which the best hotels had bought for the purpose, were kept clip-clopping between the station and the various hostelries with arriving and departing guests.

The freight build-up was less spectacular, for the railway had to compete with a fast, efficient and cheap steamer service to Glasgow. Nevertheless, freight arrivals at Oban justified the employment of three railway-owned delivery wagons 'horsed by large, strong beasts'. The *Princess Alice*, bound from Aberdeen and Stornoway to Liverpool, called unexpectedly at Oban in the third week of July and landed 600 baskets of kippered herrings which were at once sent south by train. On 27 July the *Dunara Castle* came in with large quantities of lobsters and shellfish, which were dispatched by the 6.15 train. Later in the month catches unloaded from two large boats were on sale in London before breakfast next day.

Many of Oban's inhabitants revelled in the excited flush of optimism that the railway brought with it. Builders and decorators had inquiries from hoteliers eager to extend or redecorate their premises to cope with the new tourist invasion. A company was promoted to build the grandiose Oban Hills Hydropathic Sanatorium; it was partly built, but work stopped when funds dried up. Its ruins stand today on Oban Hill. On 10 September the *Oban Telegraph* summed up the situation :

> The year A.D. 1880 is truly a red-letter year in the history of Oban. The advent of the Callander and Oban Railway has been the forerunner of a season of unparalleled prosperity and financial sunshine. The opening of the railway has developed an increase of trade in the burgh and caused a briskness in every department of our local business, particularly among our hotels and lodging houses. This class of business has had quite a surfeit of custom, and their resources have been taxed to the utmost. There has been no halt in the pressure of visitors and the cry is 'still they come'. Every train and every steamer brings fresh crowds to Oban and the great question of the day is, What shall we do with them?

The newspaper did not fail to refer to Anderson as *popular* and *affable*.

But everybody was not pleased. The harbour works were still in progress, bringing the temporary ugliness of all large works of civil engineering. Professor Blaikie, Oban's most distinguished and most vocal resident, described the railway pier as 'the most obtrusive piece of architectural hideosity that has been perpetrated in these parts'; he suggested that the area should be called in the Gaelic, *Oisinn Mosach*—Ugly Nook. A local doctor compared the C&O management to a Cook's tourist scratching his name on the face of the Appolo Belvidere.

The tourist season came to an end, the coaches were locked in their sheds, the loch steamers were beached, and the Callander & Oban trains carried a mere handful of passengers. That was to be the pattern on the railway through the years to come; four months of hectic activity, followed by eight months of modest traffic. There was always the through trade from MacBrayne's steamers, and Saturday was a good day, summer and winter; social and domestic reasons brought the people of Argyll to Oban or down to Callander in large numbers on Saturdays. In January 1881 Dugald Maclachlan, clothier and draper of Oban, announced that in order to encourage his many country friends to visit his Great Sale he would 'gladly pay 3rd class return tickets if they bought parcels of £3 and upwards' in his shop.

The first balance-sheet that Anderson produced in his new office showed that 215,000 passengers had used the line in the seven months since opening day. The revenue for the six months up to 31 January was £9,501 16s 6d and C&O trains had in that time run 117,488 miles. Three years previously the corresponding figures had been £2,863 4s 4d and 54,228.

In the 1880s the railway *soirée* was an established feature of railway life. These gatherings were held annually, when railway officers, employees and their families and friends met for a night of conviviality and entertainment. John Anderson claimed to have organised the first railway *soirée* in Scotland, and he lost no time in arranging one for the Callander & Oban. The men who worked on the C&O were on the Caledonian payroll, but Anderson was determined to impress on them that they were *his* men, a race apart. He also wished to impress Oban with the importance of the railway. He engaged a full orchestra and well-known singers from the south and sent invitations to Oban townsfolk to come along; the place was the Argyllshire Gathering Hall, the date 4 March 1881.

Alas! the down night mail that should have arrived at Oban at 4.35 on the morning of the concert, a Friday, did not arrive in Oban until 2 a.m. on the following Tuesday. It had been caught in an avalanche of melting snow in Glen Ogle, and most of the performers with it. They went home; they had had enough. On the Friday forenoon Anderson set off for the trouble spot at the head of eighty

30 JUNE 1880

(17) *Special train about to leave Stirling with opening-day guests. The engine, ex-Scottish Central 2—2—2 No. 301, ran as far as Callander*

(18) *Opening-day banquet in Oban station. The ladies were confined to the waiting-room in the background*

C & O PERSONNEL

(19) *John Anderson (clean-shaven) and inspection party at Taynuilt, 1880*
(20) *Callander station staff about 1895*

men. But beyond Killin station the line was obliterated by snow and progress was impossible. A horseman sent to try to locate the lost train was himself overcome in snowdrifts and had to be rescued. Eventually the passengers made their own way to Killin; they had guided themselves by holding on to the telegraph wires, which were carried on stumpy poles. By Monday evening the rescue squad had cleared a path up to the train, and a light engine moved in and picked up the mails.

The *soirée* was postponed first to Monday and then to Wednesday. But urgent work remained to be done at Glen Ogle and Anderson could not get back in time. While he toiled among the snowdrifts of Glen Ogle, his proxy told the guests assembled at Oban: 'The railway was born in evil times. One commercial disaster followed another, and I can assure you that it was often to me a puzzle what to do next to make people have *faith* and subscribe the money for it.' Instead of the promised feast of talent from the south, local performers rendered items like 'Failte Bhraidalban', 'Thug mi gaol don t-Seoladair' and 'Is toigh lean a' Ghaidhealtachd'. It could not be denied that the first Callander & Oban Railway *soirée* had an atmosphere all its own.

'ANDERSON'S PIANO'

On 17 August 1881 the 10 a.m. local passenger train from Oban to Dalmally was passing Falls of Cruachan in the Pass of Brander when it was struck by a falling boulder. Several carriages were derailed, but the train was running slowly at the time and no one was injured. The accident highlighted a trouble that had afflicted the line since its earliest days. Much of the c & o mileage clung to hillsides, and falling stones were a constant hazard. As early as 29 December 1870 there had been a fall of stone near Lochearnhead, and there were further falls in the same area in July 1871 and August 1873. A Mr McGregor was awarded a sum of money for giving warning of a severe rock fall. He thought he was entitled to a free pass over the line for his services, but Anderson, in thanking him, refused the pass and pointed out that his act of humanity was 'only that which any other family with ordinary feeling would have done in the circumstances'.

The menace of falling rocks had of course become more acute with the opening of the Dalmally-Oban section. For three miles the slopes of Ben Cruachan, dotted with thousands of granite boulders, rose from 1,000 to 1,500 ft directly above the railway. Summer and

F

autumn were the danger times; sheep scrabbling on the slopes set small stones rolling which in turn moved bigger stones, until eventually a cascade of rocks poured down. Some bounced over the railway to land on the road lower down or plunge into the river, but all too often patrolmen found boulders on the track. What would happen if an engine-driver suddenly found himself confronted with a rock-fall while running on the narrow ledge above the Awe? Major Marindin had given very serious thought to the dangers involved over certain lengths of the line, reporting to the Board of Trade that 'owing to the difficult nature of the ground through which the line has been carried, there are some points where a run-off would be attended by more than ordinary serious consequences'.

Marindin again inspected the line a few weeks after it had been opened and one of his suggestions was that speed along the side of Loch Awe and through the Pass of Brander should be limited to 25 miles m.p.h. Consequently drivers were instructed to occupy not less than nine minutes between mileposts 52 and 55 by day, and fifteen minutes by night; speed after dark was thus limited to 12 miles an hour. Marindin was also concerned about the possible result of a derailment on the Awe viaduct. He suggested some form of outside protection, such as a low girder or timber baulk, and he sent Anderson a sketch of a girder which the LSW had placed on their Meldon viaduct in North Devon.

Immediately after the August 1881 incident, John Anderson suggested to Barr of the Caledonian a method of protecting trains from rock fails, and the signals staff worked out the details. The scheme was approved by the Callander & Oban board on 27 September 1881, and a 1,112-yd length of track in the Pass of Brander was fitted up ready to test it by January 1882.

A 9 ft fence of steel wires 12 in. apart was erected round the hillside above the railway. The wires were connected to four semaphore signals, placed so that along the protected stretch one was always in the driver's view. If a boulder hurtled over the top strand it would continue to plunge on down the mountain; but if it broke through the screen, severing even one wire, the appropriate signals would go to danger. If two or more strands were broken, one signal on one side of the break and two on the other would turn to danger. Where a signal was on the opposite side of the line from the screen, a dummy post in the screen was fitted with lever, balance-weight and trigger, from which a wire crossed over to the signal post. If a wire in the screen was broken, the trigger was actuated and set the signals at danger.

The engineers tested the installation by deliberately rolling stones down the mountain. It was found that some stones slipped through the fence because there was too much play in the wires. Intermediate posts were put in to reduce the distance between posts to 6 ft. The screen was re-tested, found satisfactory, and brought into use in March 1882. The following summer's experience decided the board to extend the screen through the entire danger area in the Pass of Brander, the completed screen, 5,659 yd long, coming into use on 17 April 1883. In the extension ten wires were used, 10 in. apart, with additional wires at vulnerable spots. Each of the sixteen signals, except the one at each end of the protected stretch, had two arms, one for each direction; the signals were, all but one, sited on the south (or loch) side of the track. As an extra precaution, any rock within the screen that looked unsafe was wired back to the screen itself. Drivers finding a boulder signal at danger had to proceed with caution until they located the obstruction or reached a clear signal.

A special grade of signal watchman was created, the men employed looking after the boulder screen and its signals. A hut was built at Falls of Cruachan to accommodate the stores, lamps and oil needed. In 1895 the screen was fitted with commutators and connected with alarm bells in the signal box, in the signal watchmen's houses at Awe Crossing, and in the homes of the foremen platelayers at Falls of Cruachan and Bridge of Awe. A break in the wires resulted in an audible warning being given to all concerned, day or night. Part of the signal watchman's duty consisted of testing the signals: he would send a special bell signal meaning 'watchman's inspection or test'. When occasion demanded the signalman at Loch Awe had to send to the staff at Falls of Cruachan the special bell signal, 'Be ready for accident or snowstorm'. A short length of protective screen, with a signal at each end, was installed at Craignan-Calleach on Loch Lubnaigside, near the sixth milepost from Callander.

Old-timers on the C & O referred to the boulder screen as 'Anderson's piano' because the wind whistling through the taut wires produced a musical hum. The device worked well over the years, though it was not infallible and in any case the wires were apt to snap in frosty weather, giving a false alarm. On several occasions rocks bounced on to the track without actuating the warning signals: the 6.5 a.m. passenger train from Oban to Glasgow on 8 August 1946 narrowly escaped disaster when the Class 5 heading

SCOTLAND

The Home of Health, Pleasure, and Picturesque Scenery. ◢ ◢ ◢

Summer Tours to

OBAN "THE CHARING CROSS OF THE HIGHLANDS."

By Rail throughout, *via* Beattock, Stirling, Callander, and Loch-Awe.
Return Fares from London (Euston)—First Class, 132/-; Third Class, 63/-.

By Rail to Glasgow, Gourock, or Wemyss Bay, *via* Beattock, thence by Steamer, *via* Ardrishaig and Crinan Canal.
Return Fares from London (Euston)—First Class and Cabin, 130/3; Third Class and Steerage, 65/9.

Grand Circular Tour — By Rail to Glasgow, Gourock, or Wemyss Bay, *via* Beattock, thence by Steamer, *via* Ardrishaig and Crinan Canal; returning by Rail, *via* Loch-Awe, Callander, and Stirling.
Return Fares from London (Euston)—First Class and Cabin, 132/3; Third Class and Steerage, 65/3.

(Fares subject to alteration)

Tickets for these Tours are issued at all the principal London and North-Western and Lancashire and Yorkshire Stations and Town Offices throughout England. Full particulars on application.

Passengers making these Tours can travel via Edinburgh (Princes Street), in both directions, without extra charge or inconvenience, and, after visiting the places of interest in and around Edinburgh, resume their journey North, West, or South from Princes Street Station, where the Caledonian Railway Company have a magnificent new Hotel.

it struck a stray boulder. Engine and coaches were derailed on the edge of a 100 ft drop, but fortunately remained upright.

TEETHING TROUBLES

The first few months of operation revealed flaws in the Callander & Oban organisation. The engines that the Caledonian provided to run passenger trains were unsuitable, and the trains failed to keep time. With the long sections involved, one train out of time in the morning could upset the timetable for the rest of the day along the whole line. The 9.25 a.m. from Callander was the worst offender; if it was running only twenty minutes late it had to be held at Connel Ferry until the arrival of the 12.45 from Oban, which had to connect with the Limited Mail at Stirling. It was not uncommon for the 9.25, due in Oban at 12.28, to be an hour late. This in turn delayed the connecting steamers.

Only twenty days after the line was opened Anderson was reporting to the directors: 'It is next to impossible to work the trains over 71 miles of single line with staff and absolute block.' Before the end of the year an experimental section at the Oban end was equipped with Tyers Train Tablet. It proved successful and in April 1881 the extension of the tablet system to Callander was authorised.

Anderson also suggested that in the interests of time-keeping some of the longest sections should be broken by intermediate crossing places. Thus came into being the very distinctive Callander & Oban house-and-signal-box combined. The signal box was in effect a sort of bow window in the front of the house; the block bells were repeated in the domestic quarters of the building. Eventually crossing places were established at Glenlochy in the twelve-mile section between Tyndrum and Dalmally, at Awe Crossing in the nine-mile section between Loch Awe and Taynuilt, at Glencruitten Summit between Connel Ferry and Oban, and at St Brides between Callander and Strathyre. Anderson wanted to establish a passenger station at St Brides but was thwarted by the local landowner.

Imperfections in the alignment of the track, not uncommon in a railway that was still settling, caused some minor derailments and narrow escapes, though no serious accidents. The facing points leading to the pier at Loch Awe were the scene of two derailments in one week in August 1881. On 24 August, on the 6.20 Oban-Glasgow train, 0—4—2 No. 704 was in charge of seven coaches when all its wheels were derailed. The second accident on the facing points occurred on 30 August, and involved the 5.30 a.m from Oban. It was made up of twelve coaches and was booked to leave with one engine; however, the engine going to work the Loch Awe ballast train and another bound for Dalmally to work back the 6.45 coupled on, ahead of the train engine. The 5.30 stormed up Glencruitten with three engines at its head, the middle one being 704. James Turner, the driver, had taken charge of it for the first time on the previous day. The ganger at Loch Awe was walking down a woodland path on the way to work when he heard the cavalcade entering the station. Suddenly there was a bump followed by a whistling for brakes. The ganger emerged from the wood just in time to see 704, all engine and tender wheels off the road, in the process of ripping up 80 yd of track. 'It was too rough to apply my own brakes,' replied Turner when he was asked why he whistled for brakes. The wheels of the third engine were also derailed. An inspection of 704 revealed that the tyres of the leading wheels were considerably worn, and the right leading wheel was carrying 11½ cwt less weight than the left; either factor could have initiated a derailment. As a precaution a check rail was fitted at the offending curve.

A serious accident was averted by a hairbreadth on 6 June 1886. The train involved was a double-headed twelve-coach excursion from Falkirk to Oban, handsomely turned out; almost all the coaches were new, and the engines were a 4—4—0 No. 181 piloted by a 2—4—0 No. 237. The train crew included not only two guards but the traffic inspector of the Callander & Oban and the permanent-way inspector of the Luib-Oban section. When the special stopped at Callander, John Drummond, the carriage examiner, passed down the right side of the train inspecting the vehicles and was just about to start walking up the left-hand side when, to his surprise, the train set off, at the scheduled time of 7.32. This lapse of the established routine was unfortunate, for on that occasion Drummond would probably have found that all was not well.

A tablet failure delayed the special for 1h. 11m. at Lochearnhead. The two engines took fourteen minutes to take water at Tyndrum, which they left at 10.14, 1h. 25m. late. They topped the summit in Glenlochy and began the long curving descent to Dalmally; a sharp brake application brought the train's steady 30 m.p.h. down to 12 for the Succoth viaduct, then speed began to rise again. It was touching 25 m.p.h. when there was a sudden jerk and the train crew felt an abrupt brake application. The leading driver looked back to find that his train had broken in two, and the five rear vehicles were tilted over in the ditch at the side of the line. A quick inspection revealed plenty of excitement among the passengers, but there were only two complaints of injury.

The permanent-way inspector soon located the point of initial derailment: there was powdered stone on the rail surface and broken fragments of stone on either side. Any sinister implication to this discovery was dispelled by the almost simultaneous discovery that something had been trailing along the sleepers and ballast from a point 60 ft short of the point of derailment. Further examination showed that a stay rod on the left-hand side of one of the carriages had broken loose; the stay rod, 14 ft long, was attached to the front and rear axle guards by two bolts at each end. It seemed clear (and Major Marindin subsequently accepted the explanation) that the rod had broken away and the trailing end had scooped a piece of ballast on to the rail immediately in front of a wheel, causing the derailment.

The gods were on the side of the Callander & Oban that day. The train had run for 200 yd beyond the point of derailment before the five rear carriages turned over. Within the 200 yd were a high embankment, a culvert over a rocky stream, and a bridge over a sheep-creep. At the point of final derailment the train was running on a ledge round a hillface with a drop to one side. The derailed vehicles had fallen on the other side and come to rest against the soft earth of the embankment. The much-delayed excursionists spent 1h. 10m. at the accident scene before resuming their journey to Oban in the forward portion of the train.

During the first year of operation through to Oban the first section of the railway between Callander and Killin had to be re-sleepered. But the original rails lasted into LMS days. The line was re-laid throughout between 1928 and 1938. Floods in November 1884 swept away a bridge over the River Nant near Taynuilt.

FISH

In the spring of 1881 the Caledonian, with supreme optimism, suggested to Anderson that he should negotiate with the Highland Railway for a share of the Stornoway fish traffic. At first sight it did not seem likely that the Callander & Oban could compete with the Dingwall & Skye; a steamer could sail from Stornoway to Strome in seven hours whereas the voyage to Oban took sixteen hours. But the Highland Railway's complacency played into Anderson's hands.

Until 1877 the Highland had carried fish from Stornoway to

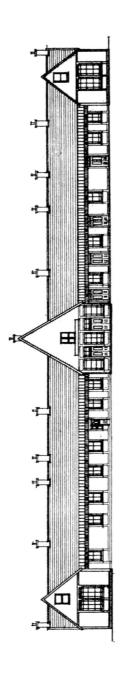

Elevation of Callander station and detail of the eaves

Strome in its steamer *Ferret*. That was the only route by which fish could be brought to a mainland railhead and the Highland took full advantage of its monopoly position, demanding a minimum load of 50 tons of fish per trip, or a cargo bringing a revenue of not less than £25. If a fish cargo fell short, the Stornoway fish-curers had to make good the difference. When in 1877 the Highland Railway withdrew the *Ferret*, the fish-curers had to find vessels for the Stornoway-Strome passage at their own expense. But the Highland still included the seventy miles from Stornoway to Strome in the mileage it claimed from the Railway Clearing House in estimating its share of the Stornoway-London rate; and this charge it passed on to the fish-dealers. In fact, the Highland was charging for goods it did not carry. The Stornoway curers protested against this iniquity and on several occasions sought a rebate on the sea portion of the trip; Inverness remained deaf. The fish-merchants also complained that the fish-handling facilities at Strome were rudimentary and that valuable time was lost in transhipping cargoes.

All this was well known to John Anderson, who now presented the c & o's case to the Stornoway merchants. To compensate for the longer sea voyage he offered cheap rates, quick handling and rapid dispatch from Oban. He provided fish-handling cranes, auctioneers' stands and offices free. The Stornoway men jumped at the chance to thwart the Highland. Three steamers started on the Stornoway-Oban run and it was soon proved that, in spite of the longer voyage, a fish cargo dispatched *via* Oban could be at Dunblane, the meeting-point of both routes, two hours sooner than a comparable cargo sent *via* Strome. On 10 June 1881 the Lochalsh correspondent of the *Oban Telegraph* reported: 'It is becoming painfully evident to those amongst us who are interested in the Highland Railway Company that your Oban line is virtually absorbing the whole of the important fish traffic of the western seaboard.' And a representative of the Stornoway fish trade wrote in a letter to *The Scotsman*: 'We cannot speak too highly of the Callander and Oban line where courtesy and attention to the requirements of the trade have been so much a contrast to that of the management of the Highland.'

Belatedly, the Highland fought back. It offered improved rates, and employed Joseph Wood of Aberdeen to run an express steamer between Stornoway and Strome. On its first trip it carried only eighty boxes, but in the long run Strome's superior geographical position could not be ignored; with improved handling facilities at the port and faster trains the Highland won back much of the traffic. The rates *via* Oban remained cheaper, however, and a worthwhile proportion of the traffic continued to come to the C & O.

The brisk burst of 1881 fish traffic was handled at a pier only partly finished, and Duncan Watson, the contractor, complained that he could make little progress. For six consecutive days he could do no work at all, so heavy were the consignments. Anderson suggested that he try a night-shift, but that proved no better.

Anderson made fish into a fetish. He mixed with the dealers and learned the talk of the trade. Up to that time there had been little scientific investigation into the habits of fish shoals. The herring season traditionally was in the summer, with no herrings caught in winter. But lately a theory had been advanced by the east-coast fishermen that herring were to be found in western waters in winter, and investigation proved them correct. They sailed their boats round to the west coast and drew rich harvests from Loch Hourn. The local fishermen were furious at the invasion, especially since some of the pirate boats used the recently-legalised but still-despised trawl net; they attacked the invaders and their gear with such effect that they sailed for home.

When Anderson heard about this episode he pressed the east-coast men to return and fish the rich west-coast grounds nearer to Oban where the C & O would provide a quick and economical outlet for their catches; Anderson had his eye on the winter traffic which his railway so much needed. And the rapacious trawl would ensure that the loads were heavy. At length the east-coast men sent boats round to Skye. The results were spectacular. 'Day after day,' reported the *Glasgow Herald* on 2 January 1883,

Loch Bay has been yielding enormous supplies of splendid herring. One trawl net drags ashore 200 crans. On Tuesday last 70 tons or thereabouts of beautiful fish were landed at Oban pier and there is every evidence that a noble fishery with enormous possibilities is being developed within reach of the railway's jaws.

The *Herald* urged the fishermen to exploit the waters round Mull (within sight of Oban) where 'the seas are so filled with fish that a rowing boat has difficulty in making progress through them'. 'We want half-a-dozen Mr Andersons,' declared a jubilant fish-dealer. Of course there were voices raised against the indiscriminate use of the trawl; one of the old school of fishermen protested : 'Anderson, in his endeavour to stimulate temporary traffic for the railway, is only helping to kill the goose with the golden eggs.'

The affair of Anderson and the mackerel came later. From his knowledge of the trade Anderson believed that there was a hitherto-untapped seasonal run of mackerel off Barra shortly after the main mackerel fishing season at Kinsale was over. When, in 1896, a fish dealer at Castlebay, Barra, made a trial run with one mackerel boat, Anderson wrote to him:

> At your leisure I wish you would tell me everything that took place as far as you know about the mackerel fishing, as I want to record what the trials were. You will remember that I wrote you that I believed the trials were made far too late in the season, and that they should have been made in the month of March or April at the latest. What do you say?

Armed with all the available information Anderson wrote to the Fishery Board, suggesting that a full-scale scientific investigation be made into mackerel fishing on the west coast. He made much of the point that the Kinsale boats should be induced to come over and fish the Scottish waters, and he claimed that his suggestion was made because of his desire to foster the prosperity of the West Highlands. In its reply the Fishery Board asked Anderson point-blank if he was writing as a private individual or as the secretary of a railway that was interested in getting the mackerel traffic. When Anderson admitted that he was after the traffic, the Fishery Board demanded a contribution towards the expense of conducting the proposed experiment. The episode closed with Anderson regretting that he had no power to part with C & O cash for such a purpose.

OPPOSITION

Anderson had always been apprehensive lest a rival railway be promoted in what he regarded as his territory. In the decade following the opening to Oban three schemes were advanced. William Campbell of Inverness appeared in 1881 with his 'Direct Inverness & Glasgow Railway'. The preliminary announcement described the proposed route through the West Highlands from Inverness to Glasgow, and added: 'It is intended that as soon as the contracts for the construction of the main line are let, locomotive and carriage workshops on a large scale will be established in Inverness for the construction of all descriptions of railway stock.' The DI & G had more than a touch of the Glenmutchkin about it, and faded away.

Very different was the Glasgow & North Western Railway scheme of 1882. This was well-conceived and substantially backed. The promoters offered a West Highland route from Glasgow to Inverness that would be some forty miles shorter than the existing route by the Highland and Caledonian railways. The line was planned to come up the east side of Loch Lomond and climb Glen

Falloch to Crianlarich following in part the track of the Caledonian Northern Direct of 1845. There it was to cross the C & O and run parallel with it up Strathfillan before striking across Rannoch Moor to Glencoe, going on by the shore of Loch Linnhe to Fort William and through the Great Glen to Inverness. The Highland Railway had most to lose if the G & NW materialised, but the Caledonian and the Callander & Oban, whose interests were also threatened, supported the Highland's case. The G & NW bill was considered before a Parliamentary select committee in April and May 1883 in one of the most protracted and expensive hearings in railway history. Ironically, many of the bill's supporters based their case on the obvious benefits that the Callander & Oban had brought to the West Highlands; ironically, too, some Oban townspeople supported the bill because the G & NW promised a junction with the C & O at Tyndrum, which would make the Oban-Glasgow journey twenty-seven miles shorter than by the C & O and Caledonian route via Stirling.

An ensuing aside during the hearing came when a Mr McTavish, general dealer of Inverness, was being examined. Mr Pope, one of the counsel, asked him: 'You are not the McTavish who was the director of Professor Aytoun's Glenmutchkin Railway?' McTavish solemnly answered: 'No.' At this point another lawyer interjected: 'It was Sir Theodore Martin who wrote the Glenmutchkin Railway.' 'I beg your pardon,' retorted Pope, 'it was Professor Aytoun. I have it in my bag.' 'At all costs they wrote it between them,' conceded his adversary. 'Sir Theodore Martin drew the prospectus for he told me so himself.' A third legal gentleman then remarked amid laughter: 'It only shows that Sir Theodore Martin was the agent of the line.'

The G & NW bill was not proved. The C & O paid £1,817 8s 10d for its participation in the case—unproductive spending that it could ill-afford. At the next half-yearly meeting of shareholders the directors recommended that no dividend be paid.

Fort William and the surrounding district of Lochaber felt the want of a railway to the south, and the failure of the G & NW scheme was a disappointment. In 1889 a new but slightly less ambitious railway was promoted locally: this was the West Highland Railway. The line was to start at Fort William, but instead of following the path of the G & NW down Loch Linnhe and through Glencoe to Strathfillan it was to strike east through the heart of Lochaber to Tulloch, where it was to turn south, cross the highest part of the Moor of Rannoch, and drop down to Tyndrum. From there it was to go down Strathfillan, cross the C & O at Crianlarich and continue by Glen Falloch and the west side of Loch Lomond, Loch Long and the Gareloch to a junction with the North British Glasgow-Helensburgh line at Craigendoran. A western extension was to take the West Highland Railway from Fort William to a new port on Loch Ailort.

The West Highland menaced the Callander & Oban at several points. The proposed port on Loch Ailort would be better placed than Oban to serve the Hebridean fish trade; the passenger traffic from Fort William and district, which now reached the south *via* MacBrayne's Fort William-Oban steamer connection, would be wholly lost; passengers from Strathfillan would be offered a more direct route to Glasgow; and the new line would be cheaper and shorter for the sheep traffic sent through Tyndrum.

The C & O's feeble answer to the West Highland was to promote the Glen Falloch Railway. This in effect was a branch line from Crianlarich down Glen Falloch to Ardlui at the head of Loch Lomond. Steamers were to provide a link to Balloch at the foot of the loch, and Caledonian trains would complete the journey to Glasgow. The proposed capital of the Glen Falloch Railway was £50,000. The Clydesdale Bank advanced the £2,500 required for a Parliamentary deposit, and Anderson entered into negotiations with the Dumbarton County Council over the acquisition of certain roads.

The C & O bill was considered by the same committee that was studying the West Highland bill. The committee accepted the West Highland bill (without the western extension) and threw out the C & O attempt. At the next board meeting the C & O directors resolved that the West Highland Railway 'as authorised by the House of Lords be opposed in the House of Commons and that every means be taken to throw it out'. The C & O promised that if the West Highland bill were rejected it would immediately build a line from Connel Ferry through Ballachulish to Fort William, thus providing a through rail link between Edinburgh, Glasgow, Stirling, Callander and Fort William. On paper the offer looked attractive. Whereas the West Highland builders were starting from scratch, fully two-thirds of the C & O mileage was built and in operation. Furthermore, the country between Connel Ferry and Fort William had much more revenue potential than the bleak, unpopulated miles across the Moor of Rannoch. Unfortunately, the C & O line had to brave three sea lochs, all of which called for major bridges. Again, the West Highland was a Lochaber conception, and its promoters were determined that their line would serve Lochaber. The West Highland won the day.

The construction of the West Highland Railway brought traffic to the C & O. Lucas & Aird, the contractors, rented ground at Tyndrum for storage purposes, and C & O trains kept it well plenished. Rails and bridgework came up from Glasgow over C & O metals, and stone for the viaducts and ballast for the permanent way came from the Cruachan Quarries where the C & O had a siding. The C & O specified that the West Highland must leave room for three lines of track in spanning its line at Crianlarich.

The West Highland was opened in August 1894. On the day that the North British, who worked the line, published its timetable in the Scottish press, showing east-coast connections to Fort William, the Caledonian published, in the same columns, a revised timetable showing west-coast connections to Fort William *via* Oban. The 8.30 p.m. from King's Cross conveyed a through carriage, due in Fort William at 12.15 the following afternoon. The corresponding west-coast train was the 8 p.m. from Euston, which had its passengers in Oban by 9.25 the following morning. The connecting steamer left Oban at 10 a.m., called at Ballachulish at 11.30 and reached Fort William at 12.30. In spite of the 35-minute wait at Oban and the 2½-hour steamer trip, passengers by the new direct rail route saved only 45 minutes on the journey.

The east-coast companies advertised a service from London to Oban *via* Fort William! The steamer connecting with the 8 p.m. from King's Cross arrived in Oban at 3.35 the following afternoon. In the up direction the 4.5 p.m. train from Fort William reached King's Cross at 5.50 a.m. The competing service by the west-coast route left Fort William (steamer) at 3.30 to connect with the 6.40 train from Oban which reached Euston at 8.10 a.m. This service, however, lasted only from 1 September until 13 October. There were four sailings between Fort William and Oban each weekday, all of them connecting with trains at Oban.

True to form, Anderson sought out and exploited every possible means whereby his company might benefit from the new railway. The West Highland agreed to detain its trains at Crianlarich by a fixed number of minutes to facilitate exchange of passengers. When Anderson recommended to his board the extension of passenger and goods accommodation at Oban, the lengthening of a loop at Glenlochy, and the provision of an additional water tank at Dalmally, he was able to give as his reason the increase in traffic following the opening of the West Highland Railway.

CRIANLARICH JUNCTION

Lucas & Aird applied for permission to make Crianlarich Junction, linking the West Highland to the Callander & Oban, on 18 November 1889. Initially, the Callander & Oban agreed to the construction of the spur provided that it itself was put to no expense or inconvenience. The spur was intended for the exchange of traffic between the two railways only; there was no question of regular services being run over it or of running powers being granted to either of the companies. Once the West Highland was ready for traffic the junction was likely to bring traffic to c & o metals; after all, the West Highland promoters had made much of the fact that their line would enable sheep and cattle to be transported from Lochaber to the great markets of Perth, Stirling and Falkirk *via* Crianlarich and the c & o.

The West Highland plan was to lead off the spur at the north end of its Crianlarich station and drop it down to a junction west of the Crianlarich (c & o) station. This plan apparently was approved by the c & o at first, but by the beginning of 1892 the board was insisting that the junction be realigned and brought in through the c & o station. This would have presented serious engineering difficulties, and was rejected by the West Highland and North British boards. The c & o then asked the West Highland to build and pay for a station at the junction, a request which was also rejected. The line was constructed as originally planned by the West Highland at a cost of £2,384 11s 8d. The two signal boxes, Crianlarich East and Crianlarich West, were both built at West Highland expense. It was agreed that they should be staffed, and the spur maintained, by Caledonian men paid by the West Highland. On 11 October 1894, Formans & McCall reported: 'The junction between the main and the Callander and Oban Railway is now ready for inspection.'

But three more years passed before the junction was brought into use—three years and five months after the opening of the West Highland. There was trouble with a landowner who considered that the junction encroached more than it should on his ground; the railway and a solicitor representing another landowner haggled for months over a matter of £100 on the price of the land; and there were differences between the two railway companies on how precisely the junction was to be worked. Meanwhile, a symbolic rail length was removed from the completed spur, the gap in the rails remaining for three years as a mute witness of the incompetence, sloth and bungling of the parties concerned.

Meanwhile, the Lochaber cattle went all the way down the West Highland to Glasgow and then back over the North British to Falkirk, Stirling and Perth. It was a costly business for the shippers who, after they had received their transport accounts following the Perth autumn sales of 1895, complained bitterly to the West Highland and demanded to know what had happened to the promised cheap direct route. The answer that the Marquis of Breadalbane gave them may have been near the truth. The Marquis was displeased with the West Highland because of its conduct on his property. In spite of its undertaking to the contrary it had tried to make a passenger station out at Gorton on the Moor of Rannoch; and now there was the affair of Crianlarich Junction.

In August 1895, Breadalbane asked the West Highland station-masters in the area if they had information about the opening of the junction. They had none. He then wrote to the secretary of the North British on the subject, and received a formal reply. He wrote again demanding precise information and was told that the junction would be opened 'after the tourist traffic ceased'. At the beginning of the winter, with the junction still not functioning, a third letter from the Marquis brought the reply: *'No information can be added to that already furnished.'*

Breadalbane, not without reason, was furious.

> Possibly the real motive of the company in not opening the junction (he wrote) is that it is more profitable to themselves to carry to the north via Glasgow over the North British Railway system than to give the public the opportunity of taking advantage of the shorter route. Had I for one imagined that the West Highland Company intended to make a junction with the Callander and Oban, but not to open it, I certainly would not have supported the line, as without a connection at Crianlarich it is of comparatively little use to the farmers and others north of Crianlarich who are desirous of sending stock to the east and north.

When the junction at last was opened, on 20 December 1897, the townsfolk of Oban, realising that there was now a direct railway route to Glasgow that saved 17 miles over the journey *via* Callander, began agitating for a regular through service between Oban and Glasgow over the C&O and WH. The fight went on intermittently decade after decade. Oban got its service—when an irreparable landslide blocked the Crianlarich-Callander section on 27 September 1965 and made running *via* the West Highland obligatory. There had been summer tourist trains *via* the West Highland to Oban before that date, but they were timed to suit visitors from the

IN THE PASS OF BRANDER

(21) *Boulder screen and signals*
(22) *Awe crossing*

EXCURSION TRAFFIC—1

(23) *Falkirk-Oban excursion derailed at Succoth, 13 September 1886. The stock was ex-works*

(24) *McIntosh 4—6—0 No. 54 heading a through excursion composed of West Coast stock from the north of England, about 1908*

south, and not the people of Oban.

INVERARAY

Ever since the abortive Ardrishaig & Lochawe scheme of 1870, residents in southern Argyll had shown interest in establishing a rail link with the national network. But any railway serving the small communities on Lochfyneside and in the isolated Kintyre peninsula would be long and straggling and unlikely to produce much revenue. At one time the Town Council of Campbeltown considered financing a line from the town to the C & O at Dalmally, but nothing came of it. In 1895, C. L. Orr Ewing, M.P. for Ayr burghs, engaged an engineer at his own expense to survey two routes out of Inveraray. One was to link Inveraray with the C & O near Dalmally; the other was to go round the head of Loch Fyne and strike east across the mountains before descending Glen Croe to Loch Long, where it would join the West Highland Railway. The engineer reported on the second alternative, but the West Highland refused to give support.

However, in 1896 both the West Highland and the Callander & Oban promoted lines to Inveraray. The little town at the head of Loch Fyne was no great prize to the railway promoter. It was the political capital of Argyll, but its glory lay in the past; by 1896 it was a sleepy backwater dominated by the castle, whose ducal occupant was not well-disposed towards railways that threatened to come within sight of his ramparts. The West Highland line from Arrochar was to reach a terminus at St Catherines, on the east side of Loch Fyne opposite Inveraray, with a ferry linking the terminal and the town. By not taking its line right into the town the West Highland thought (rightly) that it would please the Duke of Argyll and forestall serious opposition.

The Callander & Oban Inveraray branch was to leave the main line above Dalmally and run along the hillside to enter Glenaray at Accurrach. The railway was to rise to a summit of 600 ft at Cladach then follow the east bank of the River Aray and drop down to the head of Loch Fyne. As a sop to the Duke of Argyll it was to disappear into an unnecessary tunnel, 366 yd long, under the duke's policies. It was to be 14½ miles long and to cost £142,568.

Both the C & O and the West Highland schemes were engineered by Formans & McCall. The distance from Inveraray to Glasgow *via* the West Highland was 54 miles, by the C & O 107 miles. The duke had no difficulty in having the preamble to the C & O bill not proved

G

on the grounds that the proposed railway would spoil the amenity of his estate. The West Highland bill received the Royal Assent but, wisely, the company abandoned the project.

Ben Cruachan from Taynuilt

CHAPTER VI

A Village Railway

THE KILLIN LINE

The line that ran from Killin Junction down to Killin village and Lochtay Pier is usually referred to as the Killin *branch*. It was nothing of the sort. For all its 5¼ miles it was the Killin Railway Company, a railway in its own right. It opened for goods traffic on 13 March 1886, for passengers on 1 April 1886, and functioned as a separate independent company until the early summer of 1923. It was promoted in Killin village, managed from Killin village, and operated mainly to serve the needs of the villagers. At the half-yearly meetings of the shareholders, the draper and dressmaker, shoemaker and shepherd (quite literally) foregathered in the Drill Hall, Killin, to hear their board (composed entirely of kenspeckle local characters) report on the affairs of *their* railway.

Loch Tay is a typical, mountain-girt Highland loch lying in one of the great valleys that traverse Central Scotland from east to west. It is 14½ miles long and a little over a mile wide at its widest point. At the east end of the loch is Kenmore village and not far away Taymouth Castle, the seat of the Marquis of Breadalbane. Close to the west end of the loch stands Killin village. In the 1880s the mail coaches from Aberfeldy passed along the north shore of the loch on their way to and from Killin and points west. A service of cargo and passenger vessels on Loch Tay augmented the district's transport facilities. Breadalbane was very conscious of the fact that the steamers were starved of traffic and that the best possible feeder would be a railway direct to the loch's shores. There had been talk of the Highland bringing a line through from Aberfeldy to Kenmore, but nothing came of it. The Callander & Oban line was within sight of Loch Tay in its descent from Killin station to Luib, but the C & O had been content to service the villages round the loch from the station high on the hill.

In 1881 Breadalbane asked the Callander & Oban to consider building a branch from the neighbourhood of Luib down to Killin village. The board refused—a surprising decision for a company so tourist-orientated. Killin, a picture-book village built on a wooded peninsula between the rivers Dochart and Lochay, possessed one of the most spectacular waterfalls in the Highlands, while Loch Tay and its steamers offered interesting scope for the kind of rail and steamer excursions which the railway had been finding so profitable elsewhere.

Breadalbane next took his inquiry to the Caledonian, which included a Killin branch among other proposed new railways in its omnibus bill of 1861. Several major English railways claimed running powers over the proposed line, and Breadalbane envisaged an invasion of excursion trains from England: 'There will be no room on the short line for all the trains, and the inhabitants of Killin village might have to walk from Killin village to the junction on the tops of the carriages.' The villagers were spared this interesting experience, for the Caledonian bill was rejected.

If the people of Killin were to have a railway it was plain they would have to build it themselves. And that is what they proceeded to do. The first meeting took place in Killin under the chairmanship of the Marquis of Breadalbane on 19 August 1882. The marquis had already been in touch with John Strain, the engineer of the Tyndrum-Oban section of the Callander & Oban, and he was able to give the villagers a fair picture of the railway that would serve their needs. The line would climb out of Killin for four miles on a gradient of 1 in 50 to meet the Callander & Oban as it dropped down from Glen Ogle; the proposed junction on the hillside would be about 2½ miles below the existing Killin station. An eastward extension of the line would take it 1¼ miles from the village to a pier on Loch Tay.

Strain thought the railway could be made for £18,000. Its estimated annual income was £1,648 7s 6d and its cost of running £1,283 7s 6d, leaving a modest £365 for division among the shareholders. Breadalbane held up a letter from a local resident, Donald Currie, offering to take up shares to the value of £1,000; the marquis urged his audience to contribute, and he himself promised to subscribe a pound for every pound given by the people of the district.

Mr A. R. Robertson of the Bank of Scotland was appointed secretary. When Robertson wrote up the minutes of that first meeting, he apparently was unsure of the title of the new railway: he headed the first page in large, bold script 'The Killin and Lochtay Railway', then drew his pen through the words 'and Lochtay'.

By the time the next meeting was held—on 2 September—

Callander and Oban. *Top*: No 44796 runs into Callander with an up Oban train past a Caledonian dummy signal in July 1958. The station is now a car park. *The late W. Oliver/Colour Rail*
Bottom: Nos 73108 and 73072 waiting for departure from Oban with a return excursion to Glasgow in May 1961. *M. Mensing/Colour Rail*

Ballachulish services. *Top*: In September 1960 the daily goods from Ballachulish with aluminium among its traffic leaves Connel Ferry bridge. This is almost the view seen by motorists waiting for the signal for their turn to cross the bridge. *F. Sparen*

Bottom: Familiar sight for many years, branch engine No 55263 at Glencruitten summit with the 0825 Oban to Ballachulish in May 1961. *M. Mensing/Colour Rail*

Robertson had become doubtful of the wisdom of proceeding. In the three weeks since the first meeting only £370 had been subscribed, and he thought that even the most intensive canvass of the district would produce no more than £4,000, including Currie's £1,000. After all, Robertson was the village banker and he knew better than anyone else the financial strength of the district. But the promoters were determined to have their railway. If they could not attract cash they would barter shares for materials and services. Breadalbane undertook to give all the land and sleepers needed in return for shares. Negotiations with the Callander & Oban and the Caledonian resulted in the rails being secured in exchange for shares, and the Caledonian agreed to work the line for 55 per cent of the gross receipts.

Anderson bought 1,200 shares (at £10 each) on behalf of the C & O. The subscription list grew as castle and cottage contributed their quota. In the shareholders' book, beside the name of Breadalbane, was inscribed the names of Peter Graham, draper; Janet McLaren, dressmaker; Alexander Cameron, saddler; John Cameron, shoemaker; Donald McPhail, crofter; the village grocers Findlay McNaughton and Duncan Robertson, and many of their fellows. Nobody was against the railway, so the delay and expense of obtaining an Act of Parliament was unnecessary; only a Board of Trade certificate was needed. Robert Menzies of Edinburgh agreed to act as law agent in preparing the company's application for the certificate, and he proposed to collect his very modest fee only if the application were successful. The lack of both money and certificate did not deter the Killin Railway from inviting tenders from construction contractors, which were opened on 1 August 1883. The Board of Trade certificate was received on 8 August.

Nine tenders were received; most of the offers were round the £20,000 mark, but one from Macdonald of Skye at £13,783 8s was a clear £3,000 or 21 per cent lower than the nearest competitor. Strain was consulted, and he thought the railway could not be built at the price; he had misgivings about the competence of this unknown and untried contractor. But the lure of the low price induced the promoters to accept Macdonald's offer. Every penny counted in the Killin Railway office. Robertson was discovering, as Anderson had done before him, that people who had promised to take shares were less ready with forwarding the actual cash. The minister of Glenlyon, who pleaded that he had been misled when approached to buy shares, was curtly pulled up. 'I cannot take it upon myself to relieve you merely because you say you were

THE KILLIN RAILWAY COMPANY.

REPORT BY THE DIRECTORS

AND

STATEMENT OF ACCOUNTS,

TO

31st JANUARY, 1884.

THE KILLIN RAILWAY COMPANY.

NOTICE IS HEREBY GIVEN, That the HALF-YEARLY ORDINARY GENERAL MEETING of the SHAREHOLDERS of THE KILLIN RAILWAY COMPANY will be held within the DRILL HALL, KILLIN, on WEDNESDAY, the 26th day of March current, at One o'clock Afternoon, in terms of the Statute.

AND

NOTICE IS ALSO HEREBY GIVEN, That immediately after the Ordinary Business of the said Meeting shall have been transacted, an EXTRAORDINARY MEETING of the SHAREHOLDERS will be held for the following purposes, viz.:—

1. To authorise the Company, under the powers conferred by the Killin Railway Certificate, 1883, to raise Capital by the creation and issue of Shares or Stock to the amount of £27,000.

2. To authorise the Company, under the powers conferred by the said Certificate, to borrow on Mortgage or to create and issue Debenture Stock to the amount of £9,000.

The Transfer Books of the Company will be closed from Wednesday the 19th current, until after the Meeting.

By Order,

BREADALBANE, *Chairman.*
R. A. ROBERTSON, *Secretary.*

COMPANY'S OFFICE, Killin, 3rd March, 1884.

M'Corquodale & Co. Limited Printers, Glasgow and London.

Notice of Killin Railway shareholders' meeting

misled,' wrote Robertson. 'Perhaps you will let me know who misled you and in what manner it was done.'

Robertson estimated that by accepting Macdonald's offer the total cost of the railway would be £28,552. He found that the subscription list could be summarised as follows:

Cash, including Breadalbane's contributions	£8,200
Shares for equivalent value of land	£2,726
Shares for equivalent value of sleepers	£1,210
Shares for equivalent value of rails	£3,465
Money raised by loans	£5,200

The total assets, therefore, amounted to £20,801, leaving £7,751 still to be found. The directors considered abandoning the Loch Tay extension and bringing the steamers up the river to Killin Hotel. But the saving on the railway was likely to be offset by the cost of canalising the river. At the other end of the line the Caledonian made things difficult by rejecting the Killin Railway's scheme for a £2,000 junction and insisting on a layout costing £4,500. Robertson protested: 'The directors cannot hope to raise this sum in the district, as every source is exhausted.'

DEBACLE

Macdonald started work in the summer of 1883 and hoped to hand over the completed railway in time for the summer traffic of 1885. The formation of the roadbed involved the removal of some 100,000 cubic yards of earth. The line had to cross both the Dochart and the Lochay and the bridges presented special problems. Strain had experimented with mass concrete bridges and culverts on the last phase of the Oban line. The medium was still novel; nevertheless, he decided to put a concrete bridge across the Dochart. The structure was on a 45-degree skew; it was to have five semi-circular arches each with a span of 30 ft on the square and 42 ft 5 in. on the skew. For the Lochay, where the sub-soil was soft, a timber bridge of nine 20 ft spans was planned. The pitchpine beams were to rest on piles of native larch driven 40 ft into the ground. Macdonald was uneasy about the concrete bridge; he asked that it be replaced by an iron girder bridge, but Strain refused. Macdonald also asked in vain if he could make temporary use of the company's rails for his construction line.

When on 27 August 1884 Strain went over the line he was disappointed with the lack of progress. The piers of the Dochart viaduct had been erected, but there was no sign of the concrete work, which *had* to be finished before the first frost; this could be expected within two months. The cement for the concrete had not even arrived. The reason for this became apparent a few days later in a telegram to Macdonald from J. C. Johnson & Co. of the Gateshead Cement Works: '*Wire secretary of railway to send us the guarantee you promised which has not yet arrived. Nothing can be done until we get this.*' The Killin board duly guaranteed the price of 50 tons of cement so that work on the Dochart viaduct could go on. The cement duly reached Killin station, but the stationmaster would not release it until the Killin company guaranteed that the cost of transport—£12 5s 2d—would be met. Strain sent a report to the board on the contractor's shortcomings, ending: 'It is now for the directors to consider what can be done within the terms of the contract to ensure the completion of the line by the beginning of next summer.' The directors passed a copy of Strain's report to Macdonald, who replied that he was confident that he could finish the railway on time.

But poor Macdonald was too far on the way to bankruptcy for redemption. Already he had lost £1,000 on the Dochart viaduct alone. It was not that he was dishonest or professionally incompetent; his materials were excellent, his workmanship good. But he had hopelessly underpriced the job, and the money that came to him from time to time was insufficient to pay the weekly wages of the navvies and buy all the materials. By November 1884 he was in a glorious administrative muddle; creditors pressed him, and one of them precipitated a crisis by placing an arrestment on his funds. Work on the line all but ceased: no supplier would deal with Macdonald unless the Killin Railway office underwrote the transaction. Among the items for which Robertson had to guarantee payment were '4 bolts of oats, 1 of beans, 1 of Indian corn and 1 bag of bran'—presumably fodder for the contractor's horses.

A vivid picture of conditions on the works was given in a letter from Robertson to Breadalbane on 10 November 1884.

My Lord,
    The men are at work today on the bridge—a strong squad of masons, but there are none as yet working in the cuttings. They may, however, begin in the course of the day. I am afraid a large number of them are away altogether. Indeed, I am told that all the men that Macdonald paid in full the other day—that is, the roughest lot—are away, and that only those who have still money to get from him remain. Last week the carpenters were at work on Junction Station as often as weather would permit. The carters also. The masons a little, and a few labourers were at work. There I am paying for the week and

work as arranged. If this plan, however, is to last any time I am afraid we will require a check time keeper of our own as manager.

John Strain put the blame for the débâcle squarely on the shoulders of the village railway promoters. In a forthright letter he told them they had got what they deserved by accepting the lowest tender. He held the board morally responsible for allowing the navvies' wages to go in default. 'The company should in my opinion advance on Macdonald's receipt the wages in arrears,' he wrote. 'The men should not suffer for the directors accepting an offer for which they were advised the work could not be done.' Strain was not disposed to blame Macdonald unduly. He reminded the Killin board :

> At the worst the company have got a great deal of work well and cheaply done, they have got the use of the plant and materials on the ground to complete the work, and at the end they will rank as creditors on Macdonald's estate for any difference between the actual cost to them and Macdonald's contract sum.

Up to that time the Killin Railway had paid Macdonald £10,316 8s.

The contractor's creditors met the railway management in the company's office at Killin on 11 December 1884. The original contract was terminated, and John Best of Glasgow was appointed to supervise the construction of the line on behalf of the creditors. The Killin Railway advanced £1,000 as an indication of good faith. Work on the line went on. Partly because of bad weather, partly because of shortage of labour, progress was slow. On 23 February 1885 Strain reported that 71,900 cubic yd—or 73 per cent—of the earthworks had been completed, and 84 per cent of the bridges, cattle creeps and culverts. But he warned the directors that unless the work was carried on with vigour there would be no hope of the line opening for the summer. The summer passed, and still the line was not ready. The concrete arches of the Dochart viaduct were each built in a single day, the concrete being spread in 3 in. layers until the arch had attained a thickness of 2 ft.

Although the Caledonian had undertaken to work the line, the Callander & Oban had the biggest say in the direction of its affairs. Robertson took his orders from Anderson. When the line was nearing completion the Killin secretary was faced with the job of acquiring the many necessities that even a 5¼-mile railway must have. He asked James Martin of Glasgow for 'everything necessary for the working of the offices of the stations'. He hastened to add that he would not require any furniture, just dating-machines and ticket-cases; and only two of the latter for he had already obtained

and ask if Lord Breadalbane and Committee
could meet with the Directors in Glasgow on
Friday and to wire answer.

Mr Menzies explained that the plans
must be lodged with the Board of Trade not
later than 15th November to enable the Company
to proceed with the line this season and that
application cannot again be made before
the month of June. The meeting agreed that
failing a satisfactory arrangement with the
Callander and Oban Company being at once
completed application to the Board of Trade
should be postponed till Summer

Breadalbane

At Killin the 25th November 1882, which day the
Committee met
    Present Lord Breadalbane, Chairman
            John McNaughton
            Charles Stewart
            Robt. Menzies
            John Willison.
            Dond. Crerar
            John Cameron
            Dr. Hodges
            A. A. Robertson

The minutes of last meeting were read and
approved of

Mr Menzies gave a verbal report of Sub-
committee's meeting in Glasgow with the Caledonian Company Directors from which it

Page from the minute book of the Killin Railway Co.

one second-hand case. Some of Robertson's letters to Oban reveal
him as an amateur in railway matters:

> The train staff boxes have arrived all right. I am afraid they should
> have been painted and lettered before they were sent here, as we have
> none here that can do this. Should I send them to Glasgow? May I
> ask if you will get the tickets printed? I do not know what number to
> order, and you will have to get passenger tickets printed at any rate.

The line was to be worked by staff apparatus, and the management assured the Board of Trade that only one engine would be at
work. Robertson's knowledge of signalling must have been rudimentary, for when Anderson intimated that a second wire would be
erected on the Killin Railway posts, he thought that two wires
meant two engines! He complained to Anderson that the Board of
Trade might now insist on the installation of tablet apparatus and
that the money already spent on staff equipment would be wasted
'except for the levers'.

Nameboards were required for the stations, but first the names
had to be chosen; the first suggestion was Killin Junction, Killin
and Killin Pier, but the surfeit of Killins (there was also the c & o
Killin at the head of Glen Ogle) made the directors decide to call
the pier station Lochtay. John Anderson objected to this, but
Breadalbane replied, 'I cannot understand Mr Anderson's objection
to the word Lochtay. The Callander and Oban have a station, Loch
Awe. If he wishes it can be put Killin Pier—Lochtay. But we really
must have the Loch Tay somewhere, so as to let the tourists see that
the Railway goes to the Loch.' Robertson sent a copy of Breadalbane's letter to Anderson with the comment: 'This, I take it, settles
the matter.' It did.

When the Caledonian stores department delivered the nameboards for Killin Junction, they were found to exhibit the single
word 'Junction'; Robertson was told that as the original c & o Killin
station would be closed when the Killin Railway opened, the Killin
nameboards could then be paired with the Junction boards.

Robertson had hoped to inherit the Killin crane, but as Anderson
had it removed to Connel Ferry he had to order a new one from
Buttars of Glasgow at a cost of £53 8s. He was luckier with the
Killin goods shed; it was blown down in a gale, and the c & o
re-erected it at Killin Junction, thus sparing the Killin Railway the
cost of a new one.

The rails for Killin Junction arrived at Oban by sea and were sent
to the site by rail. But seventy-two 24 ft lengths went through to
Glasgow, where the Glasgow Railway & Electrical Appliance

The Killin Railway Company.

SECOND CALL OF ONE POUND STERLING PER SHARE.

No...............

KILLIN, 18th February, 1884.

Sir,

    The Directors of this Company have made a Call of One Pound Sterling per Share, which you are required to pay to the Bank of Scotland, Killin, *on Saturday, the 15th day of March next.*

    Interest at the rate of five per centum per annum will be charged on the above Call *after the said 15th day of March,* till paid.

I am,

SIR,

Your most obedient Servant,

_____*Secretary.*

To _____

Call on _____Shares, £____ _____

Interest, _____ __ _____ __

Received, _____ £_____ __

_____*Banker.*

N.B.—This letter must be sent to the Banker at the time of making the payment.

Cheques, when not on Killin or London, must include Commission.

Company fashioned them into points and crossings and sent them back to Killin Junction.

On 8 September 1885, without consulting the engineer, Robertson informed the Board of Trade that the line was finished and ready for inspection. When Strain came on the scene he pointed out that the railway was not at all ready to meet the critical gaze of the Board of Trade inspector, and Robertson cancelled his letter. A new date—28 January 1886—was fixed for Major Marindin to visit Killin. He was due at Callander at 9 a.m. and a special train was laid on to take him to Killin Junction. Again luck was against the Killin. A fierce snowstorm swept the district and blotted the railway from view. Robertson was obliged to inform the Board of Trade that 13 February would be the earliest date when he could receive the inspector.

During the dislocation that followed the snowstorm Anderson wired Killin that he had 140 tons of coal on the c & o consigned to Killin and villages round Loch Tay; since all roads were blocked Robertson might as well convey the coal from Killin Junction over the unopened railway to Killin village, using Best's engine. A brisk traffic in coal ensued. Almost at once a cry of despair came from the farmers in the area: their animals were dying for lack of hay. Could the railway help? Robertson wrote to Oban, 'What do you say?' Anderson said yes to the hay traffic, even suggesting that a Caledonian engine be used. Robertson, with the Board of Trade in mind, thought that he would have to lock up Best's engine while any Caledonian visitor was on the line, and that that would give the contractor an excuse for delaying the works; so Best's engine carried the hay, to the delight of the farmers.

Best, in later years, told with relish what happened when Major Marindin's inspection party reached the Dochart viaduct. The inspector told a workman to bore a 1¼ ft hole in one of the arches. He stood by to view the proceedings, expecting that the drill would bite through 2 ft of concrete in twenty minutes, as it usually did with masonry bridges. But at the end of twenty minutes the hole in the concrete was still only 7 in. deep.

The ceremonial opening of the Killin Railway took place on 13 March 1886. It was a surprisingly grand affair. Invitations went out to senior railway officers and civic dignitaries, and most of them accepted. Among the guests who boarded the special train at Callander that day was David Jones, locomotive superintendent of the Highland Railway. The engine was a little blue Caledonian 0—4—2 saddle-tank, one of two designed and built at St Rollox the previous year for the Killin line. Adorned with evergreens, it must have looked a brave sight as it battered its way up the Pass of Leny that bright spring morning. Breadalbane brought his guests up Loch Tay by steamer, a special train taking them to Killin Junction to join the main party. The combined trains carried all the visitors back to Killin village, where the day was being celebrated as a holiday. A meal was followed by the back-patting speeches inseparable from such occasions. John Strain claimed that the Dochart

LOCH TAY.

viaduct was the most ambitious work ever attempted in mass concrete. At this point a fellow-guest whispered audibly to the engineer: 'Spain!' Whereupon Best said, 'The success of the line has already borne fruit in other countries, and I am now engaged in constructing a railway in Spain of which the Killin Railway is just a model.'

The railway was, as already said, opened for passenger traffic on 1 April 1886. On the same date the original C & O Killin station was renamed Glenoglehead. It ceased to be a passenger station from 1 April 1889, but passengers could have most trains stopped there by notifying the guard at Killin Junction or Lochearnhead. This facility was withdrawn on 30 September 1891. Until the end of 1916, passengers for Killin travelling by the early-morning down train on Sundays only could alight at Glenoglehead, where the train stopped to set down mail. From then on Glenoglehead functioned as a private halt for railway servants and as a crossing place.

THE WEE TRAIN

The characteristic sound of Killin was the never-ceasing rush of the waters of the Dochart over its rocky bed. To this was added a new sound—the blast of the Killin engine as it climbed away from the village on its regular runs to Killin Junction. The 'wee train' quickly established itself in the affections of the villagers. Its comings and goings became a part of the place. On quiet nights, when the wind was in the west, villagers could hear above the ever-present roar of the waters the labouring beat of an Oban bogie as it lifted its train towards Glen Ogle summit four miles away, after its stop at the Junction. Then would come the growing rumble of the wee train as it wound its way gingerly down the glen and into the village.

Killin Junction station consisted of an island platform with the Killin line on its northern face and the Callander & Oban up line on its southern face. A single platform served the C & O down line. The expense of running the station was shared equally by the Caledonian and the C & O. There were two signal boxes, West with twenty-two levers and East with twenty-six levers. The Killin Railway paid half the cost of working the West box and the whole cost of the East box.

The original working agreement with the Caledonian, which was to be paid 55 per cent of the gross revenue with a guaranteed minimum of £2,377, was for three years. By a new agreement, which came into effect on 1 April 1888, the Caledonian undertook to work the line at cost for five years, and to contribute £525 to the Killin Railway in cash for the payment of the secretary's salary and interest on loans. The Caledonian would deduct operating costs from the gross revenue and send the balance to the Killin Railway. Of the money received the Killin Railway was allowed to pay 1 per cent to its ordinary stock. But it had to remit to the Caledonian a proportion of the £525 cash payment. If anything was left over the Killin kept it. The agreement was renewed at five-yearly intervals, but by a 1909 amendment the Caledonian agreed to pay salary and interest charges up to a maximum of £525 per annum.

Doubt existed in the district as to the status of Killin Junction station. People living in the vicinity not unnaturally expected to be allowed to use it, but the Killin Railway never intended Killin Junction to be anything other than an exchange point. A clear ruling was given in answer to a petition from residents in Glen

Dochart for a bridge across the line at the Junction: 'No access to
Killin Junction is provided by the railway company for the public
except by rail, and the Junction is intended wholly for the inter-
change of passengers and other traffic arriving there.'
A generous timetable was provided.

		am	am	Up am	am	pm	pm	pm	pm
Lochtay	dep.			8.55	11.35	2.15		5.50	
Killin	arr.			8.59	11.38	2.18		5.53	
	dep.	6.45	7.35	9.1	11.40	2.23	4.15	6.0	6.50
Killin Jct		6.58	7.48	9.15	11.53	2.37	4.28	6.13	7.33

		am	am	Down am	am	pm	pm	pm	pm
Killin Jct	dep.	7.12	8.4	10.25	12.30	2.50	4.55	6.30	7.12
Killin	arr.	7.25	8.18	10.38	12.44	3.3	5.8	6.45	7.26
	dep.		8.20	10.40	1.40		5.26		
Lochtay	arr.		8.24	10.43	1.44		5.29		

The 11.35, 2.15 and 4.15 up trains and the 12.30, 2.50 and 7.12
down trains were mixed. No goods trains were shown in the working timetable.

Killin station consisted of a single platform with a simple office
building. It had no loop, and trains terminating there adopted a
special procedure for running round. After an arriving train had
dropped its passengers the engine propelled the empty stock up the
branch for a short distance; it then uncoupled, ran back through the
station, and reversed into the goods yard at the east end. The
coaches were allowed to run by gravity down through the station
and were stopped at a point beyond the goods yard. The engine
then emerged from the goods yard, coupled on to the coaches and
pulled them forward to the platform ready for the next departure.
All coaches, from the opening of the line, were fitted with the
Westinghouse brake.

The trains that ran forward to Lochtay pier connected with the
steamers; there was no local public service between Killin and
Lochtay—at least, not officially. Lochtay station had a single platform and rounding loop, and a siding led on to the pier which could
handle freight as well as passengers. The line passed through the
station to terminate in a small engine-shed built into the hillside
above the loch. When the engine required coal and water it ran
down to Lochtay, sometimes light and sometimes taking its coaches.

Robertson thought that a cottage should be built for Watt and
Dick, the driver and fireman, beside the shed, but Breadalbane
insisted that they find lodgings in Killin. However, cottages were

EXCURSION TRAFFIC—2

(25) Ex-CR No. 123 and ex-NBR No. 256 'Glen Douglas' crossing the Lochy viaduct with a special train in May 1962

(26) Ex-GNS No. 49 in Glen Lochy with a special train on 14 April 1960

THE KILLIN RAILWAY

(27) *Lochtay station and pier, 1886*
(28) *Killin 'pug' No. 263*

soon provided for the footplatemen at Lochtay pier, at a rental of 1s 9d per week each. Watt does not appear to have been a model tenant, for in March 1888 Robertson wrote to the Caledonian accountant, 'What is to be done about Watt the engine driver? We have not yet received any rent from him?' John McLeod, the surfaceman, who rented the cottage beside the Dochart viaduct at a rental of 15s a year, was two years behind with his rent, and Robertson asked the Caledonian to deduct the arrears from his wages.

The wee train had been functioning for only a few months when the monthly cash remittances from the Caledonian stopped. 'My Lord,' an alarmed Robertson wrote to Breadalbane, 'the Caledonian Railway Company are now retaining in their hands the traffic receipts from our line. The question arises—how are we to pay the interest on our bonds at Martinmas—and other expenses?' The Caledonian had been paying the Killin company every month a proportion of the traffic receipts. But brief experience showed that in a year the Killin revenue was not likely to reach the £2,377 guarantee given to the Caledonian, and the Caledonian decided that it had the right to retain the entire takings. Not a penny-piece reached the Killin office. In what he called a semi-private letter, Robertson told Robert Menzies, who had just become a director: 'I am placed in an awkward fix in regard to the payment of your interest,' and suggested that he should pay this and other expenses out of the capital account—a dubious if not a downright illegal exercise.

Robertson urged Gibson of the Caledonian to meet the Killin directors to discuss the financial crisis at the earliest possible date. But Gibson, not sharing the Killin's sense of urgency, replied that such a meeting was impossible as the solicitor of the company was in London. A second urgent letter brought the news that Gibson had lumbago and could not attend to business. Robertson's third letter demanded a meeting in Glasgow on a specified date and castigated the Caledonian for perfidity. He added: 'P.S. Will you please send me a free pass to Glasgow and back.' Robertson also had the greatest difficulty in gaining the ear of his own chairman. To Porteous of the Callander & Oban office in Glasgow he confided: 'I am to call a meeting of my board in a few days, that is to say if I can possibly get Lord Breadalbane to name a day.' Eventually a meeting with the Caledonian oppressors was arranged at which Menzies and Robertson were to be present.

The correspondence files show how the two Killin men laid their

H

plans. Robertson wrote to Menzies in Edinburgh: 'One thing he [Lord Breadalbane] wished me to say was to try and *smooth* the Caledonian men as much as possible. It is very necessary that you should have a talk with me beforehand, and we will not have time in Glasgow. Could you come by way of Larbert and we could be on from there together?' Of course he added, 'If you apply to Mr Gibson he will no doubt send you a free pass.' So the case against the Caledonian was built up in a Caledonian train between Larbert and Glasgow, at Caledonian expense. Even the autocrats of Buchanan Street knew that a railway could not exist without money, and they agreed to release the few pounds necessary to pay the Killin's day-to-day expenses. 'They would allow us a slump (*sic*) sum for two years,' reported Robertson to Breadalbane. 'We must just try and get as much out of them as possible.'

Early in 1887 the Killin Railway Office published the results of the first ten months of operations—from 1 April 1886 to 21 January 1887.

	£	s.	d.
Passengers	517	6	9
Parcels, horses, carriages	102	7	0
Goods	444	19	8
Minerals	206	16	1
Live stock	46	9	5
Mails	33	4	6
Total	£1,351	3	5

General charges for 10 months

	£	s.	d.
Secretary's salary	50	0	0
Auditor's fees	10	10	0
Fee for registration		13	6
Fee for assessor		5	0
Fire insurance	3	8	10
Auditor's travelling expenses		12	0
Repairs		17	9
Postage and telegrams	2	7	1
	£68	14	2

Government duty	£5	2	1

Rates and Taxes			
Poor and school rate as proprietor	9	5	10
Poor and school rate as occupier	9	15	10
Road taxes as proprietor	5	9	6
Road taxes as occupier	4	3	1

Through to Edinburgh no more. *Top*: In May 1961 Nos 45043 and 45162 at Connel Ferry with the 1205 Oban to Glasgow and Edinburgh (division was at Stirling). *M. Mensing/Colour Rail*
Bottom: After the infamous rockfall in Glen Ogle, track lifting began that same month, December 1966. Here it is seen in progress at Balquhidder station whose site is now a caravan park. *F. Spaven*

Long Forgotten. *Top*: It is 24 July 1958, the summer season in full swing and there is little thought that this scene (No 44798 leaving Callander) will not continue. *Colour Rail*

Bottom: But even at this time No 57246 did seem somewhat anachronistic at Killin, the short through platform serving as the branch's effective end. The line continued to the engine shed beside Loch Tay where in pre-war days there was a pier and occasional 'boat train'. *J. G. Wallace*

In his first report to the Board of Trade under the Regulation of Railways Act, Robertson stated that his company had operated at least six trains a day summer and winter without accident. The trains seldom had more than ten vehicles and usually had five or six. The report explained: 'Our composite passenger carriage is sufficient for the winter, and two passenger vehicles for summer. It is hoped, therefore, that the Board of Trade will not interfere with the working of the line.'

Robertson never took major decisions, and seldom minor ones, without consulting the Castle. (He signed his letters 'I am, My Lord Marquis, Your Most Obt. Sert.') When Anderson suggested that the Killin Railway might augment its revenue by organising a parcels delivery service in the village Robertson was enthusiastic, but Breadalbane vetoed the scheme on the grounds that a second porter would have to be employed at Killin station. Later the marquis relented and a village parcels service was started with the following scale of charges:

14 lbs		...	1d
15 lbs — 28 lbs		...	2d
29 lbs — 36 lbs		...	3d
57 lbs — 112 lbs		...	4d

The easiest way for the farmers on Loch Tay to send sheep to the Perth sales was to drive them to Aberfeldy and send them by the Highland Railway. Robertson persuaded his farming friends and bank clients to route their sheep over the Killin Railway, the C & O and the Caledonian, which was something like going round three sides of a square. The Killin line was ill-equipped for handling sheep, and soon Robertson was writing to Oban to paint a pathetic picture of sheep waiting at stations without adequate shelter. 'When I wrote several lots of sheep were standing about the stations,' he complained, 'and the farmers were *swearing* and declaring they would in future go by Aberfeldy to Perth.'

Robertson also kept pleading with Anderson to make repairs to Killin Railway property. 'The Junction station is letting in the water badly on stormy days at the doors and windows,' he reported in January 1887. 'I see also the water from the urinal makes its way into the waiting room at Killin station. Should they [the station buildings] not now receive a coat of varnish so as to preserve the wood?' Anderson, for his part, was for ever pressing the Killin Railway to enlarge Killin station. That would have been a capital development, financed wholly by the Killin Railway. There was some trouble over who had to foot the bill for repairs to railway houses at Killin and Lochtay. After a lengthy triangular correspondence between Killin, Glasgow and Oban, and a meeting between Anderson and Robertson at Oban, the Killin secretary received a typically Andersonian letter: 'I don't think there is any absolute finding to give as to these improvements as it seems to me the difficulty is where the money is coming from.'

In the first winter blocks of ice floating in the Lochay splintered the wooden piers of the Lochay viaduct, and the village blacksmith was told to put in protecting plates of iron 'at a cost of not more than £6'. Later there were complaints about the dirty condition of

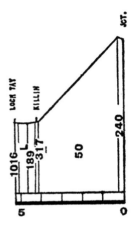

Gradient profile, Killin Railway

Killin platform; this was not surprising, in view of the fact that, to augment its income, the railway company had given the Western District of the County of Perth permission to deposit the village refuse at the station. The depositors were asked to place the material 'in such a way as through time will enable a double line of rails to be laid at the platform'.

The relationship between Robertson and Anderson is illustrated by a letter which the Killin secretary sent to Oban in January 1888 concerning a misdemeanour by a Killin villager. On a stormy night that month Malcolm McLaren went up to Glenoglehead (Killin old station) with his horse and cart to collect the mails from the evening train. Usually, the gate leading into the station yard was open, but on this occasion it was closed and padlocked. McLaren could not risk leaving his horse unattended outside the station, in case the sudden arrival of the train should frighten it. So he took the gate off its hinges and led the horse into the yard. Anderson was furious when he learned of the damage to C & O property, and he threatened McLaren with dire penalties. Robertson, taking up the case, wrote a most abject letter pleading for McLaren. 'He is now very sorry for what he has done and makes humble apology. I may mention that in Malcolm's family they now have serious trouble. This should further tend towards mercy to him.'

In 1892 Robertson was dismayed to receive from Anderson a bill for £53 11s, the wages of a C & O pointsman employed at the Junction during its construction. Robertson replied that he had settled all his debts regarding the Junction six years previously, and he refused to pay. At the same time he submitted an account to Anderson which he considered was overdue: the advertising rights of the Killin stations were let at £5 a year, and Robertson considered that he was entitled to half the revenue from Killin Junction. Anderson replied that the Killin Railway was not entitled to any payment *because Killin Junction did not belong to it.*

Robertson's letters over the next few days show his consternation at this news: 'I do not understand how this can be, seeing we paid for its erection, and this is the first time I heard of it being claimed by the C. and O.,' he wrote to Breadalbane. 'This is news to me,' he told the Caledonian. 'We paid for the erection of this, and I do not understand how it became the property of the C. and O. Can you explain this?' Poor Robertson had to accept the fact that the station his company had built on C & O ground was indeed C & O property.

THE FINAL YEARS

The wee train puffed up and down the village railway through the years. In summer the visitors came in hundreds, either to stay in Killin village or to sail on the loch steamers. In winter few people needed to travel and the single-coach train saw only a handful of passengers.

There were times on the sleepy little line when even the secretary was out of touch with current happenings. On 24 October 1917 the engine shed at Lochtay was destroyed by fire. In a quiet country district this was a talking-point for days, but MacEwan, who had succeeded Robertson as secretary, knew nothing about it until five days later when he was handed a letter from Oban asking if he had claimed the insurance money! 'I regret to report that the Engine Shed at Loch Tay Pier Station was totally destroyed by fire on the

7th June 23

Dear Sir,

In accordance with your instructions I now beg to send you inventory of this Company's property to be forwarded to you at the beginning of the week. I note that the cash books ledger and Journal are to be sent to the Accountants of the London Midland & Scottish Railway Coy at Euston, on demand.

Yours faithfully
E, MacEwen Secy

J. J. Hanning Esqr.
Secretary
Caledonian Railway Company
Glasgow.

The last letter from the Killin Railway office

morning of 24th inst.,' he reported to Breadalbane. 'This was reported to the Callander and Oban Railway Secretary and I only got to know of it through them on the 29th inst., and at once wrote to the Insurance Company.' The company paid the full amount of the policy, but the shed was under-insured, and MacEwan wondered if the Caledonian would be prepared to make up the substantial sum required for a new shed. He sent the insurance company's cheque for £120 to the Caledonian, and some days later he was able to tell Breadalbane, 'They have cashed our cheque.' This he apparently took as a sign that the Caledonian would rebuild the shed without asking further questions.

In the winter and spring of 1922-3 a melodrama was enacted at Killin. The poor Killin Railway had fallen on evil times. It had not paid a dividend for twenty years, and its debts amounted to £12,000. Moreover, the Marquis of Breadalbane had died on 19 October 1922, and his trustees were not disposed to regard the village railway in the same paternal light as had its late noble chairman. MacEwan the secretary and the two remaining directors, Campbell Willison and Alan Cameron, did what they could to keep the moribund concern functioning.

It is plain from the Killin Railway correspondence of the time that the three men in Killin had only a hazy idea of what the railway political events of 1922-3 entailed for them. They thought that the Caledonian was the absorbing power. Then, when correspondence began to arrive in their office from London, they got the impression that they were being taken over by the LNW. Eventually terms for the take-over of the line were received from an organisation calling itself the London Midland & Scottish Railway Company. The Killin directors met to consider them, and they seethed with indignation.

On 18 January 1923 the following letter from the enclave in the Perthshire hills arrived on a desk at the Euston headquarters of the country's mightiest railway empire.

Killin Rly Office,
17 January 1923,

Dear Sir,

Your letter of 8 inst was duly submitted to my Directors who have instructed me to reply that they regret they cannot accept the terms offered.

Yours faithfully,

E. MacEwan, Sec.

Arthur Watson, Esq.,
LMSR, General Manager's Office,
Euston, London.

The LMS had offered to accept all the Killin's debts, and in addition pay £1 in cash for every £100 of Killin stock. The Killin directors thought the offer insulting, and resolved to demand £10 for every £100 of stock. Watson passed the Killin affair over to Donald Matheson, late of the Caledonian but now deputy manager (Scotland) of the LMS, and in a few days he assured the Killin board that better terms would be forthcoming. In his reply to Matheson, MacEwan stated the Killin's case. He admitted that 1921 had been a disastrous year because of restrictions placed on the line due to the coal strike, but he saw financial salvation in the recently revived timber traffic. 'In addition,' he told Matheson, 'the linking up of the Highland and Caledonian railways should mean a large increase in the revenue derived from tourist traffic over the Killin Railway and the Loch Tay steamer.' And he went on,

> The Killin Railway is a necessary link in the system worked by the Amalgamated Company, the construction of which today would cost four times what the directors are asking for it as a going concern. On receipt of Mr Watson's amended offer indicated in your letter my Directors will be prepared to reconsider a modification of their claim.

A few days later MacEwan was writing curtly to Matheson : 'Please communicate by letter any new proposal which you may desire to make and I will lay the matter before my board'—he meant that he would tell his fellow-director about the offer.

Meanwhile, Euston behaved as if Killin had already surrendered. MacEwan was instructed to supply an inventory of station fittings, and he filled in a personal questionnaire, in which he revealed that he was sixty-three and that his salary from the Killin Railway Company was £30 per annum. When asked to complete an inventory of his office furniture he replied that every item belonged either to himself or to the Bank of Scotland 'from whom the Killin Railway has had free quarters during its forty years of existence'.

On 9 March 1923, William Cameron and MacEwan met LMS representatives in Glasgow and were offered £7 10s in cash for each £100 of Killin stock. They rejected the offer, and decided to fight for their independence. On 15 March, MacEwan sent a strongly-worded letter to Matheson :

> I am to ask that you will be good enough to let me have your reply to this proposal (a renewed demand for £10 per £100 of stock) by Monday morning first, as the time for the Company to lodge their case with the Tribunal, 24 March, is nearly out, and if the case is to go forward Law Agents and Accountants must at once receive their instructions, and counsel in Edinburgh and London consulted with a view to the case being in the clerk's hands by the 24th.

This was ambitious talk for a two-man, 5¼-mile railway with impressive debts and no money.

The LMS raised its offer to £8. MacEwan arranged a meeting of shareholders in Killin; the chairman carefully explained to the half-dozen present that he had consulted experienced lawyers and accountants and after fully considering all the facts the board was of the opinion—although the decision was a matter for the shareholders—that the LMS offer should be accepted. The shareholders approved but expressed the hope that the new proprietors would give the Killin directors, who had charged nothing for their services to the railway, free passes. A free pass was also requested for the secretary, who was losing his income. The meeting then closed, and the last entry was inscribed in the minute book of the Killin Railway Company: 'A hearty vote of thanks accorded to the chairman brought the meeting to a close.'

To the end the secretary sought to impress everybody with the importance of his railway. In sending written copies of the accounts to Matheson he apologised with the remark, 'I am without a typist,' implying that perhaps the typist was ill. But the Killin had never owned anything as newfangled (or expensive) as a typewriter. On 1 June, MacEwan took the ominous step of instructing the village joiner to make a strong case in which to despatch the seal and books of the company to the LMS.

The village railway was no more, though Killin would have a train service for many years yet. The pattern of traffic changed little under LMS rule. Following the withdrawal of the Loch Tay steamer services in 1939, the stretch of line between Killin station and Lochtay pier lay unused, except by the branch engine going to its shed. The line was opened temporarily in the 1950s for freight traffic to the Loch Tay hydro-electric power scheme.

Freight service was withdrawn between Killin Junction and Killin on 7 November 1964. On 27 September 1965 a landslide in Glen Ogle stopped all traffic on the main line. The 'wee train' came up from Killin village to the Junction as usual that morning; but as Killin Junction was an exchange platform only, there was nothing to exchange that day, and the train ran on to Crianlarich. The bus service through the village began next day, 28 September 1965, including the school bus which left Crianlarich at 7.25 a.m. and ran via Killin to Callander, from which it returned at 4.5; and the rail service ended.

The Ballachulish Branch

ON TO INVERNESS ?

Two weeks after the West Highland Railway opened in 1894 two quite separate survey groups were in the Great Glen looking for a railway route to Inverness. The West Highland wanted to take a line from Fort William up by the chain of lochs to the Highland capital. The Highland Railway concluded that the best defence against such an assault on its citadel was to promote a railway from Inverness down the Great Glen to Fort William. And into the picture came the Callander & Oban, with a grand plan to build a coastal and cross-country line from Oban through Fort William and up the Great Glen to Inverness. This, in part, was a revival of the c & o's 1889 scheme to win a route to Fort William in opposition to the West Highland Railway.

The country between Oban and Fort William had long been a source of anxiety to the local authorities responsible for communications. In the 30 miles between Connel Ferry and North Ballachulish the sea made three deep and narrow indentations into the land. To get from one side of Loch Etive to the other by road from Connel meant a detour of 35 miles, a five-mile detour was required at Loch Creran further north, and there was no road round the head of Loch Leven. Passengers crossed the water by a primitive ferry. The Callander & Oban had to plan formidable bridges to carry their proposed Oban-Inverness line over these salt-water channels.

In March 1891 the Argyll County Council had invited the c & o's co-operation, should it be planning a railway north of Connel, in providing dual-purpose bridges. The Council letter was considered at a board meeting and 'continued for further investigation'. When three years later the c & o decided to build an Oban-Inverness line, it decided to make it, including the bridges, at its own expense and undertake its working. The board meeting of 23 October 1894 resolved not to solicit subscriptions from other railway companies, and in particular not to extend the existing Caledonian-Callander &

Oban agreement to include the new line. 'Callander and Oban to work itself,' was the terse phrase recorded in the minute book. It was a bold decision in view of the C & O's financial history.

Sir John Wolfe Barry, one of the most eminent civil engineers of the day, was commissioned to survey the line. Barry's estimate of the cost was £9,000 per mile, without the land, the total cost being well over a million pounds. He informed Oban that his fee for surveying the route would be £30 a mile plus one-eighth per cent of the estimate. The most the C & O could afford to spend on the survey was £1,500, which was insufficient for the whole line. Anderson instructed Barry to carry the survey northwards until the money ran out: he got as far as Banavie.

Meanwhile, Anderson opened negotiations to acquire an abandoned prison as a site for the C & O station in Fort William. With Barry he met the Argyll County Council to discuss dual-purpose bridges and shared expenses. But at his next board meeting Anderson asked: 'Is the company to be bound to build dual-purpose bridges, or only if councils contribute, or shall nothing be said on the matter?' Nothing was said on the matter. When the bill was drafted the Callander & Oban claimed the right to link with the Highland Railway at Inverness; it also demanded access to the West Highland Railway pier on the Caledonian Canal at Banavie, and running powers over the recently-authorised West Highland extension to Mallaig. Davidson & Syme of Edinburgh were retained as legal agents, and the bill was presented in Parliament on 18 September 1894.

By that time a certain amount of order had been restored to West Highland railway politics. The North British and the Highland agreed not to promote railways in the Great Glen for ten years. At the same time the Caledonian gave its blessing to a West Highland Railway scheme to continue from Fort William down the shore of Loch Linnhe to Ballachulish, over part of the route of the proposed C & O line to Inverness. Thus arose the curious spectacle of the two old enemies, the North British and the Caledonian, opposing the Caledonian protégé, the Callander & Oban. The Oban intrusion into the Great Glen was a blatant violation of the treaty made by the big companies, and the promoters were threatened with implacable opposition if they persisted.

Undismayed, Anderson called a special meeting to discuss the Inverness line. Breadalbane was in London and refused to come to Oban, so the directors had to travel down to his Cavendish Square home. When they arrived the marquis was not available: he was at

Osborne on the Isle of Wight as guest of Queen Victoria. A telegram brought him back for an evening meeting, but when he produced a letter he had received from the Caledonian affirming that that company would oppose the C & O bill, even Anderson could see that the position was hopeless. Two days later, on 8 February 1895, the bill was withdrawn.

BALLACHULISH

Following the collapse of the Inverness scheme, Ballachulish became the focal point for railway promoters in the West Highlands. Ballachulish was a village of 1,800 people, most of the wage-earners working in the granite or slate quarries. The West Highland Railway proposed to reach it by a line from Fort William and a bridge across Loch Leven. The Callander & Oban produced a truncated version of its Inverness scheme, involving the building of a line across Loch Etive and Loch Creran to connect Connel Ferry with Ballachulish. Both schemes were avidly canvassed in the district. The slate-quarry interests did not like the idea of a bridge across the mouth of Loch Leven : the bridge was to have three fixed spans each of 144 ft and a swinging span of 80 ft, and it was feared that it would interfere with the cargo steamers serving the quarries. Some of the people of Ballachulish wanted nothing to do with either railway. One wrote about the proposed two-pronged assault on 'this poor, unprotected village of ours'.

The question of the railway to Ballachulish might well have set Fort William and Oban at loggerheads. Oddly enough, Fort William strongly opposed the West Highland line. The people of Lochaber had had a long and difficult battle to get a railway, and had generally rejoiced when the first train arrived at Fort William. Yet only two years later Donald Boyd, one of the two men who had founded the West Highland Railway, could write :

> The railway company have already assumed the airs of an autocrat who controls the situation and have indeed acted in a very high-handed fashion towards the rising city of Lochaber. The town indeed is to be treated as an appendage of the railway which has already seized the best part of the foreshore and cut the town off from the sea. The West Highland Railway seem to think that owing to their having graciously gone to the assistance of the town of Fort William they have a right to treat it as they please. It is as if the man who dragged another out from before the engine of the West Highland line claimed the right to half-choke him in the ditch. She is to be killed as a seaport, and handed over bound hand and foot to the West Highland Railway. She is to be choked as a tourist resort to become instead a grimy railway terminus. A wretched line like that indicated is not

worth giving up anything valuable for, seeing that the day cannot be far distant when a through line to Oban will be constructed without losing sight of the public interests, vested and sentimental. Let them boldly resist thraldom.

The people of Fort William had themselves to blame for their plight. The C & O had threatened to obliterate Oban's waterfront and had been repulsed by public clamour. The West Highland had come into Fort William along the shore of Loch Linnhe, in the process cutting off the town from the waterfront, and only a whimper of protest had been heard. Only when the line was finished did they realise they had made a mistake in allowing the railway to intrude where a picturesque promenade could have been created. And now the West Highland proposed to continue the line further down the lochside in front of the pleasant villas at the south end of the town.

The rival parties took their respective bills to Westminster and the local press kept their supporters well informed about their progress. The *Oban Telegraph* reported:

> The swearing arena of the House of Lords committee rooms has been largely patronised this week by well-known gentlemen from Oban and the vicinity; for the West Highland and Callander and Oban Railways have stripped once more to the buff, and their respective partizans are taking God to witness with customary fervour. . . . Mr John Anderson of the Callander and Oban looked anxious but in prime fighting trim; while Mr Kennedy of the West Highland meaneth to do or die.

During the hearing the chairman of the Ballachulish Slate Company admitted that he had been 'squared' by the Callander & Oban: he had agreed to support its line on receiving a promise that the station refreshment room at Ballachulish would not sell alcoholic liquors!

The West Highland and the Callander & Oban won their Acts for lines to Ballachulish on the same day—7 August 1896—but the West Highland was refused permission to build a bridge across Loch Leven. The railway was never built. The Callander & Oban's line was described in the Act as:

> Railway No. 1 25 miles, 5 furlongs, 5 chains commencing 145 yards west of the booking office at Connel Ferry to a point 760 yards from the north-east corner of Ballachulish Hotel in the Parish of Lismore and Appin, and Railway No. 2 a line 2 furlongs, 2 chains, 730 yards west of Connel Ferry to a point 300 yards from the south end of Connel Bridge.

Railway No. 2 was a spur from the Callander & Oban to enable trains from Oban to proceed directly on to the bridge. The earthworks were partly built but never completed. The original stations proposed (substantially different from those eventually built) were : Ledaig, Cregan Ferry, Portnaervish, Cuil, Ardsheil (with pier), and Ballachulish. Early in planning it was intended to take the line through Port Appin and across the mouth of Loch Creran; a company was promoted to build a hotel at the mouth of the loch. The hotel was built, but it never opened, as the railway did not go that way; it was eventually occupied as a private house. The company bought land at Fearlochan on the south side of Loch Creran for a proposed station, at Cuil for a pier, at Duror for a station, and for a ticket platform at North Connel.

Sir John Wolfe Barry and John Forman (engineer of the West Highland Railway) were appointed joint engineers, and John Best was awarded the contract for the railway works. The construction of the two large bridges was entrusted to the Arrol Bridge & Roofing Company Limited, H. M.·Brunel and E. Crutwell being associated with the engineers in designing them. The estimated cost of the Connel Bridge was £42,837 and of Creagan Bridge £11,642 7s 9d. The estimated cost of the line was £210,000, of which the Caledonian was authorised to contribute £150,000; five years were allowed for its completion. The first sod was cut without ceremony at Connel Ferry on 16 September 1898 by the resident engineer, Mr A. J. Pringle.

CONNEL BRIDGE

The bridge which the engineers undertook to build across Loch Etive was second only (in Great Britain) to the Forth Bridge in length of main span. The site was at the narrowest part of Loch Etive, over a waterway 690 ft across. The channel exhibited certain peculiarities. At low tide there was under the bridge what could be described as a salt waterfall : the Falls of Lora, of Ossianic legend. Over a distance of 100 yd the tide ebbing from the loch poured over a 4 ft drop. At certain states of tide the current moved at between 10 and 12 knots. Since the erection of temporary staging was impossible the bridge had to be designed with the piers close to each shore and clear of the current. The central span was to be built out as a continuation of cantilever spans carried on the main piers. In essence the bridge consisted of two main legs resting on each pier leaning outwards towards the middle of the channel and outwards towards the base when viewed in cross-section. The main legs were held back by booms anchored to abutments at the shore end by anchor girders buried 50 ft deep in solid masonry.

Construction began in 1898 with the erection of three 38½ ft masonry approach arches at each end of the bridge, and the building of the two main piers, which were constructed within coffer dams in shallow water on solid rock. The erection of the steelwork began at both ends in May 1890 and was completed in June 1903. Apparently progress during the first summer was disappointing, for Anderson reported to the board, 'Mr Arrol has not fulfilled his promise about Connel Bridge,' and he called for a report within ten days. The labour force employed was small considering the size of the contract; in December 1901 only 32 men were employed at Connel, but 115 were employed at Germiston Works, Glasgow, in producing 2,600 tons of steelwork for the bridge. By March 1902 these numbers had dropped to 25 and 110 respectively.

In the construction of the steelwork the anchor bearers were embedded in the masonry beneath heavy base plates. The main legs and back struts were then begun, and built outwards and upwards from the point of anchorage. Along the abutments and masonry arches and on to the main piers the work was carried out by cranes running on staging. In the centre gap where staging was impracticable the crane was mounted on an eight-wheel trolley heavily ballasted at the shore end and with the jib projecting at the other end so that it could be operated a considerable distance in advance of the work without overbalancing.

A single line of rails was laid on longitudinal sleepers of Jarrah wood carried in the troughs of the rail bearers and filled in with asphalt. The usual method of scarfing the rails so that they would slide past each other with any movement of the bridge due to variations in temperature could not be used: with traffic moving along the single line in both directions, the scarfed joint would present what was virtually a facing point to trains travelling in one direction. At the junction of the middle span with the cantilever span a 3 in. gap was left in the rail and a joint rail was placed close to the web, the top surface of the joint rail curving gradually towards the centre of the gap. When the wheels crossed the gap the outer half of the tyres was supported by the joint rail. An asphalt footway—not a roadway—was provided alongside the railway, separated from the track by a lattice fence.

Creagan Bridge, too, was successfully completed. It had two main spans each of 150 ft 4½ in. with a heading of 40 ft above high water. The centre pier was made up of two 12 ft cylinders 20 ft apart between centres, sunk into the solid rock and filled with concrete. A footway was carried on cantilever brackets outside the main girders on the eastern side of the bridge.

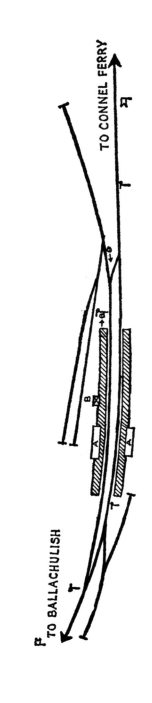

Layout of Benderloch, 1955

C & O STATIONS

(29) *Killin Junction, looking east, in 1965*
(30) 0—4—4T *No. 55195 at Ballachulish with the 3.55 p.m. to Oban
on 19 July 1954*

C & O BRIDGES

(31) Bowstring girder bridge in the Pass of Leny
(32) Creagan bridge, Ballachulish branch

Apart from the bridges there were no outstanding engineering features on the line. Gradients were easy except for a short stretch of 1 in 60 between Ballachulish Ferry and Ballachulish, and two short lengths of 1 in 70 and 1 in 80. The rails were laid on locally-produced larch sleepers, delivered at the site creosoted at 4s 7d each. The track was ballasted with ash and sea-pebbles.

THE BRANCH IN SERVICE

The branch was opened for traffic on 24 August 1903, when the following timetable came into operation.

Up

	am	am	am	pm	pm
Ballachulish *dep.*	6.20	9.30	11.0	2.50	4.30
Ballachulish Ferry *arr.*	6.26	9.36	11.6	2.56	4.36
Kentallen	6.39	9.49	11.20	3.9	4.49
Duror	6.52	10.2	11.35	3.22	5.2
Appin	7.11	10.21	11.55	3.41	5.23
			pm		
Creagan	7.23	10.38	12.15	3.53	5.35
Benderloch	7.46	11.3	12.38	4.16	5.58
Connel Ferry *arr.*	7.57	11.15	12.49	4.27	6.9
Connel Ferry *dep.*			12.53		
Oban *arr.*	8.45	11.55	1.14	4.52	6.30

Down

	am	am	am	pm	pm
Oban *dep.*	7.55	9.40	11.20	4.5	7.0
Connel Ferry *arr.*	8.12	9.58	11.36	4.22	7.18
Connel Ferry *dep.*	8.30	10.3	11.42	4.38	8.50
Benderloch	8.41	10.14	11.53	4.49	9.1
			pm		
Creagan	9.4	10.37	12.16	5.12	9.24
Appin	9.16	10.49	12.28	5.24	9.36
Duror	9.35	11.8	12.47	4.43	9.55
Kentallen	9.48	11.21	1.0	5.56	10.8
Ballachulish Ferry	10.1	11.34	1.13	6.9	10.21
Ballachulish	10.7	11.40	1.19	6.15	10.27

Connel Ferry station was rebuilt to cope with the new traffic. There was an island platform on the westbound side and a bay at each end of the eastbound platform. Branch trains normally left from the bay facing west. Once they gained the north shore of Loch Etive the passengers found themselves in true tourist country offering a magnificent range of coastal and sylvan scenery. The line skirted Ardmucknish Bay to reach Benderloch, the first crossing place, giving entrancing views across the Firth of Lorne to Mull.

J

The train cut across a peninsula to Loch Creran, slipped round its wooded shores for five miles and crossed the loch at Creagan Narrows to reach the island platform at Creagan station. Just before plunging into Strathappin came a fine panoramic view across Loch Creran to the Benderloch mountains. After Appin, with its two-platform station, the railway regained the coast and passed by the ruins of Castle Stalker, up the shore of Loch Linnhe to Duror at the head of Cuil Bay. A four-mile run through the wooded valley of Kentallen brought it to salt water again at Kentallen pier. Then the route was round Loch Leven, past the single platform at Ballachulish Ferry to the two-bay terminus in Ballachulish village.

The railway revolutionised transport in Benderloch and Appin. To get to Oban the people of Appin had had to use the infrequent steamers or embark on a journey involving two ferries, two coaches and a train. On the railway they could reach Oban in two hours. A Saturday visit to the Oban shops, once a rarely-enjoyed luxury, became a commonplace. As at Killin, the branch took its place in the life of the district. The stations became meeting-places, the trains mobile community centres where gossip was exchanged. At one time a GPO mail box was carried in the guard's van of the mid-morning up train, known as 'The Mail', and local folks would go to the stations to post their letters. Mail for destinations in the south could gain eight or twelve hours over a letter left at the village post office. The box was transferred to the main-line train at Connel Ferry, removed at Stirling and taken to the GPO.

The last Oban-Ballachulish train on Saturday nights was a merry one. More often than not it was held at Connel Ferry to await the arrival of the late-running train from the south. Then the branch passengers would seek the licensed hospitality of the nearby *Falls of Lora*. Frenzied toots on the locomotive whistle were needed to persuade the revellers to return to the train. The more helpless among them felt secure in the knowledge that at their particular branch station there would be waiting an understanding porter and his barrow!

The friendly spirit engendered by the railway was long marred by the vexed question of the footpaths on the Connel and Creagan bridges. These would have been a godsend to local pedestrians, but nobody was allowed to use them. The Callander & Oban offered the path on Creagan bridge free to the county authority if it would make approach paths from the main road. This it refused to do. Anderson met the Argyll County Council and offered the Connel Bridge footpath for an annual rental of £800. This was considered excessive. 'Impossible to negotiate,' Anderson wrote in his minute book after the meetings. The C & O had paid for Connel Bridge and it was its policy that people who used it should pay for the privilege. Meanwhile it forced would-be users of the path to cross by train and charged them the equivalent of two miles of travel. Tell-tale tracks on the embankments at Creagan and North Connel told of clandestine walks over the bridges; Anderson had a close-set palisade fence built along the line at North Connel to discourage intruders, and from the Caledonian legal department he sought advice on prosecuting trespassers.

Despite constant pressure from the local authority, from the local Member of Parliament, the press and the rising motoring organisations, the C & O kept to its policy over Connel Bridge. In 1909, however, it did augment the passenger service on the bridge, introducing a shuttle service by motor charabanc. This vehicle, about which more will be said in a later chapter, was fitted with flanged wheels and otherwise adapted for railway use at St Rollox. It ran between Connel Ferry, North Connel (opened 7 March 1904) and Benderloch. Of the ten booked services between 7.45 and 7.30, four went through to Benderloch. An odd feature of the service was that it offered ten charabanc trips on Sundays (five of which terminated at Benderloch), although the company did not run Sunday trains on its main line.

The charabanc could also carry motor cars to and from Connel Ferry and Benderloch; when a driver wanted to take his car across the bridge he loaded it on to a flat wagon which was kept in the bay at the east end of Connel Ferry station. The rail motor on its next trip picked up the loaded wagon (or sometimes two wagons), pulled it out of the bay, and then propelled it through the station and over the bridge, pulling it on the return trip. The single fare for a car was 15s, the driver and passengers sitting in their vehicle during the crossing. It was common to see a holiday-bound family perched on their open tourer with their luggage piled around them rumbling across the bridge. On trips terminating at North Connel the rail bus was signalled as a ballast train working in section.

With the increase in motor traffic the Connel car-carrier became overworked in the summer and delays were common. The C & O was pressed to make the bridge available for vehicles running on their own wheels, but the Caledonian engineer reported, 'It is impossible to form a roadway for vehicles on the bridge.' A petition presented in 1912 for the opening of the footpath only was ignored. The exasperated local authorities held endless negotiations with the railway company. In 1913 the C & O offered to open the bridge for pedestrians and bicycles only at an annual rental of £250. The offer was rejected.

Then, a month or two later, a local man, MacAlpine Downie, applied to the Board of Trade to operate a chain ferry between Connel Ferry and North Connel; and suddenly the C & O discovered that it was possible after all to construct on the bridge a roadway for vehicles. Indeed, unwonted haste was displayed in completing the arrangements to receive the motor traffic. The company already owned land at the south end of the bridge, but considered that a better approach road could be made over other land. The secretary was instructed by the board: 'Pay £100 cash for the land required and erect necessary fencing if this is agreed to within fourteen days; failing agreement proceed with alternative plan on our own ground as the work must be proceeded with rapidly.'

The company spent £2,022 3s in adapting the footpath on the bridge to take motor vehicles and in providing an interlocking signalling system to prevent road and rail traffic from being on the bridge at the same time. The bridge was opened for pedestrians, motor and other traffic on 22 June 1914, toll charges for motors ranging from 7s 6d to 10s. Up to 8 August receipts from tolls amounted to £233 4s 6d; in the corresponding period of the previous year the car-carrier earned £254 7s 10½d. At first the bridge was open during daylight only, but after November 1914 crossings could be made outside the normal opening hours for an extra fee of 1s up to 10 p.m. and 2s after 10 p.m. The bridge-keeper kept the surcharge.

A storm of course blew up in the district over the toll charges, and on 29 July 1914 the Sheriff of Inverness held a public inquiry at Oban. The motoring interests maintained that the C & O was holding road-users to ransom. The railway retorted that in building Connel Bridge it had spent an extra £11,700 so that the structure could take a roadway as well as a railway, and it was entitled to recover some of the cost. At current charges the motor traffic using the bridge was likely to yield only £650 a year. The road-users insisted that the bridge had been built to its present width to achieve stability, and they wanted the tolls reduced to 5s or 2s 6d. But the inquiry left the C & O master of its own bridge.

For many years the Connel Bridge tolls occupied more space in the correspondence columns of the local press than any other topic. The bridge built up a massive fund of ill-will for the railway. Protests and pleas were useless. The man in the toll box was a law unto himself. Anything exhibiting a hackney plate he refused at any price. A shepherd could take his flock across, but he had to lead the beasts *one at a time*. A funeral cortège could not cross as such : coffins had to be removed from the hearses and carried across the bridge on payment of the appropriate toll; alternatively, the coffin could be taken by train, again on payment of the specified rate. There was an occasion, and it was in LMS days, when special dispensation was obtained—some say from Euston—to allow a funeral party to cross the bridge. When the son of the departed called at Connel Ferry station to pay the toll dues the stationmaster busied himself with the sheaf of papers which this unusual traffic had produced. As he handed over the receipt he said, 'And now, Mr ——, I hope you are not going to make a habit of this.'

DECLINE

Like its kind all over the country, the Ballachulish branch suffered a slow decline between the 1930s and '60s. On paper, passenger figures looked impressive, but analysis showed that about 700 of the weekly recorded passenger journeys were accounted for by about seventy schoolchildren who travelled to and from Oban High School. The new Glencoe road, brought into use in the early '30s, offered an easy route to the south, and rail freight and livestock figures slumped. Motorists took the new road to avoid the tyranny of the Connel tolls.

From 14 June 1965 the Ballachulish branch became a passenger line only, which meant in effect that it existed mainly to serve the schoolchildren. The last passenger train ran on 26 March 1966. Connel and Creagan bridges became the responsibility of the Secretary of State for Scotland, and tolls were removed. Part of the abandoned railway roadbed was to be incorporated in a county road-improvement scheme; work on removing the track began on 28 March.

The service ended on a jarring note. Large crowds headed by the Provost of Oban and the County Convenor of Argyll turned out to view the last train and by all accounts there was much merriment. The *Oban Times* was moved to comment that 'one might easily have supposed that the line was being opened rather than closed'. At the next council meeting a councillor who was also a railway-man protested at the carnival atmosphere that had surrounded the closure, and vainly asked his council colleagues to dissociate them-selves from the unseemly demonstration. But the schoolchildren celebrated the end of their line with understanding and dignity. On the last Friday they presented their guard with a gift bought with money they had collected among themselves.

Connel Ferry Bridge

CHAPTER VIII

The Halcyon Years

TOURIST'S DELIGHT

Argyll was tourist territory before the railway came. In a season one coach operator alone, Campbell of Ballachulish, imported seventy horses to handle the summer traffic. But coach travel was expensive, and the total number of passengers carried was necessarily small. The railway opened tourism to the masses. The coach and boat proprietors who had seen ruin in the railways found instead unprecedented prosperity as their services were incorporated into well-planned, ingenious tours fed by rail-borne passengers.

Through the years the Callander & Oban offered excursions in infinite variety, and at low cost, from brief evening outings to elaborate tours spread over several weeks. Their itineraries ranged from simple return journeys between two points to elaborate programmes involving numerous trains, steamers and coaches. A two-day excursion to Ireland *via* Oban was one of the novelties offered at C & O stations. The line received through excursionists from the north of England, and day trippers from London bound for Staffa and Iona.

A handbook of Caledonian Railway tours published in 1911 listed forty-one tours throughout the system, and thirty-two of them involved the C & O. For instance, Tour No. 68, price 18s 9d, ran from Edinburgh (Princes St) to Balloch Pier, *via* Glasgow (Central) and Dumbarton; Balloch Pier to Ardlui, per steamer on Loch Lomond; Ardlui to Crianlarich, through Glenfalloch, per coach; Crianlarich to Oban, per Callander & Oban Railway; Oban to Gourock or Glasgow (Broomielaw), *via* Crinan Canal, Kyles of Bute and Rothesay, per the steamers of David MacBrayne Ltd; and from Gourock or Glasgow (Central) to Edinburgh, per Caledonian Railway. The ticket-holder could take the whole season to his tour, or he could do it non-stop. A footnote referring to certain tours at the eastern end of the line explained: 'The route via Callander is the only one by which tourists can follow the chase as described in *Lady of the Lake*.'

The steamer fleets on the inland lochs played a major part in the Callander & Oban tour pattern. Indeed, it was the advent of the railway that made it possible for the vessels to be placed in the remote mountain-enclosed waterways; most of the vessels were built in the shipyards of the south, dismantled, and taken by rail to the lochs. In May 1876, a year before the railway reached Dalmally, Anderson got an estimate of £28,000—more than the C & O could afford at that time—for an extension of the line from Dalmally to Loch Awe, where he was anxious to secure ownership of the pier. In 1879, when the company's pier was finally under construction at Loch Awe, it decided not to run steamers of its own on the loch, but to offer every facility to the private operators.

The turning point for the loch steamers came in 1882. In that year the Marquis of Breadalbane put the steamer *Lady of the Lake* on Loch Tay and her sister, *Countess of Breadalbane*, on Loch Awe. The two were somewhat similar in appearance. *Countess of Breadalbane* was 99 ft 9 in. long and 14 ft wide, had a depth of 7 ft and weighed 95 gross tons, while *Lady of the Lake* was 92 ft 5 in. long and 12 ft 8 in. wide, had a depth of 7 ft 1 in., and grossed 68 tons. Each vessel could carry about 100 people. Also in 1882 Breadalbane put the cargo ship *Sybilla* on Loch Tay; she was built of oak grown on Breadalbane's estate. A second cargo vessel, the *Carlotta*, was added to the Loch Tay fleet in 1883. The Loch Awe boats were operated by the Dalmally Hotel Company and the Loch Tay boats by the Loch Tay Steamboat Company Ltd.

Early success attended the Loch Awe venture. When the *Countess* was only seven years old her owners felt justified in spending £1,500 in refitting her and in installing a new 285 h.p. triple-expansion engine. A large assembly of notables gathered at Loch Awe to sail on the refurbished *Countess* on her inaugural voyage. The chairman of the owners claimed that the vessel was capable of 14 knots, and he was rash enough to state in Anderson's presence that the *Countess* could get from Loch Awe to Edinburgh quicker than Anderson's trains, which he considered to be slow. Anderson did not fail to lecture the guests on the theme that the vessel owed its success to the existence of the railway :

> I remember about 21 years ago standing on a little knoll where there was only a shepherd's house, along with Mr Blyth, contemplating what might have been. The question was then, what can we do to attract the multitudes to this unsurpassed scenery? Compare the state of matters today with those prevalent at that time. The multitudes have already come, and I hope to see the day when trains will be running as Mr Blair has said. But the first thing to do is create a

dividend and this can only be done gradually. (Applause.) Since the time I have mentioned when standing there with Mr Blyth our dreams have been realised. There was then only one steamer on the loch, which was engaged in towing timber; now there are three public and five or six private steamers. It is a source of great satisfaction to me to think that this large company has assembled to inaugurate the new arrangements, and I hope they will prove eminently successful, and such as to return the shareholders a high percentage. (Loud applause.) That is the most important matter of all.

Loch Etive is an arm of the sea, but it has many of the characteristics of an inland loch. On 26 November 1879 the Callander & Oban first considered erecting a platform and pier on the south side of the loch at Achnacloich between Taynuilt and Connel Ferry, and a steamer, *Glen Etive*, first sailed from the pier on 20 June 1881. *Ossian* followed in 1885. The Loch Etive steamers plied between Achnacloich and Lochetivehead, providing the water link in the Glen Etive and Glen Coe tour. The tour involved a train journey from Oban to Achnacloich, steamer from there to Lochetivehead, and coach (later motor bus) up Glen Etive and down Glen Coe to Ballachulish; from there passengers returned in the early days by coach and after 1903 by train to Oban. The trip could also be done in the reverse direction. At one period the tour had its own 'Loch Etive Boat Train', complete with carriage nameboards, and an engine and three-coach set kept specially spick and span. Other vessels that plied from Achnacloich were the wooden ship *Loch Etive Queen*, acquired in 1923, the MV *Rena*, formerly the *Southampton Belle*, and *George Wishart the Martyr* in 1924. Later came TSMV *Darthula II*.

Longevity was a feature of the Loch Tay and Loch Awe boats. *Countess of Breadalbane* sailed for fifty-four years. She became the property of the Caledonian Steam Packet Company Ltd (the marine arm of the Caledonian Railway) in 1922, and when she was broken up in 1936 she was replaced by the TSMV *Countess of Breadalbane*. The new *Countess* was built by Denny of Dumbarton. She was 90 ft 9 in. long, 18 ft 1 in. wide, 7 ft 2 in. in depth and had a gross tonnage of 106. Two sets of six-cylinder high-speed diesels gave her a speed of 10½ knots, and she could carry 120 passengers. Also in 1936 private owners put MV *Growley* on Loch Awe. Another notable vessel in the Loch Awe trade was TSS *Caledonia* which plied from 1895 until 1918.

Lady of the Lake sailed for forty-seven years on Loch Tay. She also had become the property of the Caledonian Steam Packet Company in 1922; she was broken up at Kenmore along with

PLEASURE SAILING ON
LOCH-TAY

By the fine Saloon Steamer "LADY OF THE LAKE.'

Commencing 1st June

CHEAP RETURN TICKETS

ARE ISSUED DAILY FOR THE

RAILWAY TRIP AND THE SAIL

AS UNDER:—

GOING.	a.m.	a.m.	RETURNING.	p.m.	p.m.
Edinburgh (Prin. St.) ....lve.	7 0	9 25	Kenmore ....lve.	12 40	4e 0
Glasgow (Buch. St.) ,,	8 0	10 10	Loch-Tay Station ,,	2 15	5e50
Loch-Tay Pier ...... ,,	10 39	1 44p	Glasgow (Buch. St.)arr.	5 18	8e40
Kenmore ....arr.	12 30p	3 30	Edinburgh (Prin. St.) ....,,	5d25	9e27

RETURN FARES, 3rd and Cabin—Edinburgh, 7/6 ; Glasgow, 7/-
Tickets available for day of issue only.

d During June arrives Edinburgh (Princes Street) at 5.43 p.m.
e During June leaves Kenmore at 4.20 p.m., Loch-Tay at 6.20 p.m., and arrives Glasgow
(Buchanan St.) at 9.40 p.m. and Edinburgh (Princes St.) at 10.4 p.m.

PLEASURE SAILING ON
LOCH-AWE.

CHEAP RETURN TICKETS

ARE ISSUED DAILY FOR THE

RAILWAY TRIP AND THE SAIL

AS UNDER:—

(By Rail and Steamer "COUNTESS OF BREADALBANE.")

GOING.	a.m.	RETURNING.	p.m.
Edinburgh (Princes St.) ...lve.	7 0	Ford (Head of Loch-Awe)lve.	2 30
Glasgow (Buchanan St.)... ,,	8 0	Loch-Awe Station .... ,,	5b13
Loch-Awe Station ....arr.	11 21	Glasgow (Buchanan St.)...arr.	8b40
Ford (Head of Loch-Awe) ,,	1 45p	Edinburgh (Princes St.)... ,,	9b27

RETURN FARES, 3rd and Cabin—Edinburgh, 8/- ; Glasgow, 7/6
Tickets available for day of issue only.

(By Rail and Steamer "CALEDONIA.")

Commencing 1st June.

GOING.	a.m.	RETURNING.	p.m.
Edinburgh (Princes St.) ...lve.	9 25	Port-Sonachan (Loch-Awe)lve.	3b45
Glasgow (Buchanan St.)... ,,	10 10	Loch-Awe Station .... ,,	5b13
Loch-Awe Station ....arr.	1c30p	Glasgow (Buchanan St.)...arr.	8b40
Port-Sonachan(Loch-Awe) ,,	2c40	Edinburgh (Princes St.) ... ,,	9b27

RETURN FARES, 3rd and Cabin—Edinburgh, 8/- ; Glasgow, 7/6
Tickets available for day of issue only.

b During June Passengers leave Port-Sonachan at 4.15 p.m., Loch-Awe at 5.54 p.m., and
arrive Glasgow (Buchanan St.) at 9.40 p.m. and Edinburgh (Princes St.) at 10.4 p.m.
c During June arrives Loch-Awe at 1.50 p.m. and Port-Sonachan at 2.50 p.m.

Sybilla in 1929. *Carlotta* had suffered a like fate in 1923, improved roads in the area having made the loch service unprofitable. The destruction of those vessels left *Queen of the Lake*, which had been added to the loch fleet in 1907, to handle the traffic. She was built by the Ailsa Shipbuilding Co. Ltd of Troon and taken to Killin in sections by rail. The sections were loaded on a barge which was towed by *Sybilla* to a slipway near Kenmore, where the vessel was re-erected and launched on 19 June 1907. Her length was 110 ft 1 in., breadth 20 ft 1 in., depth 9 ft 3 in., and her gross tonnage was 152. She was a popular boat, especially with charter parties and evening excursionists.

In addition to the MacBrayne packet sailings to the islands, Oban offered a variety of sailings from time to time. Captain Paterson's steamers *Manx Lass*, *Countess of Bantry* and *Princess Louise* cruised to places like Loch Melfort, Lismore and other points within easy reach of Oban. In 1896 through tickets were issued from Callander & Oban stations to Portrush in Ireland *via* Oban in connection with the steamer *Queen* which sailed on alternate days during the summer. The return fares from Oban to Portrush were 15s cabin and 8s steerage. The vessel also carried cargo, including livestock, fodder, poultry and butter. The Callander & Oban board seems to have had some misgivings about this service; Anderson was told to arrange that the railway company would be relieved of any responsibility for accidents to passengers on the steamer.

Some years after the Irish venture, which failed for lack of patronage, an avertisement headed 'Grand Highland Yacht Cruising Up to Date' announced cruises by the steamer *Erne* from Oban. The connecting train left Glasgow at 5.10 a.m. The *Erne* left Oban for Ballachulish at 10 a.m. and the travellers enjoyed a three-hour coach drive to Glencoe before rejoining the yacht for the return cruise to Oban. The cost of the excursion from Glasgow was 20s. A footnote on the advertisement reminded patrons that they could charter the *Erne* for Mediterranean cruising during the winter.

The C & O made no attempt to exploit Loch Earn, leaving a local bus operator to put TSMV *Queen of Loch Earn* on the loch as an added inducement to his clientèle to patronise his tours. Soon after his business was absorbed by Alexander & Sons of Falkirk the vessel was withdrawn.

SCHOOL TRAIN TALES

The advent of the C & O in 1880 had a profound effect on the higher education of the children living in the area served. There

GRAND CIRCULAR TOUR

EMBRACING

Strathallan, Strathearn, Strathyre, and Loch=Earn and Loch=Lubnaig

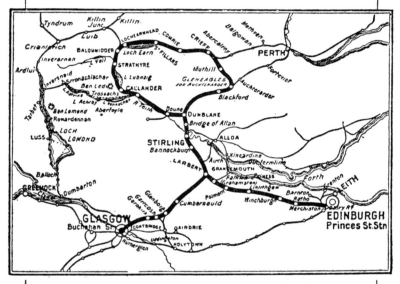

Tickets are issued daily at **Edinburgh** (Princes Street) and **Glasgow** (Buchanan Street) Stations for a Tour through Strathallan, Strathearn, Comrie, St. Fillans, Loch-Earn, Balquhidder, Strathyre, Callander, or *vice versa*, at the following Fares :—

		1st Class.	3rd Class.
Edinburgh (Princes Street),	...	17/2	9/4
Glasgow (Buchanan Street),	...	12/8	7/5

were two high schools, one in Oban and one in Callander, and the county march between Tyndrum and Dalmally was an educational as well as a political and geographical watershed. Pupils from Dalmally westward and from Ballachulish southward went to school in Oban; pupils from Tyndrum eastwards through Killin and Strathyre went to Callander. In stage-coach days the children had no alternative but to lodge near their schools; with the coming of the railway they could travel between home and school daily, although some of them had long journeys. The boys and girls became an accepted part of the weekday scene. They travelled in ordinary trains in compartments labelled *For Scholars*—perhaps a pretentious description of the at-times rumbustrious occupants.

When old school friends meet, stories of the school trains rank high in their reminiscences. There was the day in the 1950s when the morning train from Ballachulish made an emergency stop on the driver suddenly discovering a washout almost under his wheels. The scholars, most of them gazing at the homework they should have done the night before, were thrown in heaps on the compartment floors along with their exercise-books. At least they had a day off school. Then there was the chemistry experiment that got out of hand in a compartment and resulted in the sending of '*stop and examine*'. And there was a crisis at one of the fruit stalls on the line when its coffers were found to contain pennies 'converted' to florins through the enterprise of certain of the students of chemistry. A ten-year-old boy was imprudent enough long ago to steal a corkscrew from a carriage. His mother discovered the outrage at once, and dispatched her erring son to the police station to hand over the stolen property. But that did not prevent him from being hauled before the magistrates and charged with stealing the corkscrew, 'the property of the London and North Western Railway'. The magistrate left the accused in no doubt what his ultimate fate would be if he persisted in his life of crime.

Another *cause célèbre* concerned the boy who *swore* in a C & O school train. On 4 March 1898 an anonymous correspondent wrote to the *Oban Telegraph*:

> Through your valuable paper I would like to ask if anything can be done to correct the general behaviour and suppress bad language indulged in by boys who go by the morning train to Oban for the purpose of attending the Secondary School (Anglice, grammar school) there. I would suggest the placing on that train of a railway officer in plain clothes, and letting him look into matters. Meanwhile I know passengers avoid that train as they would avoid any bad company. Verb sap.—XYP.

NEW TOUR
No. 32.

The Bens, the Glens, and the Lochs

LOCH-AWE, DALMALLY, AND INVERARAY.

Going *via* Stirling, Callander, and Dalmally, and returning *via* Inveraray, Kyles of Bute, and Gourock.

					a.m.
Cal. Ry.	EDINBURGH (Princes Street)	...	...	leave	7 0
	GLASGOW (Buchanan Street)	...	...	,,	8 0
	DALMALLY	...	...	arrive	11 14
	OBAN..	...	...	leave	9 10
Motor.	LOCH-AWE	...	...	arrive	10 0
	Loch-Awe Station and Hotel	...	...	leave	10 45
	Dalmally Station.	...	...	{ arrive	11 15
				{ leave	11 20
	Inveraray	...	...	arrive	1 0
Tm. Str.	Inveraray	...	...	leave	2 15
	Gourock	...	...	{ arrive	6 20
				{ leave	6 30
	GLASGOW (Central)	...	...	arrive	7 25

Going *via* Gourock, Kyles of Bute, and Inveraray, and returning *via* Dalmally, Callander, and Stirling.

					a.m.
Str. Tm.	GLASGOW (Central)	...	...	leave	8 12
	Gourock	...	{ arrive	9 7
				{ leave	9 10
	Inveraray	...	arrive	1 15
Motor.	Inveraray	...	leave	2 30
	Dalmally Station	...	{ arrive	4 10
				{ leave	4 15
	Loch-Awe Station and Hotel	...	...	arrive	4 45
	DALMALLY	...	...	leave	5b14
	LOCH-AWE	...	,,	5b26
Cal. Ry.	OBAN...	...	arrive	6b48
	LOCH-AWE	...	leave	5 54
	DALMALLY	...	,,	6 2
	GLASGOW (Buchanan Street)	...	arrive	9 40
	EDINBURGH (Princes Street)	...	,,	10 4

b On Saturdays leaves Dalmally at 5.26 p.m., Loch-Awe at 5.34 p.m., and arrives Oban at 6.32 p.m.

Fares for the Round

(Including Coachmen's and Conductors' Fees).

					1st and Cabin.	3rd and Cabin.
Glasgow	...	...	...	...	20/3	16/-
Edinburgh	...	...	...		27/9	20/-

(Fares subject to alteration).

A member of the Oban School Board went post-haste to John Anderson, who had immediate inquiries made. 'I have found not a vestige of truth in the statement so far as I can learn from the officials on the line. They have no complaints to make whatever,' he reported. At the next meeting of the School Board the members condemned the anonymous letter-writer and affirmed that such oaths would never pass the lips of their pupils. But one member insisted that a friend of his whom he refused to name claimed that the letter was accurate. The same gentleman inquired anxiously, 'The girls and boys are not in the same compartment?' to which he got the reply, 'At the request of the Board the railway company has set aside separate carriages. We cannot be too grateful to the railway company for their kindness in all respects.'

The affair ended when XYP wrote again to the *Oban Telegraph* admitting that only one boy in one compartment was at fault, and conceding that the offending expression was 'profane rather than filthy'. 'It is at stopping-places such as the Oban ticket platform that the language complained of is best heard,' advised the writer, 'and it is as a rule connected with card-playing terms. Let card-playing be given up, and then the impulse to use any words of a painful and free character will not occur.'

C & O KALEIDOSCOPE

The story of the C & O abounds in 'incidents', many of them amusing, few of them grave. In 1891 the Callander School Board discovered that the north boundary wall of the Callander public school playground has been inadvertently constructed, seventeen years ago, with half its thickness on ground owned by the railway company. The school authority readily admitted the encroachment and offered to remove the wall and rebuild it six inches further south. After giving the matter due consideration the C & O magnanimously allowed the wall to remain where it was, provided an annual rental of 2s 6d was paid for it, in half-yearly instalments at Whitsun and Martinmas. The School Board was so relieved by this decision that it minuted its gratitude to the railway and requested that the minute be also recorded in the C & O book. The C & O, nevertheless, reserved the right to demand removal of the wall at three months' notice.

Relations between the railway and the town of Oban suffered a setback in 1884 over the affair of the Drimvargie spring well. Nobody had noticed in 1880 when the C & O came to Oban that it

Caledonian Railway Company
(CALLANDER AND OBAN LINE).

DISTRICT TRAFFIC SUPERINTENDENT'S OFFICE,

OBAN, 26 June 1915.

REFER TO
IN YOUR REPLY. S/530/4

George Pywell
15 Leighton Place
Callander

DEAR SIR,

You are hereby appointed Porter at Callander in room of _____ wages ____ per week, commending Monday 28th curt.

Yours truly,

see Johnstone please deliver.

Caledonian Railway Company
(CALLANDER AND OBAN LINE).

I/JN.

DISTRICT TRAFFIC SUPERINTENDENT'S OFFICE,

OBAN, 9th January, 191 8.

REFER TO
IN YOUR REPLY. S 7713/17
8:1:

Geo. Pywell,
Porter,
Callander.

DEAR SIR,

You are hereby appointed Passenger Shunter at Oban in room of D. McKillop, wages 23/- per week, commending 14th January, 1918.

Yours truly,

Mr. Johnstone to note and deliver.

Noted W.Johnstone

Appointment notices for George Pywell. Note that these were made from Oban and that the appointments were specifically to jobs on the C&O

had acquired the ground from which the well waters bubbled. Regular patrons of the Drimvargie waters believed they were endowed with special properties, and a mineral-water manufacturer had built a factory next to the well on which, he claimed, the high quality of his products depended. Then, in 1884 the c & o without warning built a sleeper fence between the public road and the well. Public feeling was outraged. Agitation in the press culminated in the holding of a mass open-air meeting of townspeople in Argyll Square; the demonstrators, led by a councillor and a minister of the kirk, descended on the fence and tore it down. The case went to the Court of Session, but proceedings were dropped. Later Drimvargie spring well dried up.

In 1920 there was an echo of the Crianlarich Junction dispute of thirty years before, when the Caledonian signalmen at the c & o boxes asked for porches to be built at their signal-box doors. All concerned agreed that the porches were desirable, but who was to pay for them? Eventually, the North British footed the bill.

The Callander & Oban was in constant trouble over its gas works at Oban. In 1911 the manager of Glasgow Corporation Gas Department was employed to inspect the plant and suggest remedies. He recommended getting rid of a gas compressor, which was sold to Lockerbie gas works for £10—less than a third of what it had cost the railway company in 1906. The gas plant was abandoned in 1915 and the building sold to a fish merchant.

On one occasion when the driver of a southbound train was exchanging gossip with the stationmaster during his stop at Connel Ferry he learned that the local MP's house had been burgled and his car stolen that morning. As the train was climbing away from Dalmally the driver spotted the stolen car being driven south on the adjacent road. A message dropped at the next box alerted the county police. In Glenlochy the train picked up the stolen car again, this time running parallel with the line. Engine crew and thieves in the car exchanged waves. Later the driver had the satisfaction of learning that the car was stopped at a road-block just inside the Perthshire boundary and the culprits arrested.

Safety measures were strictly observed, and for that reason there were few accidents. The guards of all down trains—including passenger trains—passing Glencruitten summit, and all up trains passing Glenoglehead, were required to signal to their drivers that they had the train under control; drivers had to whistle for this signal and not proceed without it. Guards of down trains were instructed not to leave Connel Ferry unless satisfied that their trains

K

Caledonian Railway Company
(CALLANDER AND OBAN LINE).

DISTRICT TRAFFIC SUPERINTENDENT'S OFFICE,

OBAN, 30th May 1924.

REPLY TO
S 1728/24
IN YOUR REPLY.

G. Pywell,

Porter Guard,

Callander.

Dear Sir,

You are hereby appointed Summer Passr. Guard

at Callander in room of

wages 55/- per week, commencing

2nd June, 1924.

Yours truly,

W.H. Blackstock,
per

Mr. McDonald to deliver.

D. W. Barrie.

TELEGRAPH,
Station House Supt. } TELEGRAMS, "ELENESS, PERTH."
{ TELEPHONE No. 786.

London Midland and Scottish Railway Company
(NORTHERN DIVISION)

DISTRICT TRAFFIC SUPERINTENDENT'S OFFICE,
GENERAL STATION,

PERTH, 3rd October 1924.

IN REPLY QUOTE
S. 1924.

George Pywell,
Summer Passenger Guard,
Callander.

Dear Sir,

In consequence of the withdrawal of
the Summer Train Service your appointment will
now be reduced to that of a Porter Guard at
47/6 per week, as from Monday, 29th September.

Yours truly,

D W BARRIE

Mr. McDonald to note, deliver and arrange to
enter accordingly.

Further appointment notices. Note that c & o stationery was still in use in
May of 1924. By October 1924 the Oban office had been closed and the former

had sufficient brake power; a spare goods brake-van was kept at Connel Ferry to be attached on demand.

Drivers descending Glencruitten and Glenogle had to travel slowly enough to be able to stop promptly if necessary. Special regulations governed the running of livestock trains on the long continuous falling gradient between Glenlochy crossing place and Dalmally. With a McIntosh 4—6—0 bogie engine in charge, the minimum time allowed for the descent with a twelve-wagon sheep train was fifteen minutes, with an eighteen-wagon train eighteen minutes and with a twenty-five-wagon train twenty-five minutes. With a Drummond Jumbo in charge the times for twelve, eighteen and twenty-four-wagon trains were eighteen, twenty-two and twenty-seven minutes. When cattle were being conveyed, five minutes were added all round.

Special regulation also governed the running of the Night Mail, the train that made its leisurely way between Callander and Oban in the small hours of the morning. Before retiring at night each signalman withdrew a tablet and left it lying in the box. The guard picked up the tablet and carried it through to the next station, where he left it in the box, and at the same time collected the tablet for the next section. The signalmen's first job in the morning was to replace the tablets.

Two minor outbreaks of fire are remembered. In 1923 a spark from the chimney of a labouring engine landed in a bird's nest built under the eaves of the signalman's house at Glencruitten. The resulting conflagration set the whole house on fire. And in August 1928 the gangway connection between two coaches of a southbound train was found to be on fire when descending Glen Ogle. The train was stopped and the passengers hurriedly removed, a tricky operation in such a place.

The snowstorm that sabotaged Anderson's *soirée* in 1880 was not an ominous portent. Snow caused anxiety and delays, but through many winters the line remained free of even minor blocks. Oban, protected from snow-bearing easterly winds by the mass of the Grampians behind it, and warmed by the waters of the Gulf Stream, seldom had severe falls. Glenoglehead and Glenlochy were the danger spots, where accumulated snow was inclined to slide in sudden avalanches from the steep mountain slopes and block the track.

George Pywell, an old-time C & O guard, has a vivid memory of the 1947 blizzard. He was guard of the Midnight Mail, and a Jumbo had been taken on as pilot to help the train engine to buck the drifts. The Mail was safely over Glenoglehead and up Strathfillan, and everything seemed well, when suddenly in Glenlochy the train came to a dead stand. George saw by the light of his lamp that the snow was nearly up to the carriage footboards, but he managed to struggle forward to the engine. 'We've lost Tammy,' the driver told him. Tammy was the driver of the assisting Jumbo, which had vanished. The train had hit a deep drift in the darkness, and the men guessed that the coupling between the Jumbo and the train engine had broken on impact, the Jumbo continuing on its way with its crew unaware that they were on their own.

The rules called for George to protect his train, but offered no advice on how to place detonators on rails under three or four feet of snow. The men decided to ignore the rule-book and continue on their way. But first they had to extract the Mail from the drift, and this they did by setting back a hundred yards or so and charging it. (What the passengers thought of this manoeuvre is not recorded.) After much whirring of driving wheels and churning of snow the engine broke through and the Mail began a cautious descent towards Dalmally, with George standing in front of the smokebox, handlamp trained ahead, searching for the Jumbo—which, for all he knew, might have been off the road. 'Then my lamp went oot,' said George, telling the tale later. He watched the advancing track from his rocking perch, imagining he saw the shape of the Jumbo's tender in every patch of shadow. The drifts were up to running-plate level on both sides and George remembers seeing a big hare running along the snow parallel with the train. When the Mail crew reached Dalmally, there was a much-relieved Tammy peering up the line for them.

George Pywell earned a reputation for taking good care of his passengers on their journeys across Scotland in the early hours of the morning. Funeral parties were common on the Mail, for men of the islands who died as exiles in the South liked to be buried in their native soil. Mourners could expect special solicitude, as could pilgrims bound for the sacred Isle of Iona. In 1962 an Aberdeen newspaper quoted a lady who had travelled in the Mail with a party of guildswomen as follows:

> We had to travel overnight from Stirling to Oban to catch the steamer for the island. A porter at Stirling told us that we would be all right on the Oban train as Geordie the guard would look after us. And sure enough not long after the train had left the station along came Geordie the guard to inquire about our welfare. He did everything in his power to make us comfortable and even took the trouble to tuck us in. He told us, 'I always like to make sure my passengers are settled down

for the night.' The traveller commented, 'What a nice gesture. It made all the difference to what could have been a weary trip.'

The old-time goods guards had their own vans which they furnished and decorated as they chose. A certain Callander guard had neat curtains on his van windows and polished waxcloth on the floor. One day he was horrified to find that the waxcloth had been soiled. He complained to the district superintendent, who added insult to injury by suggesting that the guard had left his van unlocked and that a cat had entered. 'Sir, you are mistaken,' replied the offended railwayman. 'I have yet to meet the cat than can tear two pages out of the working timetable.'

Then there was the story of the stationmaster who was too fond of the bottle. After many official warnings an officer was sent from Oban to hand him his dismissal notice. In due course the messenger arrived back in Oban in an inebriated condition and with a label tied to his person advising headquarters to send a man who could hold his liquor next time.

Jock Sutherland combined his hobby of nature lore with his job as a surfaceman. And where better to observe nature in the raw than on the all-season patrols of lonely lengths of C & O track? Once Jock came across a large flat stone by the side of Loch Lubnaig, its surface curiously scratched and round which were dead fish with peculiar neck wounds. Jock kept watch, and presently a wild cat crossed the line and took up position by the flat stone, looking intently in the water. There was the flash of a paw, a glint of wriggling silver, and the cat had a fish pinned on the stone.

On another occasion Jock found a woman in a lineside cottage stirring a domestic pot with what seemed to be an old dagger with a broken tip. It had been found in a peat bog and was thought to be an ornamental dagger from which the jewels had been removed; but Jock had other ideas. He sent it to Kelvingrove Museum in Glasgow where it was identified as a Bronze Age dagger, one of the only two ever discovered in Scotland.

Jock Sutherland was well acquainted with 'Anderson's piano'. 'Man,' he said, 'when the wind blew through it, it was like a harp.' Once, just after a train had passed, he saw a big boulder high up on Ben Cruachan cartwheeling down the slope. It seemed to be coming very slowly, turning over and over; at length it crashed through the boulder screen, breaking all the wires, and smashed three sleepers before plunging down into the loch.

Jock was working on the line near Craig-nan-Cailleach by Loch Lubnaig when the telegraph wires above him jerked suddenly and from round a bend came the roar of falling rock. When the surface-man and his colleagues reached the spot they found the line completely buried, and the only way round the obstruction was by boat. Rocks were still thundering down making approach to 'the Craig' impossible. The heaviest crane could not lift some of the boulders and they had to be blasted into manageable sizes. Even as the gangs worked to clear the line they were showered intermittently by falling stones.

On another occasion Jock was at work near the top of the Pass of Leny when the squad's hand-trolley ran away towards Callander, spilling its load of spikes as it went. After it came to a violent stop at Callander station the foreman made Jock push the vehicle up the Pass, gathering the spikes on the way. It was hard work on the rising gradient especially as the load increased with each recovered spike. In the end Jock buried the spikes beside the line. 'Aye, and I could still take you to the place where they're buried,' he announced, with thirteen years of retirement safely behind him.

The Pass of Leny was the scene of a spectacular runaway in 1947. The morning down goods stuck near the head of the Pass and the crew divided the train. The guard walked back to place the regulation detonators when the rear half of the train ran away; it roared into Callander station and crashed into the rear of the 7.55 a.m. passenger train. The wreckage of the goods train destroyed the covered overbridge and the distinctive clock that surmounted it.

CHAPTER IX

Timetables and Traffic

The timetable introduced in 1880 retained its shape until the end of the service *via* Callander in 1965. But as traffic increased more trains were added. By 1895 there were seven trains each way in summer and four in winter. In that year the 8 a.m. and 4.40 p.m. were described in the timetable as 'Fast Morning Express' and 'Fast Afternoon Express' respectively; the titles were, however, little more than timetable decorations for the trains were not speeded up.

Also in 1895 the C&O announced a 'New Night Express Train'. One or more sleeping-cars were attached to the 6.40 p.m. from Oban and these vehicles were combined with sleeping-cars from Aberdeen, Dundee and Perth to form a train which reached Euston at 8.10 a.m. Sleeping-car services were henceforward provided six nights a week in summer and once weekly in winter. The timetables of the period also contained short-lived novelties like a through Aberdeen coach on the 8 a.m. Buchanan Street to Oban and a through Oban coach on the 7.15 a.m. Buchanan Street to Aberdeen.

The 1905 summer timetable showed seven trains each way with one extra down service on Fridays and a corresponding up service on Mondays—the remarkable 'C&O Hotel Express'. Passengers lured by prominent press advertisements of a weekend in 'The Land of the Gael', bought a coupon entitling them to a return rail journey with accommodation and full board from dinner on Friday until breakfast on Monday in one of eight hotels in Oban, or in hotels at Ballachulish, Appin, Connel Ferry, Loch Awe, Dalmally, Lochearnhead, Killin and Callander. Fares ranged from 42s 6d for first-class rail and 'A' class accommodation in Oban to 26s 5d for third-class rail and 'B' class accommodation in Callander. The clerk who issued the ticket would make the hotel booking.

In spite of the fact that regular booked trains left Glasgow for Oban at 2.5 and 4.45 p.m., the 'C&O Hotel Express' was timed to leave at 3.55 p.m. It stopped at Larbert, Dunblane, Callander, Dalmally and Loch Awe and reached Oban at 7.30. The corresponding

Connel Ferry and Ballachulish.

Mls			a.m	a.m	SX		SO				a.m	a.m	SO	SX	
	Glasgow (Buchanan St.)lev.	4c20	8 0	1210p	—	5p10	Ballachulish N	lev.	7 30	1050	3p50	4 p 0	—
..	Edinburgh (Princes St.) „	..	6 50	1144s	—	4 23	Ballachulish Ferry	.	7 34	1054	3 54	4 4	.
—	Oban „	8 10	12 54	4 50	—	8 50	Kentallen	.	7 40	11 0	4 0	4 10	—
—	Connel Ferry .. lev.	8 45	1227	5 15	.	9 15	Duror	.	7 50	1110	4 10	4 20	.
¾	North Connel	8 48	1230	5 18	—	9 18	Appin	.	8 1	1121	4 21	4 31	.
2½	Benderloch b	8 53	1235	5 23	—	9 23	Creagan b	.	8 8	1128	4 28	4 38	.
10	Creagan b	9 9	1251	5 39	—	9 39	Benderloch b	.	8 22	1142	4 42	4 52	.
13½	Appin	9 16	1258	5 46	—	9 46	North Connel	. .	8 28	1149	4 49	4 59	.
18	Duror	9 27	1 9	5 57	—	9 57	Connel Ferry	arr.	8 31	1152	4 52	5 2	.
22½	Kentallen . .	9 35	1 17	6 5	—	10 5	Oban . . . arr.	8 55	1227	5 36	5 36	
25½	Ballachulish Ferry	9 41	1 23	6 11	—	1011	Edinburgh (Princes St.) „	2 25	4 39	10 4	10 4	
27½	Ballachulish N. . arr.	9 47	1 29	6 17	—	1017	Glasgow (Buchanan St.) „	1 34	4 23	9A31	9 31	

Killin and Loch Tay

	a.m	..	..	a.m	..	..	a.m	..	..	p.m	..	..	p.m	
Glasgow (Buchanan St.) lev.	4c20	—	—	8 0	—	—	—	—	—	1210	—	—	5 10	—
Edinburgh (Princes St.) „	..	—	—	6 50	—	—	—	—	—	1144a	—	—	4 23	—
Oban — — — — „	6 5	—	—	—	—	—	9 10	—	—	12 5	—	—	5 15	—
Killin Junction . lev.	8 12	—	—	1036	—	—	1118	—	—	2 50	—	—	7 35	—
Killin — — — arr.	8 25	—	—	1042	—	—	1130	—	—	3 2	—	—	7 48	—
Killin . . . . lev.														
Loch Tay — — — . arr.														

	a.m	..	..	a.m	..	..	a.m	..	..	p.m	..	..	p.m	..
Loch Tay — — — . lev.														
Killin . . . . arr.														
Killin . . . . lev.	7 45	—	—	10 5	—	—	1055	—	—	1 42	—	—	6 55	—
Killin Junction . arr.	7 58	—	—	1019	—	—	11 8	—	—	1 56	—	—	7 8	—
Oban — — — arr.				1227	—	—	—	—	—	4 38	—	—	9 25	—
Edinburgh (Princes St.) „	11 0	—	—	—	—	—	2 25	—	—	4 39	—	—	10 4	—
Glasgow (Buchanan St.) „	1015	—	—	—	—	—	1 34	—	—	4 23	—	—	9 31	—

* Saturdays only   † Except Saturdays
‡ Except Mondays   § Mondays only
A Arrive 9-1 p.m until 30th August
B 3-58 p.m on Saturdays until 30th August
b Barcaldine Siding (situate between Benderloch
& Creagan)—All Trains stop on notice to take
up or set down

c Central Station
N Ballachulish is the station for Glencoe and
   Kinlochleven
SX Except Saturdays   SO Saturdays only
f Waverley Station

The last LMS summer timetable, 1947: Connel Ferry-Ballachulish
and Killin Jct-Loch Tay

up train on Mondays was sandwiched between the 6 a.m. and 7.55 a.m. departures from Oban; leaving at 7.30, it stopped at Loch Awe, Dalmally, Callander and Larbert, reaching Glasgow at 11 a.m. An Edinburgh portion was carried in both directions.

In 1903 the Lochearnhead, St Fillans & Comrie Railway opened its line along the north shore of Loch Earn and completed the link-up of the Central Perthshire lines with the Callander & Oban. The new railway (a Caledonian subsidiary) came round the head of the loch and opened its own station at Lochearnhead village before coming up to form a junction at the C & O's Lochearnhead station, renamed Balquhidder. The Lochearnhead line's original claim for running powers to Oban over the C & O had been dropped when strenuous opposition seemed certain.

The former Lochearnhead blossomed from a wayside station into a busy junction, with a bay platform for the trains from the branch and two through platforms for the main-line trains, the whole controlled from two signal boxes. Travellers from Perth were now offered a choice of three routes to Oban. They could travel via Methven and the Almond Valley, via Gleneagles and Crieff, or via Dunblane and Callander. The route via Methven was 97 miles 28 chains, via Gleneagles 104 miles 76 chains, and via Dunblane 109 miles 75 chains. In 1911 the best timing was offered over the Dunblane route with the 3.37 Fridays-only train from Perth, which reached Oban in 3h. 37m. The Methven route had the best regular train, which took 3h. 55m. The best daily timing via Dunblane and via Gleneagles was 4h. 45m. over each route.

The 1911 Callander & Oban timetable showed seven down and eight up trains between Oban and Edinburgh or Glasgow. The 7.30 a.m. from Oban had a through portion for London. This train ran direct to Glasgow Central, where the London portion was attached to the midday Glasgow-London Euston express. The 6.45 p.m. from Oban also had through carriages for London. In the down direction through carriages for Oban were attached to the 8 p.m. and 11.45 p.m. from Euston, while connections to Oban were given off the 5 a.m. and 2 p.m. departures. On Sunday mornings a 9.10 from Callander reached Oban at 11.55, but this was really an extension of Saturday-night services originating in the south, and was not a true C & O train. There was no corresponding up service : an attempt to introduce one on Sundays in the 1880s met widespread opposition on Sabbatarian grounds and was not repeated in C & O days.

Goods traffic in 1911 was handled by two trains in each direction. A slow goods left Stirling at 6.30 a.m. and shunted Callander yard

between 7.35 and 9.42. It was booked out of Tyndrum at 1.5 and
Dalmally at 1.45, and arrived at Oban at 3.48. An express goods
was due to leave Callander at 2 p.m. and reach Oban at 7.45. In
the reverse direction trains left Oban at 7 a.m. and 12.45 p.m.,
arriving at Callander at 5.50 p.m. and 9.15 p.m. respectively.

The eastern end of the line was served by fast residential trains,
the principal being the 'Ben Ledi Express', which gave a morning
and evening service to and from Glasgow. A poster in purple and
gold which the Caledonian produced to advertise this train conveys
something of the atmosphere of those halcyon years.

> This is a train for men of affairs, and for the women as well, which
> taken true to time leads on to *business in the city* and *life in a country
> house* all the year round; i.e., the Caledonian railway train of true
> convenience, true comfort and true economy on measured speed,
> morning and night.

In 1909 the Caledonian made history by spending £1,667 19s 7d
on a spectacular coloured poster advertising Oban as a holiday
resort. (The c & o's share of the cost was £450 which the Caledonian
agreed to accept in six half-yearly instalments of £75.) The poster
created country-wide interest, the *Railway News* commenting:

> Such a picture could only be purchased by some millionaire and
> would be hid from view in a private gallery. Yet such a scene is at this
> moment exhibited as a poster on boardings, and we can well imagine
> many weary city toilers will mentally thank the Caledonian Railway
> Company for giving them the opportunity of feasting their tired eyes
> on this vivid reproduction of a lovely picture.

A GIANT PASSES

In that same lush summer of 1911, on 17 June, John Anderson
died, aged eighty-one. His funeral cortège, followed by most of the
leading Scottish railway officers of the day, passed through Glasgow
streets gay with flags and bunting for the Coronation of George V,
only two days away. Anderson had spent sixty years in railway
service, forty-two of them with the c & o. When he retired, on
31 July 1907, the people of Oban had presented him with his por-
trait in oils by R. S. Crawford, in recognition of his services to the
West Highlands. And the chairman of the c & o had ordered the
minute book to be inscribed as follows:

> The Directors desire to place on record their appreciation of the zeal
> and faithfulness with which he has discharged the important duties
> of Manager and Secretary during the past years, and convey to him
> their good wishes for the long enjoyment of his well earned ease.

Anderson had been given a pension of £500 per annum to which the Caledonian and London & North Western contributed. His responsibilities were divided between a secretary and a district superintendent: never again was the Callander & Oban to know a colourful, autocratic head. Anderson had left Oban, spending his last four years at Westbourne Gardens in Glasgow's west end.

ROAD RIVALRY

The railways were early in the field of road transport in the West Highlands. Shortly after the C&O was opened to Dalmally in 1877 the Caledonian Railway put a four-horse coach on the Dalmally-Inveraray run to link the C&O trains with the Loch Fyne steamers; the company also operated a coach between Crieff and Lochearn-head. These were summer services only. In the 1879 season the Caledonian lost £10 9s 8½d on the Dalmally coach, but made a profit of £41 3s 5d on the Lochearnhead coach. With the coming of the motor car the Dalmally-Inveraray run was operated by the Inveraray, Dalmally & Loch Awe Motor Car Company, the shares of which were held jointly by the Callander & Oban, Turbine Steamers Ltd and hotel-keepers in Dalmally and Inveraray. The company was wound up on 22 March 1922, when the C&O was repaid its investment of £100 plus a bonus of £17 10s. In the same year the Caledonian applied to the C&O for permission to build a garage at Oban station for cars engaged on the Oban and Loch Awe tours.

As the twentieth century moved into its second decade a new element was edging tentatively into the West Highland tourist scene—the motor charabanc. Enterprising owners began offering daring trips from Glasgow and Edinburgh into the Highlands in something of the spirit of the proprietors of small aircraft who offered pleasure trips twenty years later. Never before had the public been able to travel long distances over the King's highways in so short a time, and to go by motor charabanc rather than by the prosaic train became regarded as an adventure. Newspapers published alluring notices advertising the motor runs: 'The Trip of the Season' was the headline introducing a charabanc ride from Edinburgh and Glasgow to Oban.

The early trips made no attempt to return to their starting point on the same day; the charabancs themselves were fallible, and the roads, especially in the Highlands, were suffering from the long rot of the railway age. The motors from Glasgow and Edinburgh were

Glasgow, Edinburgh and Callander and Oban

	F	Ex Sats (TC Edinburgh to Oban)	Sats only (RC Glasgow to Oban; Ceases after 30th August)	Except Sats. until 30th Aug.; Daily thereafter (RC Glasgow to Oban)	Sats only (Ceases after 30th August)		Sats only	Sats only (Ceases after 30th August)	TC Edinburgh to Oban	Sats only	(Leave Ballachulish *3-50 p.m. †4-0p.m)	Ex Sats	Sats only		N		Sats only	Sats only	Except Saturday nights and Sunday mornings (Except Mondays)	SUNS
	a.m.	a.m	a.m	a.m.	a.m	a.m	p.m	a.m	p.m	p.m	p.m	p.m	p.m	p.m	p.m	p.m	p.m	p.m	p.m	a.m
Glasgow Buchanan St. lev.	4c20	7 15	8 0	8 0	8 0	1010	—	1150	1210	1 5	—	1 50	2 3	4 0	5 10	6 10	8 0	1015	10 0	7c15
Edinburgh (P.St.)	.	6 50	6 50	6 50	6 50	9 20	.	.	a1144	1 10	.	.	.	.	4 23	5V23	.	10 0	9 45	.
Stirling	5 45	8 12	8 50	8 50	8 56	11 3	1215	1237	1 9	2 16	—	2 45	3 4	4 58	6 1	7 10	9 3	1124	12E1a	8 35
Dunblane	.	8 25		9 3	9 9	1116	1227		1 22	2 28	.	2 58	3 17	5 10	6 14	7 23	9 25	1140	1213	8 47
Doune	—	8 32		9 10	9 16	1122	1233		1 29	2 34	—	3 5	3 23	5 16	6 20	7 29	9 31	1146	1222	8 54
Callander arr.	6 10	8 44		9 23	9 28	1135	1247		1 41	2 47	.	3 21	3 36	5 28	6 32	7 42	9 44	12 1	1244	9 11
Callander lev.	6 12	—		9 33	9 33	—	—		1 49	—	—	—	—	—	6 37	—	—	—	1248	9 15
Strathyre	.			9 51	9 51	.	.		2 7	.	.	.	.	.	6 55	.	.	.	1 9	9 33
Kingshouse Plat.	—			9A57	9A57	—	—		2A12	—	—	—	—	—	7A0	—	—	—		—
Balquhidder	6 37		9 34	10 0	10 0	.	.	1 25	2 16	.		.	.	.	7 5	.	.	.		9 43
Killin Junct. arr.	6 58		—	1023	1023	—	—	—	2 41	—		—	—	—	7 27	—	—	—		—
Killin Junct. lev.	6 59		.	1025	1025	.	.	.	2 42	.		.	.	.	7 29	.	.	.		.
Luib	7 5		—	1031	1031	—	—	—	2 48	—		—	—	—	7 35	—	—	—		1016
Crianlarion lev.	7 16		.	1042	1042	.	.	.	2 59	.		.	.	.	7 46	.	.	.	2 25	1028
Tyndrum	7 28		—	1054	1054	—	—	—	3 12	—		—	—	—	7 58	—	—	—	—	1043
Dalmally	7 54		1041	1117	1117	.	.	2 52	3 34	.		.	.	.	8 21	.	.	.	3 19	11 7
Loch Awe	7 59	—	—	1125	1125	—	—	—	3 42	—		—	—	—	8 29	—	—	—	3 38	1117
Taynuilt	8 17	.	.	1143	1143	.	.	3 18	4 0	.		.	.	.	8 47	.	.	.	4 6	1137
Ach-na-Cloich	8 26	—	—	1153	1153	—	—	—	4 9	—		—	—	—	8†56K	—	—	—	—	—
Connel Ferry	8 38	.	1121	12 3	12 3	.	.	3 35	4 21	.	5 13	.	.	.	9 8	.	.	.	4 42	1155
Oban arr.	8 55	—	1138	1227	1227	—	—	3 52	4 38	—	5 36	—	—	—	9 25	—	—	—	5 5	1215

		TC Oban to Edinburgh		Exc. Sats		Sats only	Sats only (Ceases after 30th August)		TC Oban to Edinburgh			Sats only (Ceases after 30th August)	Ex Sats (To Ballachulish)	TC Oban to Edinburgh; SC on Monday and Thursday nights only, Oban to London due 7-0 a.m.; RC Oban to Glasgow	Sats only (To Ballachulish)		SUNS	
	a.m	a.m	a.m.	a.m.	a.m	p.m	a.m	.	p.m	p.m	p.m	p.m	p.m	p.m	p.m	.	.	.
Oban lev.	—	6 5	8 10	—	9 10	—	1145	—	12 5	—	—	4 45	4 50	5 15	8 50	—	—	—
Connel Ferry	.	6 21	8 26	.	9 28	.	12 3	.	1225	.	.	5 4	5 6	5 34	9 6	.	.	.
Ach-na-Cloich	—	—	—	—	9 36	—	—	—	1233	—	—	—	—	5 42	—	—	—	—
Taynuilt	.	6 34	.	.	9 42	.	1218	.	1239	.	.	5 17	.	5 49	.	.	.	.
Loch Awe	—	6 53	—	—	10 1	—	1237	—	1258	—	—	5 36		6 8		—	—	—
Dalmally	.	7 0	.	.	10 8	.	1244	.	1 5	.	.	5 43		6 15		.	.	.
Tyndrum	—	7 30	—	—	1036	—	—	—	1 33	—	—	6 11		6 43		—	—	—
Crianlarich lev.	.	7 42	.	.	1051	.	.	.	1 43	.	.	6 21		6 53		.	.	.
Luib	—	7 52	—	—	11 2	—	—	—	1 53	—	—	—		7 3		—	—	—
Killin Junction arr.	.	8 2	.	.	1112	.	.	.	2 3	.	.	.		7 13		.	.	.
Killin Junction lev.	—	8 4	—	—	1114	—	—	—	2 4	—	—	—		7 14		—	—	—
Balquhidder	.	8 20	.	.	1130	.	1 55	.	2 20	.	.	7 0		7 34		.	.	.
Kingshouse Platform	—	8825	—	—	—	—	—	—	2B27	—	—	—		—		—	—	—
Strathyre	.	8 29	.	.	1140	.	2 5	.	2 31	.	.	.	.	7 43	.	.	.	.
Callander arr.	—	8 46	—	—	1158	—	2 26	—	2 48	—	—	7 27	—	8 0	—	—	—	—
Callander lev.	7 55	8X53	.	9 25	12 8	1 25	2 31	.	2 55	4 0	5 43	7 35	.	8 3	.	.	.	.
Doune	8 7	9 5	—	9 37	1220	1 44	—	—	3 7	4 12	5 55	—	—	8 15	—	—	—	—
Dunblane arr.	8 16	9 14	.	9 46	1229	1 54	.	.	3 16	4 21	6 4	7 37	.	8 24	.	.	.	.
Stirling "	8 28	9 25	—	9 54	1240	2 7	3 6	—	3 27	4 33	6 16	8 9	—	8 35	—	—	—	—
Edinburgh (Pr. St.) "	9V59	11 0	.	11 0	2 25	.	.	.	4 39	6V39	7 36	.	.	10 4	.	.	.	.
Glasgow (Bu. St.) "	9 15	1015	—	1225	1 34	3 8	3 58	—	4 23	5 30	7 15	9 1	—	9 31	—	—	—	—

* Saturdays only † Except Saturdays A Stops to set down on notice at Strathyre. Luggage and Bicycles not dealt with B Stops to take up when Passengers on Platform. Luggage and Bicycles not dealt with c Central Station E Will not be detained beyond 12-15 a.m. for connection with 8-22 p.m from Carlisle F Sleeping Car from London (leave 7-30 p.m) to Oban on Wednesday and Friday nights only K Stops to set down passengers on notice at Stirling N Through Carriage Edinburgh to Oban RC Restaurant Car SC Sleeping Car TC Through Carriage V Waverley Station X 8-49 a.m. on Saturdays

The last LMS summer timetable, 1947: Glasgow-Oban

advertised to arrive in Oban 'in time to allow passengers to return same day by train'. The charabanc fare was 5s 6d single. The Argyll Motor Car Company offered a charabanc trip from Campbeltown to Oban, leaving Campbeltown at 10 a.m. one day and returning from Oban at 2 p.m. the next. On 1 June 1914, David MacBrayne started a regular daily motor-bus service between Ardrishaig and Tayvallich. It is doubtful if anybody in the railway offices saw in these lumbering vehicles with their loads of dusty passengers the medium that was to change the established tourist pattern on which the c & o depended for its success.

On 29 June 1914 the charabanc announcements in the press met with a counterblast.

A UNIQUE HIGHLAND OUTING

The Public are respectfully informed that commencing on the 3rd August a luxuriously appointed Pullman Observation Car for first class Passengers will be run daily from Glasgow (Buchanan Street) on the 8 a.m. to Oban, returning from Oban at 3.30 p.m. reaching Glasgow at 7.25 p.m.

A unique opportunity of seeing to advantage the *Historic, Romantic* and *Picturesque* Western Highlands between Callander and Oban will be afforded.

For the convenience of passengers Lunch, Tea and Refreshments will be obtainable en route.

Something New in Railway Travelling

Thus was the travelling public informed of the incomparable *Maid of Morven*. Something new in railway travelling indeed! Here was the most luxurious vehicle ever set on British rails for public use, a Pullman car lavishly decorated, furnished with leather-covered easy chairs and with great bevelled windows filling the rear end from floor to roof. (It is fully described in Chapter X.) It seemed that *Maid of Morven* was destined to introduce a new era of luxury rail travel. But in the very newspaper column in which the railway company's proud announcement was published appeared an ominous notice from the Austro-Hungarian consulate in Glasgow. 'His I and R Apostolic Majesty, the Emperor of Austria and Apostolic King of Hungary has ordered a partial mobilisation of his forces (Standeserhoehung des Heeres).' On the day that *Maid of Morven* ran its initial trip Europe was ablaze with war and Britain's declaration was expected hourly. The Pullman was withdrawn after a short season, and its eventual return to c & o metals was in an age which was far removed from the leisurely, carefree days of 1914.

Layout of Tyndrum, 1955

1923 AND AFTER

The first meeting of the Callander & Oban in 1923 took place at 58 Bath Street, Glasgow, on 7 February, and the first question on the agenda was, 'Is this office to be taken for another year?' The directors decided to give up the office on 28 May. The last Callander & Oban board meeting took place at 2.30 p.m. on 14 March and lasted ten minutes. Against the item 'Next board meeting' the secretary wrote 'to be arranged if necessary'. At 2.30 on the same day a special meeting of proprietors and debenture shareholders was held 'for the purpose of considering and if so determined of approving a Preliminary Scheme in pursuance of the said Railways Act 1921 for the absorption of the Callander and Oban Railway Company by the London Midland and Scottish Railway Company.' The meeting voted unanimously for the proposal.

When the conquerors from Euston were inspecting the acquired territories west of Callander they came across the very striking fountain on Strathyre platform in the shape of a heron, carved out of Cruachan granite by Aberdeen craftsmen, and ordered its removal to Euston Great Hall. Only the vociferous protests of the stationmaster stopped this act of sacrilege.

By closing the Oban office in August 1924 the LMS took its first retrograde step. Donald MacKay, the chief clerk, had gone there with Anderson in 1880 when the office was opened. The staff, ten in number, posed solemnly for a photograph outside the office before departing for the office of the district traffic superintendent at Perth. 'It is feared,' commented the *Oban Times*, 'that the removal of the office from Oban to such a distant centre as Perth will result in a serious check to the commercial progression of the Highlands and Islands.'

Yet the line retained its character under the new ownership. It was still the Callander & Oban. The same holiday families arrived at their favourite destinations summer after summer to be greeted by the same friendly stationmasters and porters. The same signalmen could be seen peering out of their windows flanked by shelves of geraniums. The gaily-painted farm carts came to the flower-decked stations to collect passengers' luggage.

In 1928 Messrs Rankin started a daily bus service between Glasgow and Oban. The bus ran *via* Loch Lomond, and its timetable compared favourably with that of the trains. About the same time the LMS started a bus service between Oban and Taynuilt. In the

'20s the first Sunday excursions were run to Oban from the south. Similar trips to Fort William, over the West Highland Railway, after some perfunctory opposition were accepted by the people of Lochaber. Oban's inhabitants never were reconciled to the Sunday trains, shopkeepers and others making little attempt to profit from the hundreds who arrived on fine Sundays from Glasgow or Edinburgh on 6s tickets.

The Sunday trains were heavy and smartly timed. In 1931 three trains arrived in Oban within 56 minutes on Sunday afternoons; these were the 9.55 and 10.15 from Glasgow and the 10.15 from Dundee or (on alternate Sundays) Edinburgh. The 9.55 was due out of Callander at 11.14 and arrived at Oban ticket platform at 1.50, having stopped at Balquhidder and Taynuilt for water. The 10.15 from Glasgow stopped at Balquhidder and Dalmally. The Dundee train ran via Perth, Crieff, Comrie and St Fillans, picking up passengers at each point; it left Balquhidder at 1.18, and with a water stop at Taynuilt, reached Oban ticket platform at 2.51. The Glasgow trains returned from Oban at 5.35 and 6, and the Dundee (or Edinburgh) left at 6.35.

The '30s saw the introduction of evening excursions from Edinburgh, Glasgow, Perth and Dundee to C & O stations. An after-tea trip from Glasgow to Killin with a sail on Loch Tay cost only 3s 3d. On one occasion the LMS offered Glasgow passengers 'a night in Elysium' for 2s; it turned out to be an evening circuit of Loch Earn—out via Callander and Balquhidder, and home via St Fillans, Crieff and Gleneagles. This popular and ridiculously cheap excursion became one of the best patronised in an extensive programme. It was nothing to find two long trains from Glasgow going round the circle clockwise and squeezing past a train from Edinburgh and another from Dundee taking the trip counter-clockwise.

On 10 June 1931 the first-ever train to Oban via the West Highland line and Crianlarich Junction was dispatched from Queen Street station, Glasgow. It was run to connect with a special excursion to Staffa and Iona by the new MacBrayne vessel Lochfyne, and the journey was completed in eighty-three minutes less than the best Glasgow-Oban service shown in the current Callander & Oban timetable. Once again Oban agitated for a regular service by this route, but only occasional special trains were offered.

Children returning from Callander in the afternoon had their own special train, worked by the Killin engine and stock, usually two coaches. The empty stock followed the up midday train from Killin Junction to Callander, where it loaded up and departed at 4.6 p.m.

CROSSING LOCH ETIVE

(33) *Road and railway on Connel bridge*
(34) *Connel rail bus with car-carrying vehicle*

LOCOMOTIVES IN LMS DAYS

(35) *McIntosh Oban bogie at Stirling*
(36) *Drummond Jumbo No. 17428 at Luib in July 1938*
(37) *Pickersgill '191' class No. 14622 in April 1938*

From Mondays to Thursdays the train ran to Killin, but on Fridays it went through to Crianlarich first. This was to suit Tyndrum children who boarded at Callander during the week; they travelled on from Crianlarich to Tyndrum by the West Highland late-afternoon down train. The loading of the Killin school train in 1965 was sixty-one on Mondays to Thursdays and seventy-seven on Fridays. There were eight passengers daily for Strathyre, twenty-three for Kingshouse, thirteen for Balquhidder, seventeen for Killin —known as *aborigines* from their school motto *Ab Origine Fides*.

Between 1935 and 1938 the school coach was attached at Callander to the 2.25 freight ex-Stirling, which ran as a mixed train to Crianlarich. In practice the freight was suspended for months on end due to the trade depression, and the Killin engine worked the school coach to Luib where it overtook and was attached to the 1.35 freight ex-Stirling. The train ran mixed to Crianlarich where the coach was detached and returned to Callander by the 6.35 ex-Oban next morning, except on Fridays when it was run through to Oban on the freight for cleaning purposes.

Two wars left their mark on the Oban line. During the 1914-18 war the Callander & Oban handled a considerable quantity of timber. A siding was opened at Achnacloich on 16 August 1917 to deal with a timber-merchant's traffic guaranteed at £500-worth a year; timber was also cut by Loch Tay and Loch Awe and taken to Killin and Loch Awe piers respectively for transfer to rail. On the Ballachulish branch four sidings, West and East Larach, Ardshiel and Auchendarroch, totalling 36 chains, were lifted and sent to France. The government paid £884 14s 11d in compensation, which was £198 15s 11d more than the sidings had cost to install. The Ben Cruachan Quarry sidings were sold for scrap, 4,567 lineal yards bringing in £1,484 15s 6d.

The line was much harder pressed in the 1939-45 war. Important military establishments in Argyll included a naval repair base at Dunstaffnage and an airfield at North Connel. Extensive sidings were put in at the south side of Connel Ferry station, and emergency sidings were also provided at Pass of Brander and St Brides. An LNW bogie brake-van fitted with anti-gas equipment was stationed in the west-end bay at Connel Ferry station for the duration. Many of the hotels in Oban were acquired by the military for billeting, and regular heavy personnel trains from the south included complete trains of GWR stock from Plymouth. A train on the Ballachulish branch was machine-gunned during an attack on naval shipping off the coast, but no one was hurt.

L

Callander and Oban Railway Company.

REPORT BY THE DIRECTORS

TO THE

MEETING OF SHAREHOLDERS,

TO BE HELD WITHIN THE

OFFICE OF THE CALEDONIAN RAILWAY COMPANY, 302 BUCHANAN STREET, GLASGOW

On TUESDAY, the 28th FEBRUARY, 1922, at Three o'clock Afternoon.

The control of the Railways under the Ministry of Transport Act, 1919, terminated on 15th August, 1921.

The Railways Act, 1921, which received the Royal Assent on 31st August, 1921, authorises the grouping and amalgamation of Railway Companies and the absorption of small Railways by the Working Companies on terms to be arranged.

The Callander and Oban Railway Company, with the Caledonian Railway Company, will be amalgamated with the London & North Western, Midland, North Staffordshire, and Furness Railway Companies in England, and with the Glasgow and South Western and Highland Railway Companies in Scotland, forming the North Western, Midland, and West Scottish Group.

An Amalgamation Tribunal is constituted to approve or settle the terms and conditions of Amalgamation Schemes, which are to become effective on 1st July, 1923.

The Act also provides for a payment of £60,000,000, in two instalments, one half of the whole sum being subject to Income Tax, in settlement of claims of the Railway Companies arising out of the Government control of the Railways. Out of the first payment of £24,500,000 the portion due to the Callander and Oban Railway Company amounts to £16,608.

The Statement of Accounts for year ending 31st December last, shows that the sum at credit of

Revenue Account No. 9 and carried to Net Revenue Account No. 10 is	£15,306	12	8
Add the balance from last year's account,	208	12	7
Drawn from the above-mentioned Government Compensation of £16,608,	3,000	0	0
General Interest,	234	13	11
	18,749	19	2
Less Feu-Duties and Interest Charges,	15,082	5	6
leaving a balance available for Dividend of	£3,667	13	8

Of this, £3,075 is absorbed by the Interim Dividend for the half-year ended 30th June, which was paid on 3rd September last to the Proprietors of the Four-and-a-half per cent. Preference Shares 1878, leaving a balance of £592 13s. 8d. to be carried to next account.

The reduction in balance available for Dividend is due to the increased cost of labour and other working expenses, and the depression of trade.

Colonel John D. Sutherland, C.B.E., retires from Office as a Director at this time and is eligible for re-election.

HENRY ALLAN, CHAIRMAN.

GLASGOW, 14th February, 1922.

DIRECTORS.

HENRY ALLAN, Esq., 21 Bothwell Street, Glasgow,
CHAIRMAN.

Sir JOSEPH WHITE TODD, Bart., Moreuish, Killin,
DEPUTY-CHAIRMAN.

THE MARQUIS OF BREADALBANE, K.G., Taymouth Castle, Aberfeldy.

JOHN GRAHAM STEWART, Esq., Ault Wharrie, Dunblane.

COL. JOHN M. DENNY, C.B., Leven Shipyard, Dumbarton.

J. HAMILTON HOULDSWORTH, Esq., Castlebank, Lanark.

HENRY E. GORDON, Esq., O.B.E., Aikenhead, Cathcart,

WILLIAM MURRAY MORRISON, Esq., 137 Whitehall Court, London, S.W.1

COLONEL JOHN D. SUTHERLAND, C.B.E., 11 Inverleith Row, Edinburgh.

NATIONALISATION

The pattern of travel and tourism in the West and Central Highlands remained substantially unchanged until 1939. It emerged from the war changed almost beyond recognition. Many of the steamers that had provided the tourist links on salt and fresh water were laid up for the duration and never sailed again. Their places were taken by buses running over more or less parallel routes. Even the name MacBrayne, once synonymous with scarlet funnels on blue seas, began appearing on a growing fleet of scarlet buses plying the West Highland roads. In time they were joined by buses of other hues bringing tourists from far and near. Private cars, relatively rare in pre-war days, choked the West Highland roads on summer Saturdays. Heavy lorries with Grimsby and Lowestoft markings lumbered through the Pass of Brander piled high with boxes of herrings, and double-decked sheep-floats churned their way down Strathfillan and through Glen Dochart, bound for the markets of Central Scotland. During a herring boom in December 1965 (shades of John Anderson!) the *Oban Times* published a photograph showing the railway pier crammed with lorries loading the fish. The paper commented: 'Fish lorries queued from the *Railway Pier* to the bus shelter in *Station* Square.' (The italics are the present writer's.)

Nationalisation brought yet another attempt by the people of Oban to win a through service to Glasgow *via* the West Highland line: with the railway system of the country now unified there seemed at last to be no obstacle. On 23 May 1949, British Railways finally obliged, with a train leaving Glasgow (Queen Street) in the forenoon and returning from Oban in the late afternoon. It allowed people in the south to enjoy a day on the Callander & Oban with a short stay in the town, but was of little benefit to Oban residents. It was withdrawn for lack of support, but was revived in the '50s as a summer-only diesel multiple-unit with a special appeal to tourists.

Sunday excursions to Oban were not resumed after the war, but a new excursion venture, the Six Lochs Land Cruise, achieved outstanding popularity. This, usually as a six-car diesel set, left Glasgow (Buchanan Street) and went first to Callander, where passengers were allowed time for lunch. The next call was at Killin, and then the train returned to Glasgow *via* Crianlarich and the West Highland. The six lochs of the title were Loch Lubnaig, Loch Earn, Loch

Tay, Loch Lomond, Loch Long, and the Gareloch.

The rot began at the end of the summer of 1951 when the Comrie-Balquhidder line closed. The Perthshire feeder lines, once so valuable to the main route, had become sucker lines. One by one they withered away, leaving thriving towns and villages that had rejoiced at the coming of the railway a century before without a train; among them were Crieff, Methven, St Fillans, Comrie and Lochearnhead. Balquhidder degenerated from a junction station with two signal cabins into an unstaffed halt. Travellers in passing trains saw a broken, grass-grown platform, and peeling buildings with open doors revealing papers scattered over the floors of former offices.

Anyone who travelled the line in the long, crowded trains of summer Saturdays in the '50s would have concluded that the C & O was a vital, prosperous concern. Weekdays told a different story, and in winter the trains were left almost empty. At times the three-coach 6 a.m. from Stirling ran all the way with three passengers or less. The final rundown was rapid. On 7 September 1964 all freight traffic was withdrawn from the Callander-Crianlarich section, and freight to and from Oban was routed via Crianlarich Junction and the West Highland. This move foreshadowed the total closure of the line between Callander and Crianlarich and the routing of all Oban traffic over the West Highland line. The news when it came was worse than anticipated: the line was to be closed completely from Dunblane to Crianlarich, leaving Callander without trains.

There was a brief fight to save the line. The people of Callander were sentimental about the railway but, in truth, private transport catered for most of their needs. Killin put up stiffer resistance; the villagers were thinking in particular of the plight of the schoolchildren if the school train ceased to run. The Rev John R. Colquhoun, the main opponent of the closure, wrote: 'This is the clearances all over again, only they are being more polite about it this time. To talk of alternative road transport is ludicrous. There are 154 bends between Killin and Callander, many narrow bridges and the formidable gradient of Glen Ogle.'

In the last summer timetable—that of 1965—covering the original C & O route, one train each way merited the title express. The down train, the 11.55 a.m. from Glasgow Buchanan Street, ran on four Saturdays in July only, and it is interesting to compare its performance with that of the 'C & O Hotel Express' of sixty years earlier. The 1965 train, diesel-hauled, took 3h. 33m. for the Glasgow-Oban journey; the 1905 train took 3h. 35m. The Hotel Express ran from Callander to Oban in 2h. 21m. with two intermediate stops; the 1965 express, also with two stops, took 2h. 28m. Both trains ran non-stop from Callander to Dalmally, the 1905 train in 1h. 29m., the 1965 train in 1h. 32m.

The fastest up service between Oban and Glasgow in 1965 was provided by the 6.35 p.m. Saturdays Only, which took 3h. 55m. to the trip compared with the 3h. 30m. of the up 'C & O Hotel Express'. From Monday to Friday this train left Oban at 6.30 and took 2h. 20m. to reach Callander with two stops. The 1905 train, also with two stops, took 2h. 19m.

INTERRUPTION TO NORMAL SERVICE

Monday 27 September 1965 was the Autumn Holiday in Glasgow and district, and as part of their holiday programme British Railways had advertised their Six Lochs Land Cruise from Glasgow to Callander and Killin. It was to be the last such excursion, for the notices were already exhibited on the stations announcing the closure of the line between Dunblane and Crianlarich from 1 November. That morning, when intending passengers arrived to join the Six Lochs train they were greeted with a routine 'Interruption to Normal Service' notice, telling them that owing to a landslide near Balquhidder the train would run *via* the West Highland line and would not call at Callander. Unknowingly the passengers were reading the obituary notice of the Callander & Oban Railway.

The landslide had been discovered in Glen Ogle in the early hours of the morning. It was at a spot that had given trouble for years; a retaining wall had been built there after a similar blockage in 1963. In the light of handlamps the damage did not look extensive; some rock and soil had spilled over one rail and extended not quite to the middle of the track. Interim measures were taken : in the middle of the night the railway staff arranged for the remains of Roderick Walker, a former Glasgow policeman, to be transferred with his funeral party, bound for the South Uist steamer at Oban, from the Night Mail (12.30 a.m. from Stirling), which was held at Balquhidder, to a hearse; this was dispatched by road to Oban, where the *Claymore* was kept waiting. The next down train, the 6 a.m. from Stirling, was held at Strathyre to await daylight and the arrival of the civil engineers. Its passengers were taken by bus to Luib, where they joined the 6.15 ex-Oban which reversed and returned to Oban. The bus picked up the 6.15's southbound passengers and took them to Strathyre to join the stranded 6 a.m. down train, which then took up the 6.15's timing back to Stirling.

Proper inspection revealed that the landslide was massive. Many hundreds of tons of rock were likely at any time to roll down on to the railway. The damage, according to the engineers' report, would take a month to repair and cost £30,000. Since the line was due to close in five weeks only one course of action was possible. The railway between Callander and Crianlarich was abandoned and a three-stage emergency plan was introduced. Up to 2 October the Oban passenger trains left Glasgow Buchanan Street in two portions: the first, usually a DMU twin set, left at the scheduled time and ran to Callander; five minutes later the Oban portion followed, but reversed within two miles of the Glasgow terminus, and ran via Sighthill yard and Cowlairs to reach Crianlarich via the West Highland line. Meanwhile on the arrival of the DMU at Callander a connecting bus ran through Strathyre, Balquhidder, Killin village and Luib to Crianlarich, where the passengers transferred to the waiting train.

The second phase of the emergency came into operation on 4 October, when the Oban trains were transferred to Queen Street and ran to the timetables that were to have been introduced on 1 November. The DMU still ran from Glasgow to Callander with the connecting bus service to Crianlarich. In the third phase the line between Dunblane and Callander was closed, and a bus service replaced the trains.

The new railway timetable was revolutionary as far as Oban was concerned. At last, in 1965, Oban was given the service it had been demanding since 1894. 'It's Quicker by Rail now to Glasgow' said a front-page headline in the Oban Times. 'West Highland timetables are proving popular.' The trip to Glasgow was not only quicker; it was cheaper. Because of the reduced mileage passengers made the pleasant discovery that the return fare to Glasgow was down by 9s, from £3 3s 6d to £2 14s 6d. But the journey to Edinburgh, now reached via Glasgow, was longer and more expensive—an extra 9s 6d on a return ticket. The through West Coast sleeping-car from Oban to London was withdrawn. There were complaints, but the official explanation that only a handful of people used a vehicle costing £20,000 and requiring £1,500 a year to maintain was unanswerable.

The 6.15 from Oban was replaced by a 7.45 which took 3h. 30m. to reach Glasgow, as compared with the 4h. 13m. of its predecessor. (But the timing was the same as that of the 'C & O Hotel Express' of 1905 which used a route 17 miles longer.) The 12.20 departure from Oban was retimed to leave at 12.25 and ran to Glasgow in 3h. 27m., a saving of 34 minutes. In the down direction the former 7.55 a.m. from Glasgow Buchanan Street was timed to leave Queen Street at 8.35 and saved 42 minutes. The Night Mail was replaced by a 1 a.m. passenger and parcel train which ran through from Queen Street to Oban in 4h. 15m. in place of the 6h. 22m. of the old train, a saving of 127 minutes.

The changed pattern brought transport problems to individuals. Under the old system a bus left Tyndrum (Lower) for Kinlochleven at 7.40 a.m. on the arrival of the North Lorn mails by the 6 a.m. from Stirling. Among the regular passengers were two girls who were able to reach school in Kinlochleven in time for commencement of lessons at 9 a.m. Under the new system the mails went by the West Highland to Bridge of Orchy and the bus was retimed to leave there at 8.32. The girls could not reach Kinlochleven until 10 a.m., thus losing an hour of their education each day. Some of the children in Killin and Glen Dochart gave up the daily journey to Callander and became boarders in the town. It is doubtful if the Minister of Transport ever heard the complaint of one small boy when the question of the school train's withdrawal first arose: 'I can do my homework in the school train. I can't do it in a *bus.*'

Falls of Cruachan

CHAPTER X

Locomotives and Rolling Stock

THE BEGINNINGS

The first passenger trains on the opening of the Callander & Oban
through to Oban in 1880 were hauled by 2—4—2 tanks specially
designed by George Brittain. A considerable mythology has grown
round these engines. The principal myth is that their design was the
result of the trials of an LNW 2—4—2 radial tank on the Oban line.
E. L. Ahrons, in his *Locomotive and Train Working in the Nineteenth Century*, wrote: 'One of Mr Webb's London and North
Western 2—4—2 tank engines was in 1881 lent to the Caledonian
and tried on this road (the Oban), and as it did fairly well the
locomotive department of the Caledonian ordered some 2—4—2
tank engines (152 to 166) which will be mentioned later.' Two pages
further on Ahrons commented: 'These engines, Nos. 152 to 166,
built by Neilson and Co. in 1881, were originally intended for the
Oban line with its numerous curves, but did not prove very satisfactory on that service.' Unfortunately for Ahrons' theory—it could
have been nothing more substantial than a theory—the Caledonian
tanks were *not* built in 1881. They were designed in 1879 and built
in 1880. The engines were delivered at St Rollox in March and April
of that year, and at that time only one of the LNW 2—4—2 radial
tanks was in steam. Contemporary records indicate that an LNW
tank did visit the Callander & Oban, but not until the Caledonian
tanks had been in service for six months.

Another school of opinion has it that the Caledonian tanks were
not designed for the Oban line at all, but were sent there as stop-
gaps because the C & O had not made its engine requirements known
to the Caledonian until the last minute. A more picturesque story
has Anderson falling out with the Caledonian and asking the LNW
to work his line—hence the appearance of an LNW engine.

The true story of the Caledonian radial tanks can be traced from
extant contemporary records. The first mention of a special engine
for the Oban services appeared in the Caledonian Railway traffic
committee minutes of 29 July 1879 under the heading, 'Engines and

other Rly Rolling Stock required for the Callander and Oban Railway on the opening throughout in 1880.' George Brittain was informed, 'Report recommendation to next meeting.' This disposes of the tale that the c&o did not give details of their locomotive requirements until the last minute. The next meeting of the traffic committee was held on 12 August 1879. Very soon afterwards the Caledonian opened negotiations for the loan of an LNW tank, and on 25 November 1879 the minute book records: 'Reported that the LNW Co are willing to lend one of theirs for trial for a day or two. Offer accepted.' But there is no evidence that the LNW offer was taken up at that time.

The Caledonian 2—4—2 tanks were smart in appearance. They had Webb radial axle-boxes and outside cylinders, whereas the LNW engines had inside cylinders. They had the plain conical chimney favoured on the Caledonian since Sinclair's day, and the Prussian-blue passenger livery then standard on the line. The side tanks were painted in two lined-out panels; in the centre of the left-hand panel were the letters C.R. and in the right-hand panel the number of the engine. In June 1880 eight of the class were sent to the c&o ready for the opening of the line, Nos. 153, 154, 155 and 158 going to Oban and Nos. 156, 159, 160 and 161 to Callander. No. 164 also seems to have visited Oban at that time: see plate No. 3.

On 10 August 1880, six weeks after the line opened, a frantic complaint came from John Anderson: 'The present engines are not suitable for, or able for the work. Mr Smithells be requested to remove the difficulty under which we now labour by supplying proper engines.' The passenger trains had been consistently running late, and Anderson had found that the new engines were at fault. Drivers complained that they ran hot and rode roughly at high speeds. Worse still, the leading wheels had a tendency to derail: every guard's van carried a set of double ramps and with these and jacks the crew would re-rail them. With Major Marindin's warning of the consequences of derailments on the line fresh in his ears this peccadillo must have been alarming to Anderson.

On 7 September 1880 a Callander & Oban minute recorded: 'Secretary to inquire what determination has been taken as to Engines, and report that the working of the passenger trains is still unsatisfactory.' The action taken by Brittain is indicated in a minute of the Caledonian Railway stores committee meeting held on 21 September 1880. 'Tank Engine Wheels. Submitted Mr Brittain's letter of the 20th inst asking authority to order four pairs of leading wheels for the new radial axle tank engines estimated cost £44 each pair. Mr Brittain to get the wheels.' The next reference to the Oban tanks appears in the minutes of the Caledonian's traffic committee meeting held on 12 October 1880. 'Report on the Tank Engines on the C and O Line. Engines to be tried, and if found suitable to purchase one or more from LNWR if price is satisfactorily arranged.' That the Caledonian was prepared to purchase a *foreign* locomotive for the Oban services shows that it too was feeling desperate about the C & O's position.

The records make no further reference to the LNW trials. Nothing could have happened by mid-November 1880, for Anderson was then instructed by his board to 'call Mr Smithells' attention to the delay to trains, one quarter of those down being upwards of 15 minutes late, and of the up a number not quite so numerous but still too many'. J. F. McIntosh confirmed to D. H. Littlejohn that the LNW trials took place on the Callander & Oban late in 1880, Webb, Brittain and a Mr Leighton of Carlisle being among those present. The next reference to the Callander & Oban Railway in the Caledonian traffic committee minutes appeared on 20 September 1881 : 'Submitted request for 10 new engines with brake power applied.' On 12 October the board recommended that the ten engines be built. But these engines were of an entirely new design. The performance of the Webb tank on the C & O evidently was not such as to induce the Caledonian to buy LNW engines or to produce a new design based on them.

Ahrons said that the Caledonian tanks failed because the curves of the radial axle-box guides were struck from the wrong radius. He based this opinion on what an unspecified 'Scotch engineer' told him; it may well be hearsay rather than history. Anyway, Brittain admitted defeat and withdrew the engines from the Oban line. After having the leading radial axles blocked they were put to work on the Lanarkshire line where the curves were less severe. On 22 January 1889, No. 166 was derailed with five coaches on a Hamilton-Lesmahagow train at Haugh-head Junction when it broke through a check rail on a curve.

THE 2—4—2 TANKS

Built by Neilson & Co., Hyde Park Works, Glasgow, 1880. Nos. 2567-2581. CR Nos. 152-166.

Cylinders	17½ x 22 in.
Dr wheels	5 ft 8 in.
Radial wheels	3 ft 8 in.

Heating surface

Tubes (210—1¾ in.)	1,010 sq ft
Firebox	81.5 sq ft
Total	1,091.5 sq ft

Grate area	13.4 sq ft
Boiler pressure	130 p.s.i.
Tank capacity	1,200 gal
Coal capacity	2½-3 tons

Wheelbase 6ft 6 in. + 8 ft + 6 ft 6 in. = 21 ft

Length over buffers		35 ft 10½ in.
Weight	Leading axle	10 tons 6 cwt
	Dv axle	15 tons 15 cwt
	Rear coupled axle	14 tons 2 cwt
	Rear axle	11 tons 9 cwt
	Total	51 tons 12 cwt

The engines were withdrawn as follows:

No.	Year	No.	Year
152	1904	159	1910
153	1921	160	1906
154	1912	161	1901
155	1900	162	1899
156	1912	163	1903
157	1904	164	1901
158	1906	165	1903
		166	1901

Following the withdrawal of the radial tanks, train working was taken over largely by Conner's '670' class of 0—4—2s (670-679), turned out by Dübs in 1878. They were designed as goods engines, but performed adequately on the Oban passengers. They had 5 ft 2 in. coupled wheels, the cylinders were 17 by 24 in., boiler pressure 140 p.s.i., and they weighed 34 tons 12 cwt. By January 1881 only two of the radial tanks were left at Oban, 155 and 166, the other two having been replaced by 0—4—2s 670 and 674; 678 was sent to Oban in June of that year. By the same date (January 1881) only 158 remained at Callander, the 0—4—2s 671, 672 and 673 having taken the places of the other radial tanks. A further twenty 0—4—2 goods made a timely appearance early in 1881 and some of this batch went to the Oban line new. One of them, 704, was derailed twice at Loch Awe soon after delivery (see page 86). By May 1881 all the radial tanks had disappeared from the Callander & Oban. Engines at Oban in the summer of 1881 were 671, 679, 701, 702 and 700, and at Callander 703, 704, 705 and 384.

THE OBAN BOGIES

In the forty years between 1882 and 1922 three designers each produced an Oban bogie. The first one was George Brittain's successor to the ill-fated radial tanks. Built by Dübs, it was a 4—4—0 with outside cylinders, a four-wheel tender, stove-pipe chimney and rounded cab. The small tender was obligatory because of the short turntables on the line, but was also an advantage over the lengthy gradients. The Oban bogies were remarkably like the Highland Railway Skye bogies which David Jones built for the Dingwall & Skye line at the same time. Both engines had 18 by 24 in. outside cylinders, the Highland engine weighed 42 tons and the Oban engine 41 tons 12 cwt. The Brittain bogie had 5 ft 2 in. driving wheels, the Jones engine 5 ft 3 in. driving wheels.

When new, Nos. 180, 183, 185, 186 and 187 were allocated to Oban, and 179, 181, 182, 184 and 188 to Stirling.

The Oban bogies were a success from the start, and gave two decades of excellent main-line service. It was only when passenger stock became heavier and loads greater in the closing years of the nineteenth century that the engines showed signs that they were no longer up to the work. Between 1898 and 1901 J. F. McIntosh rebuilt them with Lambie class 29 0—6—0T boilers.

The Oban 4—4—0s. Built by Dübs & Co., 1882.
Works Nos. 1672-1681. CR Nos. 179-188.

	As built	As rebuilt
Cylinders	18 x 24 in.	18 x 24 in.
Driving wheels	5 ft 2 in.	5 ft 2 in.
Bogie wheels	3 ft 2 in.	3 ft 2 in.
Boiler length	10 ft	10 ft
Boiler diameter	4 ft 3 in.	4 ft 4⅛ in.

Heating surface		
Tubes	1,053.22 sq ft	975 sq ft
Firebox	93.2 sq ft	110.9 sq ft
Total	1,146.42 sq ft	1,089.9 sq ft
Grate area	14.4 sq ft	17.0 sq ft
Boiler pressure	130 p.s.i.	150 p.s.i.

Engine weight		
Bogie	14 tons 4 cwt 0 qr	13 tons 10 cwt 0 qr
Driving axle	14 9 1	14 19 0
Rear axle	12 18 2	12 8 2
Total	41 11 3	40 17 1
Wheelbase	6 ft + 6 ft 7 in. + 8 ft 5 in. = 21 ft	

Tender weight

4-wheeled						
leading axle	12 tons	6 cwt	0 qr	9 tons	13 cwt	0 qr
Middle axle				9	10	0
Rear axle	11	14	1	9	2	3
Total	24	0	1	28	5	3
Weight of engine						
and tender	64	11	4	69	2	4

The four-wheel tenders had 4 ft wheels at 8 ft 6 in. centres, a coal capacity of 4 tons and water capacity of 1,550 gallons. The six-wheel tenders which were fitted to the two engines working the Ballachulish branch between 1915 and 1920 had a wheelbase of 11 ft 5½ in., coal capacity of 4¼ tons and the tank held 1,840 gallons.

Numbers, rebuilding and withdrawal dates

CR	Rebuilt		LMS	Withdrawn
179	Oct	1900	14100	1930
180	Jun	1901	14101	1925
181	Apr	1900	14102	1923
182	Mar	1901	14103	1930
183	Mar	1900	14104	1927
184	Dec	1900		1922
185	Dec	1900		1922
186	Mar	1901	14105	1930
187	May	1900	14106	1924
188	Jul	1898	14107	1925

The improved engines were not powerful enough to take the heaviest trains singlehanded and much double-heading was called for in the peak holiday months. The Oban road needed an engine with increased adhesion, but an axle-load that took account of the severe restrictions, and a wheelbase acceptable to the C & O curves. McIntosh, by then famous as the designer of dazzling 4—4—0 express locomotives for the Caledonian West Coast services, found the answer in his '55' class of 4—6—0s. In 1902 express passenger engines of this wheel arrangement were by no means common and McIntosh's choice was a bold one.

There were nine engines in the class: 55-59 were built at St Rollox in 1902 and 51-54 in 1905. Measuring 12 ft 11 in. from rail level to the top of the chimney cap, they were extremely handsome. The sight of them in their shining blue livery threading the glens and lochsides with strings of brown-and-white carriages was something to remember. They did all that McIntosh asked of them.

With the appearance of the '55' class the Brittain bogies were relegated to the lighter trains or to assisting the new engines on the principal expresses. Two of them went to the Ballachulish branch at a later date.

In 1906, McIntosh built at St Rollox five engines with the same wheel arrangement, wheel base, coupled wheel diameter, cylinders and motion as the '55' class. But he gave them a boiler of the same diameter as his famous '903' class. The new engines (918-922) were intended to run the express goods on the West Coast route, and they soon became known as the 'Carlisle goods'. They weighed 60 tons 8 cwt—three tons more than the Oban bogies. To help with the heavy holiday traffic in July 1914, Nos. 918, 920 and 921 were sent to Oban. Plate 6 shows the interesting combination of a '918' piloting a '55' on an Oban-Glasgow train. In 1930 two of the McIntosh bogies, 52 and 53, were given boilers from two scrapped members of the '918' class, 920 and 919, the idea being to increase the power of the McIntosh engine.

The third-generation Oban bogie, William Pickersgill's outside-cylinder 4—6—0, arrived at the very end of the Caledonian's history. It was the last design to leave the St Rollox drawing boards, and it would have been pleasant to record that it was a success. It was not the abject failure that the first-ever C & O design had been, but there was little to be said in its favour. Eight of the engines were built (191-198) in December 1922 at the Queen's Park Works of the North British Locomotive Company (works numbers 22955-22962) and shortly became LMS 14619-14626. They were sluggish in action, and the drivers preferred the ageing McIntosh bogies.

	'55' class	'191' class
Cylinders	19 x 26 in.	19½ x 26 in.
Driving wheels	5 ft	5 ft 6 in.
Bogie wheels	3 ft 6 in.	3 ft 6 in.
Boiler pressure	175 p.s.i.	185 p.s.i.
Heating surface		
Tubes (275)	1,800 sq ft	(275) 1,707 sq ft
Firebox	105 sq ft	116 sq ft
Total	1,905 sq ft	1,823 sq ft
Grate area	20.63 sq ft	21.9 sq ft
Boiler		
Length	14 ft 0⅛ in.	14 ft
Diameter	4 ft 7 in.	4 ft 8⅛ in.
Wheelbase	5 ft 9 in. + 6 ft 9½ in.	7 ft + 5 ft 5 in.
	+ 5 ft 3 in. + 6 ft	+ 6 ft 2 in.
	= 24 ft 9½ in.	+ 6 ft 2 in.
		= 24 ft 9 in.

Weight

	tons	cwt	qr	tons	cwt	qr
Bogie	14	11	0	16	19	0
Leading driver	15	16	0	15	3	0
Driver	13	11	0	15	14	0
Rear driver	13	10	0	14	19	2
Total	57	8	0	62	15	2
Tender weight						
Leading wheels	12	8	0	12	10	0
Centre wheels	12	8	0	12	11	2
Rear wheels	12	10	0	12	15	2
Total	37	6	0	37	17	4
Weight of engine and tender	94	14	0	100	12	6
Length over buffers	54 ft 1 in.			55 ft 5 in.		
Water	3,000 gal			3,000 gal		
Coal	4½ tons			4½ tons		

A surprising visitor to the c & o was one of Pickersgill's large 4—6—2 passenger tanks, No. 954. In 1921, for a brief exciting period during the coal strike, the Oban line managed to keep going by burning a mixture of wood and nutty slack in some of the engines. Temporary wood supply depots were set up at places where timber was readily available. Surfacemen were given the task of cutting down and stacking trees growing inside the railway boundary fence. On the Ballachulish line a Jumbo was to be seen stopped at a woodpile, and while the fireman replenished the tender the driver, standing astride the boiler, swept the chimney with a brush.

But the ascent of Glencruitten was a problem for the wood-burners. They might well have spewed the entire contents of their fireboxes over the countryside on the three-mile climb, and the 4—6—2, burning 'goods' coal, was sent to Oban to assist them. The engine was well over the axle load for the c & o, and before it left St Rollox it was considerably stripped down and the bits and pieces placed in a wagon. The tank was hauled dead to Oban, with four runners between it and the train engine on the Leny bridges. For a few weeks passengers were treated to the whiff of woodsmoke on their journeyings.

THE DRUMMOND CONTRIBUTION

Dugald Drummond came to St Rollox in 1882 just as Brittain's new Oban bogies were settling in. Drummond, therefore, was not called upon during his eight momentous years at St Rollox to provide motive power for the Oban line, but he did produce at St Rollox in 1885 two 0—4—2 saddle tanks for the opening of the Killin Railway. These engines had outside cylinders 14 x 20 in., and 3 ft 8 in. coupled wheels, with 2 ft 6 in. trailing wheels. The length of the engine over the buffers was 27 ft 8¼ in. The saddle tank held 800 gallons, and the bunker had a capacity of ¾-ton, later increased to 1¼ tons by the addition of side rails. The engines like the Killin line coaches were fitted with the Westinghouse brake as a Board of Trade condition of their working on the steeply-graded Killin Railway. They weighed 31 tons 4 cwt 2 qr in working orders. They were numbered 262 and 263, and eventually became LMS 15000 and 15001. The saddle tanks remained on the Killin Railway until 1895.

Several of Drummond's 0—4—4 tanks built between 1884 and 1891 appeared on the Oban line. Among them were 175 and 229 (built in 1884 and 1886 respectively) which worked there between 1914 and 1922, and 194 (built 1891) which was on the line in 1928.

Drummond's most prolific design was that for his 0—6—0, the famous Jumbo; the first of these was produced in 1883 and 244 were eventually in existence. They had 18 x 26 in. cylinders and 5 ft driving wheels. Though they worked all over the Caledonian system, including the Oban line, it was not until 1936, when they were well into their fourth decade, that the C & O Jumbos gained their greatest accolade. That summer the locomotive on an excursion train failed, and the only replacement immediately available was 0—6—0 17412 (CR 745). The Jumbo gave such a good account of itself on the passenger train that excursions and holiday specials henceforth became part of its regular duty. There were few finer sights on the C & O in the late '30s than two Drummond Jumbos rattling along with a nine- or ten-coach Sunday excursion. Sometimes they piloted more aristocratic engines, at other times they handled the lighter trains alone.

There was a curious episode in 1889. Two years previously Drummond had turned out the first of a dozen 'coast bogies' for the fast Glasgow-Greenock services; the engine was a 4—4—0 with 5 ft 9 in. driving wheels and the usual 18 by 26 in. inside cylinders. On 27 April one of the class was used to haul a special train for railway officers and press representatives from Glasgow to Loch Awe and back. The object of the outing was to introduce new passenger stock to be placed on the Oban run on the following Monday. Dugald Drummond himself was present—he acted as croupier when the party stopped at Tyndrum for a meal on the way back—and the

MAID OF MORVEN

(38) *Rear view when new. The heavy curtains impeded the passengers'*
view and were later removed

(39) *Interior view looking towards observation window*

EX-HIGHLAND RAILWAY ENGINES AT WORK

(40) 'Clan Cameron' and 'Clan Fraser' climbing Glencruitten bank
with the 5.15 p.m. from Oban in July 1938

(41) 'Skibo Castle' in Strathfillan with the Oban goods in 1941

(42) 'Clan Mackinnon' leaving Stirling with an Oban-Glasgow
train in June 1937

journalists were given the impression that the engine used for the demonstration trip would be regularly employed on the new Oban trains. But this was not so. The class was represented later on the Oban line, but it played only a minor role.

AFTER THE GROUPING

A visitor to Oban shed on a Sunday in 1923, when almost all the engines of the local stud would have been there, would have found that all three classes of Oban bogie were still in use. There were four of the old 4—4—0s (1181, 1186, 1188 and 1185), five McIntosh bogies (55, 56, 59, 52, and 54), and three of the new Pickersgill bogies (194, 195 and 196), along with one coast bogie (1085) and a Jumbo (200). Three tanks of different vintages made a specially interesting sight: 9 (Lambie), 1224 (Drummond) and 4 (Lambie).

The position remained more or less unchanged during the '20s, but as the loads increased and the older engines deteriorated mechanically even more double-heading became necessary. The LMS looked round for alternative motive power, and found it on the former Highland Railway. The Highland engines had been designed for tasks similar to those on the Callander & Oban, but by the early '30s were being replaced by new LMS machines. The early 'Castles' were near-contemporaries of the '55' class, but some of the later members still had useful life. The Cumming superheated goods 4—6—0s of 1917-18, and the last Highland design of all, the 4—6—0 'Clans', were possible candidates for transfer to the C & O.

The eight 'Clans' (four built in 1919 and four in 1921) had 21 by 26 in. cylinders, 6 ft driving wheels, a boiler pressure of 175 p.s.i., and a weight of 62.24 tons in working order. The 'Castles' had 19½ by 26 in. cylinders, 5 ft 9 in. drivers, boilers pressed at 175 p.s.i., and they weighed 58.85 tons, while the superheated goods had 20½ by 26 in. cylinders, 5 ft 3 in. drivers, a boiler pressure of 175 p.s.i., and a weight of 56.45 tons. Trials of all three classes on the Oban road resulted in 'Castles' and 'Clans' being put to work. In practice the 'Castles' were only marginally better than the '55' class, but the 'Clans' were better than anything that had ever appeared on the line. The 'Clans' were classified 4P while the 'Castles' and Caledonian 4—6—0s were classified 3P.

By 1938 the McIntosh engines had disappeared—the last, 14606, was withdrawn in November 1937—and the passenger traffic fell largely to the Highland engines. Of the eighteen 4—6—0s regularly employed on the line ten were ex-Highland engines. They were distributed as follows:

St Rollox			
14763	Clan Fraser	14619	(191 class)
14767	Clan Mackinnon	14621	,,
14768	Clan Mackenzie	14625	,,
14769	Clan Cameron	14626	,,
14681	Skibo Castle	14686	Urquhart Castle

Stirling			
14762	Clan Campbell	14620	(191 class)
14765	Clan Stewart	14622	,,

Oban			
14764	Clan Munro	14623	(191 class)
14766	Clan Chattan	14624	,,

The through excursion and holiday traffic from Dundee to Oban was worked by the Perth-based 'Castles', 14691 *Brodie Castle,* 14684 *Duncraig Castle,* and 14682 *Beaufort Castle.*

In September 1939 the shape of things to come was made plain by the introduction of LMS class 5s to the line. The first engines of the class to work there were based at St Rollox: 5157, 5158, 5355, 5453, 5454 and 5455. For a short time in 1939 two of the class, 5358 and 5362, were shedded at Oban. No. 5358 worked the midday train from Oban to Glasgow on Mondays, Wednesdays and Fridays and returned with the 12.10 p.m. from Buchanan Street on Tuesdays, Thursdays and Saturdays. No. 5362 ran the 9.10 a.m. from Oban to Glasgow daily and returned with the 5.12. Both were soon transferred to St Rollox.

Four of the eight 'Clans' survived the war; the last to go was *Clan Mackinnon* in February 1950. The two 'Castles' regularly employed on the Oban line were scrapped in 1946, while 1945 saw the last survivor of the Pickersgill bogies—14621—disappear. Thereafter, most of the Oban line traffic was consigned to the capable class 5s.

There were interesting visitors to the line from time to time. No. 1123 made routine trips with the officers' saloon. The same engine, restored as CR No. 123, partnered NBR *Glen Douglas* on an enthusiasts' excursion to Oban in 1962, while GNS No. 49 *Gordon Highlander* hauled a special consisting of the two preserved Caledonian coaches. Class 2 4—4—0s and Midland compounds worked the Loch Earn circle excursions and a standard 'Mogul' brought an excursion train from G & SW territory. The rare through excursion trains from Queen Street to Oban, and the circular tour from Glasgow to Crianlarich, out by the West Highland and back by the Callander & Oban, were worked by ex-GER B12 class 4—6—0s; they included the Eastfield-based 8536 and 8502. In 1949, when BR started the once-daily service from Glasgow to Oban *via* the West Highland, B1 class engines were used.

The Ballachulish branch saw a variety of motive power. The three generations of Oban bogie took turns on the line, and during the war class 5s were known to have slipped over Connel Bridge with troop trains for Benderloch. But most of the passenger handling was done by 0—4—4 tanks.

At first, Drummond 0—4—4T engines on the branch were fitted with cowcatchers, but these were soon removed. The proximity of the road to the railway at several points resulted in the Callander & Oban receiving the warning: 'The Lorn District Committee apprehend danger to passengers at several points upon the highway in consequences of horses being frightened by the sight of trains and that they are going to apply to the Board of Trade.'

The line was rich in 'characters'. The passenger driver was James Beaton, and the goods driver, Christie, inherited Beaton's job when he retired. Beaton always turned his engine so that it ran chimney first, but Christie was quite happy to run bunker first. Both could whip the trains along at 50-55 m.p.h. on favourable stretches of line.

Almost from their introduction 0—4—4 tanks were used on the Oban road, on station duties, on the Killin line and the Ballachulish branch. In the final years of steam Oban became the graveyard of those little engines, as successive members of the various classes, displaced from closing branch lines, arrived at the shed to spend the last years, or even months, of their working lives. The last McIntosh '19' class, built in 1895, ran its last working turn, as 55124, at Oban in 1961. The last 0—4—4 to work the Killin branch was 55204. In 1961 this duty was taken over by a BR 2—6—4T and in the same year the 0—4—4s were partly displaced from the Ballachulish branch by ex-LMS and BR 2—6—0s. By the end of 1961, on the eve of the diesel take-over, there were three 0—4—4 tanks still at work at Oban: 55204, 55260 and 55217. In 1962 the replacement of the forty-five steam engines working on the Callander & Oban and West Highland railways with twenty-three Type 2 diesel-electrics and four diesel shunters began. The 2—6—0s were brought in from the Ballachulish branch for a brief period of station duties at Oban, and the 0—4—4s became redundant. No. 55204 was the last to go, in the summer of 1962.

THE CONNEL BUS

The vehicle that started the unique passenger and car-carrying service across Loch Etive in 1909 had earlier taken part in an experiment in integrated road and rail transport, operating as a charabanc between Clarkston railway station, on the Caledonian on the outskirts of Glasgow, and the village of Eaglesham. The Caledonian bought the vehicle, and the decision to run it on the Connel Ferry Bridge was taken on 11 May 1909, when McIntosh was authorised to spend £126 in adapting it for rail traction. One of its drawbacks was that it was capable of only 4 m.p.h. in reverse, and since part of its duties entailed a certain amount of propelling, the gearing was altered to improve this.

The rail bus had a 30 h.p. petrol engine, and had seats for twenty-three passengers arranged facing forward in ascending tiers. A high, over-all canopy, supported by metal struts, and a glass partition behind the driver's seat, afforded the passengers some measure of protection.

As mentioned in Chapter VII, a four-wheel wagon could be attached to carry cars. After its conversion at St Rollox the rail bus was taken to Connel Ferry under its own power, and trials were held on 30 June 1909. The public service opened the next day and the vehicle was housed in a small shed at Connel Ferry when not in use.

ROLLING STOCK

In the earliest days the c & o had to make do with whatever stock the Caledonian cared to send. It was not until 1889 that special attention was paid to providing passenger stock for the line. In that year six complete trains, each consisting of one first-class and two brake-third composites, with accommodation for 150 passengers, were put in service. The carriages were 45 ft long and ran on four-wheeled bogies. The bogie centres were set 2 in. nearer the leading axle than the trailing axle. The first-class vehicles weighed 22 tons; of their eight compartments, four offered the novelty of lavatories 'so that the passengers can have a wash and themselves made comfortable towards the close of the journey'. The third-class carriages weighed 19 tons.

The compartments were lit by Pintsch patent gas, and smoking compartments and lavatories were ventilated by a patent apparatus which made use of the motion of the train to eject foul air and inject fresh air. Another novelty was the passenger communicating device: the pulling of a knob in a compartment caused a bell to ring in the van loud enough to be heard throughout the train. An external disc, phosphorus-painted, indicated the compartment where the alarm had been raised. The alarm knob was not replace-able so that a passenger could be detected 'should he pull the knob in mere diversion'.

During the demonstration run with the new stock in April 1889 the smokers among the guests, we are assured, placed a severe strain on the ventilating device; they otherwise had a merry time pulling the alarm knobs at intervals during the day.

No further special stock was built for the Oban line until 1910, when eight-wheeled, semi-corridor bogies were constructed at St Rollox. These were the first Caledonian coaches to have sliding doors in the corridors. In the later CR days ex-West Coast Joint Stock vehicles appeared on the Oban line; they were LNW-built and had 'For use on the Callander and Oban section' painted on the solebars.

The highlight in the story of C & O rolling stock was the advent of the Pullman car *Maid of Morven* in 1914. This unique vehicle was a combined observation, lounge and kitchen car. Of wooden construc-tion and running on two four-wheel bogies, it was 61 ft 1 in. long over the buffers and had an extreme width of 9 ft. The observation compartment was 23 ft by 5¼ ft and had individual armchair seating for fourteen first-class passengers. The lounge was 13 ft 8¼ in. by 8 ft 4¼ in. and accommodated eight passengers. The internal decoration, after the Sheraton period, was lavish; the walls were panelled in finely-figured pearwood, and there were marquetry pilasters with details after Pergolesi. The Bergère chairs were upholstered in brown tapestry with a floral trellis design. The light brackets were of chased metal, and table-lamps with hand-painted silk shades were provided. A heavy pile plain brown carpet covered the floor.

Maid of Morven first ran on 3 August 1914. It was withdrawn because of war conditions on 28 February 1915, and did not reappear until 1 March 1919. The car enjoyed a few years of prestige and popularity before its patrons began to desert to the motor car. *Maid of Morven* was an observation car in more ways than one. The proletariat along the line made a habit of watching it on its daily journeys to see whom among the local notables was travelling. 'So-and-so was on the Maid' became the opening gambit of many a village gossip session. That may have been why the car's armchairs as often as not were placed with their *backs* to the wide observation windows.

Pullman dining-cars provided an elegant service in late Caledonian and early LMS days. Well remembered was *Mary Beaton*, one of the twelve-wheeled Pullman cars. The interior was beautifully panelled in figured mahogany and the decoration was Louis XIV marquetry. Furniture included a bow-fronted cabinet surmounted by a clock. There was rich green carpeting, with green morocco chairs and blinds of green silk. Blue was the theme colour in *Mary Carmichael* —a blue carpet and blue upholstered chairs offset the pearwood panelling. *Mary Seaton* had crimson carpeting, crimson chairs, ivory ceiling and walnut panelling. A patron of the line in those days, reminiscing about schoolday journeys, wrote:

> The eight o'clock breakfast car train from Buchanan Street to Oban was in winter a very comfortable train. The Pullman car *Mary Beaton* was manned by a most hospitable crew. Many a time going home for the holidays you might have only two or three people having breakfast with the result that I always did very well with at least two plates of bacon and eggs, mountains of toast and lashings of coffee.

EPILOGUE

Such was the Callander & Oban Railway. From the beginning its secretary set out to give it character and flavour, and in the face of overwhelming physical and political difficulties he succeeded. Around the time that the line was truncated, the self-same gentleman who as a schoolboy had consumed two plates of bacon and eggs in the Pullman reflected: 'It was an intensely friendly railway even in LMS days. The staff were all very much of a family. Everybody knew everybody else, and rarely had any of them been on other sections of the line, although in 1939 we were getting stationmasters from the Highland and Caledonian sections.'

John Anderson would have liked that.

CHAPTER XI

Changes and Continuity
By John H. Farrington (1988)

TWO PARTS

John Thomas was able to include in his book the events which led in 1965 to the severing of the railway whose coming had meant so much to Oban, to John Anderson, and to visitors and locals alike who had used the line over the years for business or pleasure. At the end of the previous chapter, the scene was set for the present situation on the Callander & Oban, which is in the full sense a railway no more. Rather, it is a line in two parts, one of which, between Crianlarich and Oban, is a busy railway with improving commercial prospects, though still not a paying proposition in strict financial terms. The other part of the line is of value as a transport link no more, for the abandonment of the trackbed and stations between Callander and Crianlarich has allowed the incursion of building and the elements, so that it now snakes along the glens as a quiet testimony to the determination and vision of the Victorian promoters and engineers. However, as we shall see, sections of it are being put to other uses.

It is appropriate to look separately at these distinctive parts of the original line, starting with the surviving section. A passenger travelling to Oban from the south boards the train in Glasgow's Queen Street Station. I made the journey on a September day in 1987 by kind permission of Keith Plues, area traincrew manager, in the cab of 37409, *Loch Awe* accompanied by traction inspector George Steele. Before we left, on time, at 0820, driver and inspector exchanged notes on the state of the locomotive, agreeing that the overheating light on the instrument panel was a false alarm, something that particular loco was noted for. Then, amidst the din of the rumbling diesel engine, only partly muffled by the engine compartment access door, we plunged into the tunnel and tackled the fearsome Cowlairs Incline. The noise made conversation impossible, but it was interesting to note the steady progress sustained up the 1 in 43 gradient, and all at the turn of a handle – a far cry from the days when steam locomotives belched out thick clouds of smoke, filling the tunnel so that a footplate crew could even be unaware that their forward progress had ceased and that their train was actually sliding backwards.

Our journey along the electrified lines through North Clydeside's industrial and residential sprawl was uneventful, but as we branched right at Craigendoran Junction, the railwayman's 'Gateway to the Highlands', the clouds were thickening in the west, promising real Highland weather for the later part of the journey.

The climb up the valley side through Garelochhead and on towards Crianlarich was accomplished with a little wheelspin on the now greasy rails, as a steady drizzle blotted out much of the fine mountain scenery, but it cleared sufficiently to allow splendid views over Loch Lomond to the east. At each of the stations we passed south-bound trains off the Oban and Fort William lines, including ballast, freight and passenger traffic, all hauled by Class 37s. At Arrochar & Tarbet, Driver Thompson took over for the rest of the journey to Oban. Arrival at Crianlarich, on time at 1022, marked a pause in our progress as we waited to cross and connect with the late-running 0830 passenger train from Fort William. With the benefit of information obtained by Inspector Steele, we decided that there was ample time for refreshments in the station tearoom, so like countless travellers before us we found a warm welcome and shelter from the cold, wet winds sweeping the platform. During our stay, the clouds cleared for a few minutes, revealing that the steady rain at our level had fallen as snow on the mountains – a drastic end to a poor summer in the Highlands.

As we turned onto the old Callander & Oban line, fifteen minutes late, the clouds swept down again, but the cab heaters provided a pleasant warmth in the midst of a wintry and hostile environment. We reflected on the change in working practice since the departure of steam, and though there was approval of the noisy comfort of a diesel cab on the part of driver and inspector, it was clear that the pride in achievement that used to come from working steam locomotives over the difficult Highland lines could not be found with modern motive power.

Meanwhile, we hurried on, though our chances of recovering time were slim, with frequent speed restrictions of 35mph on curves, and our running speed was typically 40 to 45mph. The train was being well-used, I noted, with ten to twenty passengers waiting at each of the stations to Oban. Most appeared to be 'locals', with shopping bags and young children, off to Oban for an outing, but a few hikers stood out with their 'wet gear' and rucksacks, no doubt driven from the hills by the weather.

An indication of the use being made of the line's scenic attraction for leisure travel was *The Royal Scotsman*, with 37084 at its head, awaiting our passage at Taynuilt. This luxuriously-appointed train attracts visitors on tours of the Highlands and includes steam haulage on the Fort William line.

As we approached Connel Ferry, the skies cleared at last, giving us a splendid view of the former railway bridge which carried the Ballachulish branch across the narrow straits of Loch Etive at Falls of Lora. We also noted the mussel farms along the shores of the loch, with their pontoons and ropes. With fish-farming, this relatively recent economic development is providing much needed employment in the Highlands, although the high-value products normally leave the area by road or air.

Then came the climb to Glen Cruitten summit with its distinctive signalbox and house combined in one building, and referred to on pages 48 and 85, and finally the 1 in 50 descent to Oban, past the siding leading to the site of the old turntable and loco shed (see plan, p66) through the short cutting and into the station with its new buildings, opened on 3 January 1986 by BR chairman Sir Robert Reid.

We came to a stop at 1141, eight minutes late, and before we had left the cab, the relief driver and shunter had taken over to run the locomotive round the stock, which would form the 1300 departure for Glasgow. We would return on that train, but first there was time to join the holidaymakers and shoppers for a walk round the harbour, as well as to walk back along the track to inspect the site of the locomotive shed.

Wearing the requisite orange vest, I made my way alongside the single line, which leaves Oban station through the cutting, and reached the site of the former signalbox for the junction with the engine shed and goods station. A single siding leaves the main line and leads through the now overgrown site of the shed yard to the present oil depot, with storage tanks situated in the old turntable well. Petroleum tank wagons stood in quiet isolation in the once bustling yard area. I recorded the scene with my camera and hurried back to the station for the return journey which was accomplished on time and for the most part in bright sunlight.

THE WEST HIGHLAND LINES

Recent years have seen many changes on the Crianlarich–Oban portion of what are nowadays collectively known as the 'West Highland Lines' (Glasgow to Oban, Fort William and Mallaig).

In 1981, Class 37 locomotives officially took over as principal motive power on the line, replacing Class 27s, which had been the mainstay of haulage since 1961. The latter did continue to work some trains until 1986 when they were banned (apart from special authorisation) due to their high failure rate and difficulties in getting them back to Eastfield for repair. An exciting appearance in the summer of 1981 was 'Deltic' 55021 *Argyll & Sutherland Highlander*, on two Edinburgh–Oban excursions. Until 1985 steam heating was still used in some trains, but the clever conversion of three Class 25 locomotives into 'Ethels' (Electric Train Heating Ex Locomotive) renumbered 97250/1/2 allowed electric train heating, and these were first regularly used on the summer 1983 Sunday Edinburgh–Oban excursions. Their principal use was on the Mk3 Euston–Fort William sleeping cars, but by 9 September 1985 all the MkI coaching stock was converted to electric heating, and Class 37/4 locomotives removed the need for the Ethels. In October 1986 Mk1a SO and FO coaching stock was introduced, and in May 1987 MkII SO and FO stock was cascaded from other regions, the SOs coming from Norwich. An example of the initiative still to be found on the West Highland Lines was the refurbishment of the MkI stock with new carpets, fluorescent lighting, wall maps and so on in 1985.

A better known, and now widespread innovation was the identification, from January 1983, of all West Highland locomotives by means of the 'West Highland Terrier Dog' transfers, while some also received full white stripes along lower body sides, head lamps, snow ploughs and repainted cab ends and interiors. To Keith Plues goes the credit for these ideas, which were adapted and applied to all Scottish Region allocated locomotives, in the shape of transfers depicting the Highland Terrier (Eastfield), Stag (Inverness), Salmon (Motherwell) and Castle (Haymarket).

A slightly more controversial innovation was the introduction in 1986 of the renovated Birmingham Carriage & Wagon-built diesel unit for Oban–Crianlarich Sunday excursion work. Its livery was a distinctive purple and white, and it was nicknamed 'The Mexican Bean'. It left the line in late 1987.

Adhesion has always been a problem on these lines, and although beyond the strict remit of the present chapter, it is worth mentioning a successful innovation dating from 1984 for applying sand. A converted diesel single unit named 'Sandra' periodically works during the autumn leaf fall period between Craigendoran and Crianlarich, applying blobs of gell-coated sand, which are subsequently spread by other trains, improving adhesion. This helped to overcome a problem which, in 1982/83, had been tackled by fitting five Class 20 locomotives with through steam heating pipes and marshalling one of them inside a Class 37 on the Glasgow–Fort William Monday sleeper for extra traction.

A significant change regarding the line's stations in recent years was the opening of the new Oban station in January 1986, and the demolition of the old station buildings, the site to be 'redeveloped' for other non-railway uses. The modern building contrasts sharply with the old station's appearance and fits BRs strategy of presenting a modern image in cases where rehabilitation and retention of old buildings is not considered practicable. Just two passenger platforms are now in regular use, the old platforms 3 and 4.

In 1985/86, with the aid of EEC finance, ScotRail's then general manager, Chris Green, authorised renovation and repainting of 'West Highland Lines' stations mainly in green and white, though the new Oban station carries the modern livery.

Loch Awe Halt was reopened in 1985, and Falls of Cruachan Halt was reopened at the low cost of £10,000 on an experimental basis for the 1988 season, with all services stopping by request, except for the 2025 Sunday Crianlarich to Oban service. The halt affords access to a tour of Ben Cruachan

Power Station. Only Oban station is now staffed, a sad reflection of the constant need to improve the cost-revenue ratios, though Crianlarich happily retains its staffed tearoom.

Signalling on the line has also seen major changes in recent years, the principal innovation being the final commissioning of Radio Electronic Token Block (RETB) signalling between Crianlarich and Oban on 27 March 1988. Together with the systems of hydromagnetic semi-automatic points and point set indicators at passing stations (brought into operation in February/March 1986), RETB has removed the need for intermediate signal boxes and staff, with financial savings. RETB had teething troubles in the area due to interference with Irish television signals, and with emergency service transmissions, but now makes its contribution to cost-savings in these times of stringent commercial imperatives for BR.

The future for the Crianlarich–Oban line looks moderately assured, but nothing can be guaranteed in a time of ever-tightening public purse-strings and, perhaps more ominously, of proposed privatisation of British Rail.

Costs were further cut by the introduction of 'Sprinter' Class 156 trains with their lower maintenance costs for the 1989 summer service. The service was then totally recast, Oban having four instead of three weekday trains but all being joined or separated at Crianlarich with 'Sprinters' from or to Fort William/Mallaig. The new service has generally been well received and gives a quicker, smoother as well as more frequent ride to Oban. But the cramped seating and poorer visibility from the Sprinters have naturally been criticised, the restricted visibility seeming especially at odds with one of the lesson's for the line's survival – its scenery.

The introduction of 'Sprinters' certainly underlines the assurances given about the future of The West Highland Lines. They can definitely hope for fairer treatment than they were accorded in some of the options discussed in the Serpell Report in 1983, where the basic illogicality of the blinkered financial approach was exposed: the line from Glasgow to Crianlarich would remain open, while the Fort William/Mallaig and Oban lines from Crianlarich would close. The fact that almost all of the traffic on the Glasgow–Crianlarich section derives from the Mallaig and Oban lines was obscured by such an approach. It is worth adding that increasing freight traffic on the main line through Crianlarich (though Oban normally sees oil freight) helps the economics of the whole of the West Highland Lines.

CLOSED SECTIONS

The line between Callander and Crianlarich has gone, but an excursion along its route by car, bicycle or on foot is a fascinating, if nostalgic, exploration in its own right. By car, it is easily possible to follow the route, calling at points of interest, in half a day, making a day trip from Glasgow or Edinburgh. However, a more leisurely progress by bicycle or partly on foot, would be repaid by much of interest, and could occupy two or more days in the area, where there are numerous hotels and guest houses with caravan sites as an option (some of the latter are on the old railway itself). Observations made here are based on field work carried out in April and October 1988. Ordnance Survey 1:50,000 Sheets 50, 51 and 57 show the abandoned line and are indispensable for detailed interpretation.

The main points of interest to follow are firstly the identification of remains and their interpretation against the history of the line told in this book, and secondly the recognition of new uses for the trackbed and station sites.

At Callander the station site has been cleared and is used as a car and coach park. A platform edge survives on the southwest side of the site, and the road overbridge at the eastern end is intact and resplendent in brown and cream paint. At Strathyre, the station has also gone completely, though at Kingshouse, Balquhidder, Luib, Crianlarich and Loch Tay there are remains of interest, though these are on private land and the normal courtesies of asking permission for access should be followed where possible. At Kingshouse, the earth and timber platform edge, and platform shelter foundations, can be picked out. Closer inspection of the north end of the embankment on my visit revealed firebox clinker and a partially fused brick, probably from a collapsed brick arch in a firebox, and evocative of some footplate crew's struggle to maintain steam for the ferocious 1 in 60 climb to Glenoglehead.

Between Callander and Strathyre, lengths of the trackbed are used as part of the Callander and Strathyre Railway Path and Cycle Route, a project which has been carried out by Sustrans Ltd, a registered charity working throughout Britain on the construction and maintenance of pathways for pedestrians, cyclists and in some cases horse-riders. The Callander and Strathyre path was funded by Stirling District Council, the Manpower Services Commission, the Countryside Commission for Scotland, Glennocky Trust and Central Regional Council. It is a splendid example of the results of co-operative effort, with a well-surfaced walkway and smartly finished gates and fencing, and clearly presented signing and information. The stretch that runs past the Falls of Leny approaches along the right bank of the river from Callander and joins the trackbed just upstream of the site of the railway bridge, giving good views of the buttresses which are all that remain of the structure shown in Plate 31. Between this point and Strathyre, the path uses the trackbed for much of the way, giving walkers and cyclists a peaceful perspective of Loch Lubnaig before restoring them to civilisation at Strathyre.

Sustrans propose to link the Callander and Strathyre path with another walkway that makes good use of the old trackbed. This is known as the Glen Ogle Trail and it uses the magnificent alignment of the railway to climb along the west side of Glen Ogle to the summit at Glen Ogle Head by Lochan Lairig Chiele, allowing a return to Lochearnhead via a path on the east side of the valley. This walkers' circuit was developed by Stirling District Council. Information boards and maps in the loch-side car parks at Lochearnhead explain the route, which affords a splendid opportunity for peaceful and easy walking in rugged scenery, including as it does the Glenogle Viaduct.

Also worth a visit (although off the Callander & Oban itself) is the well-restored station at Lochearnhead, now used as a Scout Activity Centre. The buildings, platforms and track alignments survive, and it is good to see them put to such productive use, though it should be remembered that this is not a public site.

Balquhidder station site is now host to Leitters Brae Caravan Site, but the stairway and white glazed brick retaining wall are still present alongside the A84 road, and directly opposite The Golden Larches Restaurant. The subway was blocked by a canvas screen on my visit, but platform edges and the remains of a room, including a fireplace, could still be identified on the north-western side of the site, on the old platform.

Luib station site is occupied by Glen Dochart Caravan Park owned by Bryan and Margaret Donaldson who are keenly appreciative of the site's history. They have retained in use the railway cottages on the north side of the site, and the stone plinth supporting the water tank. Platform edges also survive and are being incorporated as features of the site's development. The Donaldsons intend to provide interpretative material for visitors, explaining the former use of the caravan park.

The approach to Loch Tay station is along a narrow private road which winds through the wet land of the combined delta of the Rivers Lochay and Dochart. The trackbed has become overgrown to the point where it is hard to believe that it once carried trains of eager excursionists from the urban areas of the Central Belt, and further afield, to meet steamers on the loch. The station site is occupied by private grounds and houses, one of which uses the old station building, now painted white, as part of the accommodation. A nice touch is the use of old sleepers as gateposts.

The Ballachulish branch closed in March 1966, but parts of it remain, to be seen in the rugged landscape. Kentallen station has been converted into the Holly Tree Restaurant, while Appin station is derelict but more or less intact. Duror station has largely gone, as has Benderloch, though here the platforms remain, and housing has been built on the site.

Ballachulish station itself remains in good order under the ownership of Mr Chisholm, who uses the site as his garage premises. The track bed at the northern end of the line is planned for use as part of road construction for the new alignment of the A828.

Crianlarich (Lower) station buildings have gone, though the yard remains in use as a freight yard, principally for the loading of southbound timber, with some coal storage also in evidence. The line eastwards to Callander is now truncated a little way out of the yard and is used as a headshunt, an inglorious end for John Anderson's line!

CONCLUSION

Perhaps a danger facing the Oban line is that in a period when BR is under strong commercial pressure, the Mallaig line with its steam associations and greater scenic grandeur may overshadow the future of the Oban line.

An exhortation familiar during the Beeching era was 'Use it or lose it'. I hope that this ultimatum is too severe to apply to the Oban line at present, and certainly no formal threat to the line has been put forward. Yet it remains, like all ScotRail's passenger lines, unprofitable in the strict commercial sense. However, recent investment in infrastructure and rolling stock, and the cost savings they produce, are welcome, and the number of passengers using the line is encouraging.

John Anderson's perceptive and tireless work, chronicled so ably by John Thomas, gave us an asset which still provides a source of utility and pleasure at the end of the century. I believe it can, and will, serve us into the next century – and for the foreseeable future.

I am indebted to Keith Plues, area train crew manager, and George Steele, traction inspector, both based at Queen Street Station, Glasgow, for their help in arranging my cab trip on the Oban line. Keith Plues has also responded unfailingly to my requests for information about recent developments, and has provided photographs. David Summers carried out a valuable 'reconnaissance' of the Callander-Crianlarich track-bed before my own visits. Dave Holloway of Sustrans Ltd provided information on that company's activities in Scotland, including their achievements on lengths of the Callander-Crianlarich trackbed, and Bryan and Margaret Donaldson showed me their Glen Dochart Caravan Park on the site of Luib Station. For those wanting to keep up with further changes, the newsletters of the Friends of the West Highland Line provide information about the Oban line as well as the Fort William and Mallaig lines. The chairman, Doug Carmichael, helped in providing information for this chapter.

Appendices

1 : CALLANDER & OBAN CHRONOLOGY

1 July	1858	Dunblane, Doune & Callander Ry opened
22 June	1864	First meeting of C & O Ry held in Glasgow
17 Dec	1864	Agreement signed by Scottish Central Ry and C & O
5 July	1865	C & O Ry Act passed
29 June	1865	Scottish Central absorbs DD & C
5 July	1865	Caledonian Railway absorbs SCR
1 Sept	1865	John Anderson appointed secretary
27 June	1866	Contract for construction of Callander-Killin section awarded to John MacKay
29 Oct	1866	First sod cut
6 Nov	1866	Contract signed
1 Dec	1866	Mr Kerr appointed resident engineer
5 Nov	1867	Caledonian pressed for suspension of work on C & O
12 May	1870	C & O (Abandonment) Act passed
18/19 May	1870	Official inspection of line by Board of Trade
1 June	1870	Callander-Killin opened
12 Oct	1870	Trossachs Ry surveyed
21 June	1871	Kingshouse platform opened
Aug	1873	Opened to Tyndrum
16 July	1874	C & O (Tyndrum & Oban) Act passed
2 Mar	1875	Tenders invited for Dalmally contract
1 Apr	1877	Opened to Dalmally for goods
1 May	1877	Opened to Dalmally for passengers
27 June	1877	John Strain authorised to survey and stake out Dalmally-Oban section
22 July	1878	C & O Ry Act, 1878, passed
12 June	1880	Opened to Oban for goods
30 June	1880	Ceremonial opening to Oban
1 July	1880	Opened to Oban for passengers
Nov	1880	Tyers tablet authorised, Oban-Dalmally
3 Dec	1880	Tyers tablet approved, Dalmally-Callander
20 June	1881	Steamer sailings began from Achnacloich
6 Jan	1882	Experimental boulder screen ready for tests
27 June	1882	Boulder screen authorised for Pass of Brander
19 Aug	1882	First meeting of Killin Ry Co
2 Nov	1883	Major Marindin sanctioned use of reconstructed Callander station
8 Nov	1884	Collapse of Nant bridge
13 Mar	1886	Ceremonial opening of Killin Ry. Open for goods
1 Apr	1886	Killin Ry opened for passengers. Killin station name changed to Glenoglehead
13 Sept	1886	Derailment of Falkirk-Oban excursion train
1 Oct	1893	Awe crossing opened

16 Nov	1893	Strathyre station destroyed by fire
20 Dec	1894	Crianlarich Junction opened
7 Aug	1896	C & O Ry Act passed (Ballachulish extension)
18 Dec	1896	Lochearnhead, St Fillans & Comrie Ry claimed running powers over C & O to Oban
8 Aug	1897	Loch Awe station destroyed by fire
16 Nov	1898	Dalmally station (north side) destroyed by fire
1 Oct	1902	Opening of double line between Callander Junction and Callander Dreadnought
13 Jan	1903	Mechanical tablet exchangers approved
4 Mar	1903	Extension to Oban station authorised
7 Mar	1904	North Connel opened
1 July	1904	Lochearnhead station name changed to Balquhidder
7 July	1905	Introduction of 'C & O Hotel Express'
31 July	1907	John Anderson retired
2 Jan	1908	Scissors crossing at Callander East approved
1 July	1909	Start of Connel railbus service
17 June	1911	Death of John Anderson
6 Feb	1912	Barcaldine siding authorised
22 June	1914	Connel Bridge opened for pedestrians, vehicles and other traffic
3 Aug	1914	Pullman car *Maid of Morven* introduced
28 Feb	1915	*Maid of Morven* temporarily withdrawn
1 Jan	1917	Achnacloich closed temporarily
1 Mar	1919	*Maid of Morven* reintroduced
1 June	1919	Achnacloich reopened
	Aug 1924	Oban office of railway closed
10 June	1931	First through train from Glasgow to Oban *via* West Highland line
1 July	1931	Kingshouse Halt changed to Kingshouse
9 Sept	1939	Passenger service withdrawn Killin-Loch Tay
7 Sept	1964	Freight service withdrawn between Callander and Crianlarich
2 Nov	1964	Freight service withdrawn from Killin branch
14 June	1965	Freight withdrawn from Ballachulish branch
27 Sept	1965	Landslide in Glen Ogle. End of service between Callander and Crianlarich
4 Oct	1965	Regular service between Glasgow Queen St and Oban began
1 Nov	1965	Official closing of line between Dunblane and Callander and Killin branch. Falls of Cruachan, Achnacloich and Loch Awe closed
26 Mar	1966	Last train on Ballachulish branch
During 1981		Class 37 locomotives with steam heating boilers replaced Class 27s
January 1983		West Highland Terrier Dog emblem given to locomotives
July 1984		Edinburgh–Oban Sunday train introduced for summer season, with Glasgow engine crew working into Oban, and in return Oban men working a summer-only Shopper Service to Glasgow

26 April 1985	Reflectorised distant boards with AWS magnet on the approach side installed at Crainlarich Tyndrum Lower and Dalmally, replacing distant signals
9 Sept 1985	Class 37/4s introduced with electric train heating
3 Jan 1986	Rebuilt Oban station officially opened by Sir Robert Reid
During 1986	Class 27s banned from West Highland lines without special authorisation
	'Mexican Bean' diesel unit introduced for Sunday Oban–Crianlarich excursions
Feb/March 1986	Stop signals removed, point set indicators erected and semi-automatic points fitted, at Crianlarich, Dalmally, Taynuilt and Connel Ferry
27 March 1988	Radio Electronic Token Block signalling commissioned, Crianlarich–Oban
16 Jan 1989	Class 156 DMU's officially introduced ending daytime locomotive-hauled trains.

2 : MILEAGES

	Miles	Chains	Opened to passengers
Callander C & O Junction	0	00	1.6.1870
Callander (Dreadnought)	0	61	1.6.1870
St Brides Crossing	4	21	*
Strathyre	9	32	1.6.1870
Kingshouse Halt	11	38	21.6.1871
Balquhidder	12	38	1.6.1870
Glenoglehead (Killin)	17	50	1.6.1870
Killin Junction	19	72	1.4.1886
Luib	23	40	8.1873
Crianlarich	29	57	8.1873
Crianlarich Junction	30	20	20.12.1897
Tyndrum	34	71	8.1873
Glen Lochy Crossing	40	10	*
Dalmally	46	75	1.5.1877
Loch Awe	49	49	1.7.1880
Falls of Cruachan platform	52	65	1.10.1893
Awe Crossing	54	19	1.10.1893 *
Taynuilt	58	53	1.7.1880
Achnacloich	62	14	1881
Connel Ferry	65	30	1.7.1880
Glencruitten	68	39	1903 *
Oban	71	44	1.7.1880

Connel Ferry	0	00	
North Connel		53	7.3.1904
Benderloch	2	68	24.8.1903
Creagan	10	03	24.8.1903
Appin	13	24	24.8.1903
Duror	18	72	24.8.1903
Kentallen	22	56	24.8.1903
Ballachulish Ferry	25	50	24.8.1903
Ballachulish	27	54	24.8.1903

Killin Junction	0	00	1.4.1886
Killin	4	08	1.4.1886
Loch Tay	5	05	1.4.1886

* Crossing places only

3 : CALLANDER & OBAN NAMES

The place-names on the Callander & Oban were derived from Gaelic.
The following table gives their English meanings

Callander	*cailleanach tir*, district of reeds or husks of grain
Strathyre	Valley of the land
Balquhidder	*baile-chuil-tir*, farm on the back-lying land
Killin	*cille fhionn*, the white church
Luib	*luib*, bend, curve, angle (in a river)
Crianlarich	*crion laraich*, the little pass
Tyndrum	*tigh-an-druim*, house on the hill, ridge
Dalmally	*dail mailidh*, wet land
Loch Awe	*Ath*, ford or shallow river
Taynuilt	*tigh-an-uillt*, the house by the burn
Achnacloich	*ach-na-cloich*, the field of the stones
Connel Ferry	*coingheall*, a whirlpool (referring to the falls of Lora)
Glencruitten	Glen of the stones
Oban	*ob-an*, a little bay
Benderloch	*beinn dar loch*, the mountain between the lochs
Creagan	*creag-an*, little rock
Appin	*apuinn*, the abbey lands
Duror	*dur odhar*, grey water
Kentallen	*cinn an t-sailen*, head of the salt water
Ballachulish	*bail-a-chaolais*, village on the straits

4: NOTES ON THE STATIONS

Callander station was reconstructed in 1883. In 1902 the line between Callander Junction and Callander station (referred to as Callander Dreadnought in the official correspondence) was doubled. The old station at Callander (Dunblane, Doune & Callander Railway) remained open for a short time after 1870, but most of the trains, including Caledonian and North British trains terminating at Callander, used the c & o station. The old station was eventually used for goods.

Oban station was rebuilt in 1903, a double-line bay being added.

When *Balquhidder Junction* was formed, on the completion of the Lochearnhead, St Fillans & Comrie Railway, the staff of one stationmaster, one signalman and one porter was increased by three signalmen, one porter-guard and one porter. An engine shed, two boxes and turntable were provided. The West Box had thirty-six levers, the East Box forty-five. The waiting-room at Balquhidder was used for a time as a council chamber by Balquhidder Parish Council. It was also used as an official polling station at local and general elections.

Barcaldine siding between Benderloch and Creagan was authorised on 6 February 1912, and was built at a cost of £340, half of which was paid by Mr Ogilvy, the landowner. He had to guarantee traffic worth £40 a year, failing which he was bound to pay 7½ per cent of half the cost of the siding to the c & o. Trains stopped at Barcaldine on request.

Lochtay. The original designation was Killin Pier-Lochtay. Later the station appeared in timetables as Loch Tay Pier or simply Loch Tay.

Kentallen Pier. For many years MacBrayne's steamers called at the pier, adjacent to the station. The rather high pier-due of 5d per passenger was levied.

Tablet exchangers. Tablet exchangers were suggested by Anderson in December 1902 as a means of speeding up traffic, and were installed in 1903 at the following points: Glencruitten Summit, Connel Ferry West, Connel Ferry East, Taynuilt, Awe Crossing, Glenlochy Crossing, Tyndrum, Crianlarich Junction West, Crianlarich Junction East, Crianlarich, Luib, Killin Junction West, Killin Junction East, Glenoglehead Crossing, Balquhidder West, Balquhidder East, Strathyre, St Bride's Crossing and Callander West.

5: REVENUE FROM TRAFFIC 1870-81

Year ending 31 July	Passengers £ s. d.			Merchandise £ s. d.			Livestock £ s. d.			Minerals £ s. d.		
1871	2,833	19	3¾	1,083	7	5	227	12	3	297	18	8
1872	3,037	10	5	1,366	4	0	339	4	7	606	14	8
1873	3,173	15	0	909	8	7	510	9	11	533	5	7
1874	5,140	7	2	973	18	2	1,193	13	9	463	7	3
1875	5,357	2	5	1,205	4	7	1,356	3	2	412	1	11
1876	5,560	16	5	1,788	17	4	1,503	1	0	691	7	6
1877	6,232	18	5	1,329	8	4	1,448	6	1	815	5	6
1878	7,940	18	11	607	4	2	1,888	5	1	598	5	6
1879	7,508	0	8	2,219	18	2	2,013	18	0	858	5	4
1880	10,775	18	10	2,050	9	11	1,555	10	5	816	1	5
1881	22,423	10	3	4,274	14	7	2,247	10	9	2,748	12	5

Year ending 31 July	Parcels £ s. d.			Mails £ s. d.			Total £ s. d.		
1871	298	0	0				4,821	17	8¾
1872	429	17	9				5,906	9	1
1873	352	14	1				6,624	7	8
1874	501	8	8	56	10	0	8,464	14	6
1875	690	0	3	75	0	0	9,372	17	7
1876	641	3	6,	75	0	0	10,559	0	3
1877	711	19	0	373	2	8	11,052	15	3
1878	929	6	11	970	0	0	13,962	13	6
1879	1,085	19	2	970	0	0	14,879	7	9
1880	860	12	1	697	10	0	17,278	19	3
1881	4,076	3	2	2,520	16	8	38,751	8	9

This table shows how revenue increased as the line was extended. The large increase in livestock receipts in 1874 followed the first full year when the line was open to Tyndrum, the focal-point of cattle drovers from the West and Northern Highlands. Livestock traffic was mainly seasonal, the autumn sales accounting for most of it. For instance, in the last half of 1879 livestock receipts were £1,475 19s 3d, but they were only £79 11s 3d in the first half of 1880.

The total receipts include miscellaneous items such as rents from company properties, interest, etc. For the first three years the mail receipts were included in the parcels receipts.

6 : TRAIN MILEAGE AND COST OF MOTIVE POWER
AND ROLLING STOCK, 1870-81

	Paid to CR for engines	Paid for rolling stock	Pass and mxd train miles	Goods	Total miles
1871	£920.17.3	£323.6.3	27,028	576	27,604
1872	£969.18.10	£386.15.7	28,309	720	29,029
1873	£962.12.8	£420.13.6	27,162	1,696	28,858
1874	£2,217.4.0	£748.9.1	53,060	13,456	65,916
1875	£2,151.14.8	£887.11.0	51,410	13,242	64,652
1876	£2,388.14.8	£855.5.8	56,480	13,302	69,782
1877	£261.18.0	£958.7.0	61,802	16,549	78,351
1878	£3,347.0.0	£1,243.12.8	87,296	9,814	97,110
1879	£3,122.15.6	£1,445.8.5	94,864	16,000	110,864
1880	£3,506.13.6	£1,467.14.0	113,646	15,828	129,474
1881	£7,016.17.11	£3,061.8.0	193,287	45,328	238,615

7 : TOTAL REVENUE, BALANCE PAID TO NET REVENUE,
AND MILEAGES, 1881-90

	Balance to net revenue	Pass and mxd train-miles	Pass and mxd train-miles	Goods	Total miles
1881	£38,761.9.7	£15.969.7.4	194,387	45,328	239,715
1882	£41,801.16.7	£13,092.2.11	193,075	52,935	246,010
1883	£45,429.18.2	£18,447.4.10	186,417	47,267	233,674
1884	£45,039.10.0	£15,210.2.10	189,187	53,083	242,170
1885	£45,063.17.3	£17,260.11.0	199,122	53,445	252,567
1886	£46,606.4.10	£17,622.7.10	166,784	88,643	255,427
1887	£46,643.13.4	£18,532.12.4	187,794	61,628	249,422
1888	£46,353.13.1	£19,345.19.1	184,234	57,768	242,002
1889	£50,585.11.4	£20,154.0.5	195,113	53,499	248,612
1890	£50,731.9.3	£20,266.0.4	195,571	66,284	261,855
1905	£83,316.13.1	£39,088.3.6	321,183	90,899	412,082
1911	£82,814.17.3	£31,596.3.0	321,113	90,611	411,724
1922	£161,696.4.6	£19,822.12.5	302,295	131,977	434,272

The 1905 accounts showed the first full year's receipts from the Ballachulish branch. 1911 was a typical pre-war peak year. The 1922 accounts are for the full calendar year, the final year of the C & O. Mixed-train mileage fell steadily; in 1911 it was 148,820, but had fallen to 31,679 by 1922.

8: MILEAGES, REVENUE AND WORKING LOSS ON THE KILLIN RAILWAY FOR TWO FIVE-YEAR PERIODS, 1887-91 AND 1900-1904

	Mileage	Revenue	Loss on working
1887	19,750	£1,559.10.8	
1888	19,656	£1,372.12.1	
1889	18,745	£1,516.19.10	£241.3.8
1890	18,544	£1,482.16.2	£252.10.7
1891	16,830	£1,493.9.10	£172.0.10
1900	17,186	£1,456.8.0	£703.12.7
1901	17,268	£1,369.16.9	£1,028.5.6
1902	17,356	£1,400.3.2	£976.13.5
1903	17,462	£1,396.16.10	£1,073.18.11
1904	17,551	£1,452.12.6	£757.13.4

9: DIRECTORS OF THE KILLIN RAILWAY, 1882

The Rt Hon the Earl of Breadalbane, Taymouth Castle, Aberfeldy, chairman
Charles Stewart, Esq., Tighndruim. Killin, deputy chairman
Sir Donald Currie, Garth, Aberfeldy
John Willison, Esq., Killin
John Cameron, Esq., Killin

10: DIRECTORS OF THE CALLANDER & OBAN RAILWAY, 1923

Henry Allan, Esq., Glasgow, chairman
Sir Joseph White Todd, Bart., Morenish, Killin, deputy chairman
Henry E. Gordon, Esq., Lanark
William Murray Morrison, Esq., London S.W.1
John Graham Stewart, Dunblane
Col John D. Sutherland, CBE, Edinburgh

THE ILLUSTRATIONS

The original edition's illustrations were acknowledged as noted below. Acknowledgements of the extra illustrations are included in their captions.

Author, 1, 8, 21, 29; J. B. Aird, 2; J. F. McEwan collection, 3, 10, 15, 16, 18, 19, 22, 24, 28, 32, 35; H. J. Patterson Rutherford, 4, 5, 6; N. B. Hurst, 7; D. McDonald, 9; A. McLaren, 11, 13, 14, 20; W. A. C. Smith, 12, 14, 26, 30, 31, 33; Ian Peddie collection, 17, 38, 39; J. Templeton, 23, 27; C. Lawson Kerr, 25, 36, 37, 40, 41, 42; British Railways, 34. Alisdair M. McDonald provided the sketches on pages 31, 36, 38, 40, 44, 60, 66, 78 and 88. British Railways Board archives are responsible for the illustrations on pages 102, 106, 108, 118 and 162. The originals of the employment notices on pages 144 and 146 are in the possession of G. Pywell. The *Railway Magazine* provided the map on page 18 and the gradient profile on page 52, J. F. McEwan drew the gradient profile on page 116 and A. J. S. Paterson provided the sketches on pages 127 and 158. The sketches on pages 55, 57 and 110 are from *Mountain, Moor and Loch*, the original guide book to the West Highland Railway.

BIBLIOGRAPHY

Callander & Oban Railway Act, 1865, 5.7.1865
Callander & Oban Railway (Abandonment) Act, 1870
Callander & Oban Railway (Tyndrum & Oban) Act, 1874
Callander & Oban Railway Act, 1878
Callander & Oban Railway Act, 1896
Callander & Oban Railway minute books, 1865-1923
Callander & Oban Railway Directors' Reports and Accounts, 1865-1923
Callander & Oban Railway secretary's letter books, 1865-1874
Killin Railway Directors' Reports and Accounts, 1882-1916
Killin Railway minute books, 1882-1923
Killin Railway statement book
Killin Railway secretary's letter books, 1882-1923
Caledonian Railway minute books, selected
North British Railway minute books, selected
West Highland Railway minute books, selected
Caledonian Railway Foreign Junction Arrangement Book
Caledonian Railway working and public timetables
Caledonian Railway appendix to the working timetable
Pass of Brander Boulder Signals. A Memorandum. CR
Scotland for the Holidays. (CR). 1911
The Story of Lorn (Hugh Shedden)
Place Names of Argyll (H. J. Gillies)
Journal of a Summer Tour (J. C. Roger), 1898
Tour Through Perthshire (M. Ferguson), 1870
Clyde River and Other Steamers (Duckworth and Langmuir)

Newspapers and periodicals:

*Railway Times, Railway Gazette, Railway Magazine, Railway Engineer,
Scottish Railway Gazette, Herapath's Railway Journal, The Engineer,
Engineering, Glasgow Herald, Glasgow Argus, North British Daily Mail,
The Scotsman, Dundee Advertiser, Blackwood's Edinburgh Magazine, Oban
Times, Oban Telegraph*

C. Boocock: British Rail at Work : ScotRail. Ian Allan, 1986

K. Cordner: Invest in the West. Modern Railways Vol 45, No 480, September
1988, pp 474–477

Serpell Report: Report of a Committee on Railway Finances, HMSO, 1983

M. Roughley: 'Steam to Killin', Back Track, Vol 3, No 1, spring 1989, Atlantic

D. Kennedy: The Birth and Death of a Highland Railway, 1971. (The
Ballachulish Branch)

Index